Foreword

God continues to speak to us through His Word – the Bible. His counsel is always sure and true for all people and every generation. From its pages we find God's promises from which to draw wisdom, courage and strength.

Let us face this coming year with a renewed confidence in the Lord for indeed He promised never to leave us nor forsake us.

Our GOD is the God of fresh starts and new beginnings. He is the one True Constant in a world of change and uncertainty. He satisfies. He restores. He renews. ❧

Jess D. Curabo
Country Director
Our Daily Bread Ministries Phils., Inc.

D0681449

More Than We Ask or Imagine

Several years ago when I was going through a particularly difficult time, a minister I greatly admired pulled me aside at a conference we were attending. He said, "I would like to ask you to pray with me. Let's agree to pray Ephesians 3:14–21 for each other for the next 30 days." During the month that we prayed for each other, I had to be hospitalized for several days. Things seemed to go from bad to worse. But my relationship with God deepened, and I was affirmed of His love in a powerful and lasting way as the Ephesians passage says.

How will He answer? What will He do?

When we pray together in Jesus's name, God's power is poured out in ways that exceed our comprehension. No wonder Jesus insisted so passionately, "My house will be called a house of prayer for all nations" (MARK 11:17). If we want to see real change and true progress for the kingdom of God, we must reach for what He alone can do. Spurgeon said, "Am I to do any great work for God? Then I must first be mighty upon my knees."

Together, we are stronger than we ever could be on our own. We are not performing by our own strength but by God's, and He has promised His presence when two or more seek Him together. How will He answer? What will He do? What blessings will only come from His hand if we ask?

There is only one way to find out.

Our Father is waiting. The door to the throne room is open, and we are welcomed with love and anticipation.

Why don't we ask Him? ❧

Excerpted and adapted from *The Lost Art of Praying Together* by James Banks, ©2009 Discovery House.

God's Offer of Peace

The first book of the Bible chronicles the account of the first peaceable kingdom, Eden. Then it goes on to tell of our tragic fall into sin and rebellion (GENESIS 1–3).

The New Testament begins with four great narratives about the One who humanly descended from Abraham to pay a dreadful price for our peace—the sacrificial Lamb who died for the sins of the world.

Finally, we come to the messianic kingdom of peace that will be replaced ultimately by the eternal kingdom that God wants every person to experience. Peter wrote:

> **Ultimate peace can be ours because of the One who sits on the throne of peace.**

The Lord is not slow in keeping his promise, as some understand slowness. Instead he is patient with you, not wanting anyone to perish, but everyone to come to repentance (2 PETER 3:9).

The Bible ends with an invitation to a world desperate to experience ultimate peace. That peace can be ours because of the One who sits on the throne of peace:

No longer will there be any curse. The throne of God and of the Lamb will be in the city, and his servants will serve him. They will see his face, and his name will be on their foreheads. There will be no more night. They will not need the light of a lamp or the light of the sun, for the Lord God will give them light. And they will reign for ever and ever (REVELATION 22:3–5).

Have you accepted God's offer of peace? ●

Adapted from *What Does the Bible Say about Peace?*
© 2007 Our Daily Bread Ministries.

¹³ Brothers and sisters, we do not want you to be uninformed about those who sleep in death, so that you do not grieve like the rest of mankind, who have no hope. ¹⁴ For we believe that Jesus died and rose again, and so we believe that God will bring with Jesus those who have fallen asleep in him. ¹⁵ According to the Lord's word, we tell you that we who are still alive, who are left until the coming of the Lord, will certainly not precede those who have fallen asleep. ¹⁶ For the Lord himself will come down from heaven, with a loud command, with the voice of the archangel and with the trumpet call of God, and the dead in Christ will rise first. ¹⁷ After that, we who are still alive and are left will be caught up together with them in the clouds to meet the Lord in the air. And so we will be with the LORD forever. ¹⁸ Therefore encourage one another with these words.

This Could Be the Year

My dad was a pastor, and on the first Sunday of each new year he preached about the return of Christ, often quoting from 1 Thessalonians 4. His point was always the same: "This could be the year that Jesus will return. Are you ready to meet Him?" I'll never forget hearing that sermon at age 6, thinking, *If that's true, I'm not sure I will be among those He's coming for.*

I felt certain that my parents would be going to heaven, and I wanted to go too. So, when my dad came home after church, I asked how I could be sure. He opened the Bible, read some verses to me, and talked to me about my need for a Savior. It didn't take much to convince me of my sins. That day, my dad led me to Christ. I will be forever grateful to him for planting these truths in my heart.

TODAY'S READING
1 Thess. 4:13–18

We who are still alive and are left will . . . meet the Lord in the air. And so we will be with the Lord forever.

1 Thessalonians 4:17

In an increasingly chaotic world, what a hopeful thought that this could be the year Jesus returns. More comforting still is the anticipation that all who trust Him for salvation will be gathered together, relieved from this world's suffering, sorrow, and fear. Best of all, we'll be with the Lord forever! ❂

JOE STOWELL

Lord, keep me always mindful of Your inevitable return.
Thanks for the assurance that this world is not all we have
but that a blessed eternity awaits all who trust in You.

Perhaps today! DR. M. R. DEHAAN

¹ Whoever dwells in the shelter of the Most High
    will rest in the shadow of the Almighty.
² I will say of the LORD, "He is my refuge and my
    fortress, my God, in whom I trust."
³ Surely he will save you
    from the fowler's snare
    and from the deadly pestilence.
⁴ He will cover you with his feathers,
    and under his wings you will find refuge;
    his faithfulness will be your shield and rampart.
⁵ You will not fear the terror of night,
    nor the arrow that flies by day,
⁶ nor the pestilence that stalks in the darkness,
    nor the plague that destroys at midday.
⁷ A thousand may fall at your side,
    ten thousand at your right hand,
    but it will not come near you.
⁸ You will only observe with your eyes
    and see the punishment of the wicked.
⁹ If you say, "The LORD is my refuge,"
    and you make the Most High your dwelling,
¹⁰ no harm will overtake you,
    no disaster will come near your tent.
¹¹ For he will command his angels concerning you
    to guard you in all your ways;
¹² they will lift you up in their hands,
    so that you will not strike your foot against a stone.
¹³ You will tread on the lion and the cobra;
    you will trample the great lion and the serpent.
¹⁴ "Because he loves me," says the LORD, "I will rescue him;
    I will protect him, for he acknowledges my name.
¹⁵ He will call on me, and I will answer him;
    I will be with him in trouble,
    I will deliver him and honor him.
¹⁶ With long life I will satisfy him
    and show him my salvation."

He Will Reply

was elated when I came upon the Twitter page of my favorite Korean movie star, so I decided to drop her a note. I crafted the best message I could and waited for a reply. I knew it was unlikely I would receive a response. A celebrity like her would receive an enormous amount of fan mail every day. Still, I hoped she would reply. But I was disappointed.

Thankfully, we know God responds to us. He is the "Most High," the "Almighty" (PS. 91:1). His position is exalted and His power is limitless, yet He is accessible to us. God invites: "Call upon Me, and I will answer" (V. 15 NKJV).

> **TODAY'S READING**
> **Psalm 91**
>
> **He will call on me, and I will answer him.** Psalm 91:15

An ancient legend tells of a monarch who hired weavers to make tapestries and garments for him. The king gave the silk and the patterns to the weavers with the strict instructions to seek his aid immediately if they had any difficulties. One young weaver was happy and successful while the others were always experiencing trouble. When the boy was asked why he was so successful, he said, "Didn't you notice how often I called for the king?" They replied, "Yes, but he's very busy, and we thought you were wrong in disturbing him so frequently." The boy answered, "I just took him at his word, and he was always happy to help me!"

Our God is like that king—only so much greater. He is loving and kind enough to care about our smallest concern and faintest whisper. 🌸

POH FANG CHIA

Lord, it's amazing to me that You—the God who created the universe— care about me and want me to come to You in prayer. Thank You for loving me so much.

We always have God's attention.

¹ Praise the Lord, my soul; all my inmost being, praise his holy name. ² Praise the Lord, my soul, and forget not all his benefits— ³ who forgives all your sins and heals all your diseases, ⁴ who redeems your life from the pit and crowns you with love and compassion, ⁵ who satisfies your desires with good things so that your youth is renewed like the eagle's.

⁶ The Lord works righteousness and justice for all the oppressed.

⁷ He made known his ways to Moses, his deeds to the people of Israel: ⁸ The Lord is compassionate and gracious, slow to anger, abounding in love.

⁹ He will not always accuse, nor will he harbor his anger forever; ¹⁰ he does not treat us as our sins deserve or repay us according to our iniquities.

¹¹ For as high as the heavens are above the earth, so great is his love for those who fear him; ¹² as far as the east is from the west, so far has he removed our transgressions from us.

¹³ As a father has compassion on his children, so the Lord has compassion on those who fear him; ¹⁴ for he knows how we are formed, he remembers that we are dust.

¹⁵ The life of mortals is like grass, they flourish like a flower of the field; ¹⁶ the wind blows over it and it is gone, and its place remembers it no more.

¹⁷ But from everlasting to everlasting the Lord's love is with those who fear him, and his righteousness with their children's children— ¹⁸ with those who keep his covenant and remember to obey his precepts.

¹⁹ The Lord has established his throne in heaven, and his kingdom rules over all. ²⁰ Praise the Lord, you his angels, you mighty ones who do his bidding, who obey his word.

²¹ Praise the Lord, all his heavenly hosts, you his servants who do his will.

All His Benefits

A recurring difficulty on our journey of life is becoming so focused on what we need at the moment that we forget what we already have. I was reminded of that when our church choir sang a beautiful anthem based on Psalm 103. "Bless the LORD, O my soul, and forget not all His benefits" (V. 2 NKJV). The Lord is our forgiver, healer, redeemer, provider, satisfier, and renewer (VV. 4–5). How could we forget that? And yet we often do when the events of daily life shift our attention to pressing needs, recurring failures, and circumstances that seem out of control.

TODAY'S READING
Psalm 103

Praise the LORD, my soul, and forget not all his benefits. Psalm 103:2

The writer of this psalm calls us to remember, "The LORD is compassionate and gracious . . . . He does not treat us as our sins deserve or repay us according to our iniquities. For as high as the heavens are above the earth, so great is his love for those who fear him" (VV. 8,10–11).

In our walk of faith, we come to Jesus Christ humbled by our unworthiness. There is no sense of entitlement as we receive His grace and are overwhelmed by the lavishness of His love. They remind us of all His benefits.

"Praise the LORD, my soul; all my inmost being, praise his holy name" (V. 1). ❀

DAVID MCCASLAND

Heavenly Father, we pause to consider all we have in You. Grant us eyes to see Your provision and help us to remember every benefit You have given to us.

Love was when God became a man.

26:39 Going a little farther, he fell with his face to the ground and prayed, "My Father, if it is possible, may this cup be taken from me. Yet not as I will, but as you will."

40 Then he returned to his disciples and found them sleeping. "Couldn't you men keep watch with me for one hour?" he asked Peter. 41 "Watch and pray so that you will not fall into temptation. The spirit is willing, but the flesh is weak."

42 He went away a second time and prayed, "My Father, if it is not possible for this cup to be taken away unless I drink it, may your will be done."

27:45 From noon until three in the afternoon darkness came over all the land. 46 About three in the afternoon Jesus cried out in a loud voice, *"Eli, Eli, lema sabachthani?"* (which means "My God, my God, why have you forsaken me?").

Is He Listening?

"**S**ometimes it feels** as if God isn't listening to me." Those words, from a woman who tried to stay strong in her walk with God while coping with an alcoholic husband, echo the heartcry of many believers. For many years, she asked God to change her husband. Yet it never happened.

What are we to think when we repeatedly ask God for something good—something that could easily glorify Him—but the answer doesn't come? Is He listening or not?

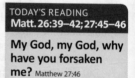

TODAY'S READING
Matt. 26:39–42; 27:45–46

My God, my God, why have you forsaken me? Matthew 27:46

Let's look at the life of the Savior. In the garden of Gethsemane, He agonized for hours in prayer, pouring out His heart and pleading, "Let this cup pass from Me" (MATT. 26:39 NKJV). But the Father's answer was clearly "No." To provide salvation, God had to send Jesus to die on the cross. Even though Jesus felt as if His Father had forsaken Him, He prayed intensely and passionately because He trusted that God was listening.

When we pray, we may not see how God is working or understand how He will bring good through it all. So we have to trust Him. We relinquish our rights and let God do what is best.

We must leave the unknowable to the all-knowing One. He is listening and working things out His way. 🌿 *DAVE BRANON*

Lord, we don't need to know the reason our prayers sometimes go unanswered. Help us just to wait for Your time, because You are good.

When we bend our knees to pray, God bends His ear to listen.

⁹ Do your best to come to me quickly, ¹⁰ for Demas, because he loved this world, has deserted me and has gone to Thessalonica. Crescens has gone to Galatia, and Titus to Dalmatia. ¹¹ Only Luke is with me. Get Mark and bring him with you, because he is helpful to me in my ministry. ¹² I sent Tychicus to Ephesus. ¹³ When you come, bring the cloak that I left with Carpus at Troas, and my scrolls, especially the parchments.

¹⁴ Alexander the metalworker did me a great deal of harm. The Lord will repay him for what he has done. ¹⁵ You too should be on your guard against him, because he strongly opposed our message.

¹⁶ At my first defense, no one came to my support, but everyone deserted me. May it not be held against them.

¹⁷ But the Lord stood at my side and gave me strength, so that through me the message might be fully proclaimed and all the Gentiles might hear it. And I was delivered from the lion's mouth. ¹⁸ The Lord will rescue me from every evil attack and will bring me safely to his heavenly kingdom. To him be glory for ever and ever. Amen.

The Lonely Season

Amid the pile of post-Christmas mail I discovered a treasure—a handmade Christmas card painted on repurposed cardstock. Simple watercolor strokes evoked a scene of wintry hills livened with evergreens. Centered at the bottom, framed by red-berried holly, was this hand-printed message:

Peace be with you!

The artist was a prisoner and a friend of mine. As I admired his handiwork, I realized I hadn't written to him in 2 years!

Long ago, another prisoner was neglected as he waited in prison. "Only Luke is with me," wrote the apostle Paul to Timothy (2 TIM. 4:11). "No one came to my support, but everyone deserted me" (V. 16). Yet Paul found encouragement even in prison, and he wrote, "The Lord stood at my side and gave me strength" (V. 17). But surely Paul felt the lonely ache of abandonment.

> **TODAY'S READING**
> **2 Timothy 4:9–18**
>
> **I have not stopped giving thanks for you, remembering you in my prayers.**
> Ephesians 1:16

On the back of that wonderful Christmas card my friend wrote, "May the peace and joy and hope and love brought about through the birth of Jesus be with you and yours." He signed it, "Your brother in Christ." I put the card on my wall as a reminder to pray for him. Then I wrote to him.

Throughout this coming year let's reach out to the loneliest of our brothers and sisters. 🕮

TIM GUSTAFSON

What lonely people can I think of right now? Newcomers to town? Prisoners? People in the hospital or in senior living centers? What can I do, no matter how small, to reach out to them?

Reach out in friendship and encourage the lonely.

²¹ The wicked borrow and do not repay,
  but the righteous give generously;
²² those the LORD blesses will inherit the land,
  but those he curses will be destroyed.
²³ The LORD makes firm the steps
  of the one who delights in him;
²⁴ though he may stumble, he will not fall,
  for the LORD upholds him with his hand.
²⁵ I was young and now I am old,
  yet I have never seen the righteous forsaken
  or their children begging bread.
²⁶ They are always generous and lend freely;
  their children will be a blessing.
²⁷ Turn from evil and do good;
  then you will dwell in the land forever.
²⁸ For the LORD loves the just
  and will not forsake his faithful ones.
Wrongdoers will be completely destroyed;
  the offspring of the wicked will perish.
²⁹ The righteous will inherit the land
  and dwell in it forever.
³⁰ The mouths of the righteous utter wisdom,
  and their tongues speak what is just.
³¹ The law of their God is in their hearts;
  their feet do not slip.

Ringing Reminders

The clock tower at Westminster, which contains the bell known as Big Ben, is an iconic landmark in London, England. It is traditionally thought that the melody of the tower chimes was taken from the tune of "I Know That My Redeemer Liveth" from Handel's *Messiah*. Words were eventually added and put on display in the clock room:

Lord, through this hour be Thou our guide;

So by Thy power no foot shall slide.

These words allude to Psalm 37: "The LORD directs the steps of the godly. He delights in every detail of their lives. Though they stumble, they will never

TODAY'S READING
Psalm 37:21–31

Though he may stumble, he will not fall, for the LORD upholds him with his hand. Psalm 37:24

fall, for the LORD holds them by the hand" (VV. 23–24 NLT). Notice how intimately involved God is in His children's experience: "He delights in every detail of their lives" (V. 23 NLT). Verse 31 adds, "The law of their God is in their hearts; their feet do not slip."

How extraordinary! The Creator of the universe not only upholds us and helps us but He also cares deeply about every moment we live. No wonder the apostle Peter was able to confidently invite us to "cast all your anxiety on him because he cares for you" (1 PETER 5:7). As the assurance of His care rings in our hearts, we find courage to face whatever comes our way. ✤

BILL CROWDER

Loving Father, thank You that every part of my life matters to You. Encourage me in my struggles so that I might walk in a way that reflects Your great love and honors Your great name.

No one is more secure than the one who is held in God's hand.

5 "And when you pray, do not be like the hypocrites, for they love to pray standing in the synagogues and on the street corners to be seen by others. Truly I tell you, they have received their reward in full. 6 But when you pray, go into your room, close the door and pray to your Father, who is unseen. Then your Father, who sees what is done in secret, will reward you. 7 And when you pray, do not keep on babbling like pagans, for they think they will be heard because of their many words. 8 Do not be like them, for your Father knows what you need before you ask him.

9 "This, then, is how you should pray:

"'Our Father in heaven,
hallowed be your name,
10 your kingdom come,
your will be done,
    on earth as it is in heaven.

Starting Upstream

My home sits along a creek in a canyon in the shadow of a large mountain. During the spring snowmelt and after heavy rains this stream swells and acts more like a river than a creek. People have drowned in it. One day I traced the origin of the creek to its very source, a snowfield atop the mountain. From there the melted snow begins the long journey down the mountain, joining other rivulets to take shape as the creek below my house.

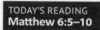

TODAY'S READING
Matthew 6:5–10

Your Father knows what you need before you ask him. Matthew 6:8

It occurs to me, thinking about prayer, that most of the time I get the direction wrong. I start downstream with my own concerns and bring them to God. I inform God, as if God did not already know. I plead with God, as if hoping to change God's mind and overcome divine reluctance. Instead, I should start upstream where the flow begins.

When we shift direction, we realize that God already cares about our concerns—a loved one's cancer, a broken family, a rebellious teenager—more than we do. Our Father knows what we need (MATT. 6:8).

Grace, like water, descends to the lowest part. Streams of mercy flow. We begin with God and ask what part we can play in His work on earth. With this new starting point for prayer, our perceptions change. We look at nature and see the signature of the grand Artist. We look at human beings and see individuals of eternal destiny made in God's image. Thanksgiving and praise surge up to Him as a natural response. ❀

PHILIP YANCEY

Dear Lord, I praise You for loving and caring for me so much.
What would I ever do without You?

Prayer channels God's supply to our needs.

31 To the Jews who had believed him, Jesus said, "If you hold to my teaching, you are really my disciples. 32 Then you will know the truth, and the truth will set you free."

33 They answered him, "We are Abraham's descendants and have never been slaves of anyone. How can you say that we shall be set free?"

34 Jesus replied, "Very truly I tell you, everyone who sins is a slave to sin. 35 Now a slave has no permanent place in the family, but a son belongs to it forever. 36 So if the Son sets you free, you will be free indeed. 37 I know that you are Abraham's descendants. Yet you are looking for a way to kill me, because you have no room for my word. 38 I am telling you what I have seen in the Father's presence, and you are doing what you have heard from your father."

The Best Kind of Happiness

"**E**verybody's doing it**"** seemed like a winning argument when I was young. My parents never gave in to such pleas no matter how desperate I was to get permission to do something they believed was unsafe or unwise.

As we get older we add excuses and rationalizations to our repertoire of arguments for having our own way: "No one will get hurt." "It's not illegal." "He did it to me first." "She won't find out." Behind each argument is the belief that what we want is more important than anything else.

Eventually, this faulty way of thinking becomes the basis for our beliefs about God. One of the lies we sometimes choose to believe is that we, not God, are the center of the universe. We think we will be

TODAY'S READING
John 8:31–38

If you hold to my teaching, you are really my disciples. Then you will know the truth, and the truth will set you free. John 8:31–32

carefree and happy only when we reorder the world according to our desires. This lie is convincing because it promises an easier, speedier way to get what we want. It argues, "God is love, so He wants me to do whatever will make me happy." But this way of thinking leads to heartache, not happiness.

Jesus told those who believed in Him that the truth would make them truly free (JOHN 8:31–32). But He also warned, "Everyone who sins is a slave to sin" (V. 34). The best kind of happiness comes from the freedom we find when we accept the truth that Jesus is the way to a full and satisfying life. 🌿

JULIE ACKERMAN LINK

Lord, we confess our tendency to rationalize everything to get what we think we want. Guide us today so that we choose to obey Your commands instead of pursuing our own desires.
There are no shortcuts to true happiness.

¹ In that day you will say:
"I will praise you, LORD.
    Although you were angry with me,
    your anger has turned away
and you have comforted me.
² Surely God is my salvation;
    I will trust and not be afraid.
The LORD, the LORD himself, is my strength and my defense;
    he has become my salvation."
³ With joy you will draw water
    from the wells of salvation.
⁴ In that day you will say:
"Give praise to the LORD, proclaim his name;
    make known among the nations what he has done,
    and proclaim that his name is exalted.
⁵ Sing to the LORD, for he has done glorious things;
    let this be known to all the world.
⁶ Shout aloud and sing for joy, people of Zion,
    for great is the Holy One of Israel among you."

Wells of Salvation

When people drill holes deep into the earth, it is normally for pulling up core samples of rock, accessing oil, or finding water.

In Isaiah 12, we learn that God wanted His people, who were living in a spiritual desert as well as a geographical desert, to discover His "wells of salvation." The prophet Isaiah compared God's salvation to a well from which the most refreshing of all waters can be drawn. After many years of turning their back on God, the nation of Judah was destined for exile as God allowed foreign invaders to conquer the nation, scattering the people. Yet, said the prophet Isaiah, a remnant would eventually return to their homeland as a sign that God was with them (ISA. 11:11–12).

> **TODAY'S READING**
> **Isaiah 12**
>
> With joy you will draw water from the wells of salvation. Isaiah 12:3

Isaiah 12 is a hymn, praising God for His faithfulness in keeping His promises, especially the promise of salvation. Isaiah encouraged the people that deep in God's "wells of salvation" they would experience the cool water of God's grace, strength, and joy (VV. 1–3). This would refresh and strengthen their hearts and cause praise and gratitude to God (VV. 4–6).

God wants each of us to discover through confession and repentance the deep, cool waters of joy found in the everlasting well of His salvation.

MARVIN WILLIAMS

What will you do to draw deeply from God's well to find His joy, refreshment, and strength?

The wells of God's salvation never run dry.

¹ Then the Lord said to Joshua: ² "Tell the Israelites to designate the cities of refuge, as I instructed you through Moses, ³ so that anyone who kills a person accidentally and unintentionally may flee there and find protection from the avenger of blood. ⁴ When they flee to one of these cities, they are to stand in the entrance of the city gate and state their case before the elders of that city. Then the elders are to admit the fugitive into their city and provide a place to live among them. ⁵ If the avenger of blood comes in pursuit, the elders must not surrender the fugitive, because the fugitive killed their neighbor unintentionally and without malice aforethought. ⁶ They are to stay in that city until they have stood trial before the assembly and until the death of the high priest who is serving at that time. Then they may go back to their own home in the town from which they fled."

⁷ So they set apart Kedesh in Galilee in the hill country of Naphtali, Shechem in the hill country of Ephraim, and Kiriath Arba (that is, Hebron) in the hill country of Judah. ⁸ East of the Jordan (on the other side from Jericho) they designated Bezer in the wilderness on the plateau in the tribe of Reuben, Ramoth in Gilead in the tribe of Gad, and Golan in Bashan in the tribe of Manasseh. ⁹ Any of the Israelites or any foreigner residing among them who killed someone accidentally could flee to these designated cities and not be killed by the avenger of blood prior to standing trial before the assembly.

True Shelter

I n March 2014 a tribal conflict broke out in my hometown area, forcing my father's household, along with other refugees, to take cover in the region's capital city. Throughout history, people who have felt unsafe in their homelands have traveled to other places searching for safety and something better.

As I visited and talked with people from my hometown, I thought of the cities of refuge in Joshua 20:1–9. These were cities designated as places of safety for those fleeing from "relatives seeking revenge" in the case of an accidental killing (V. 3 NLT). They offered peace and protection.

> **TODAY'S READING**
> **Joshua 20:1–9**
>
> **The name of the LORD is a fortified tower; the righteous run to it and are safe.**
>
> Proverbs 18:10

People today still seek places of refuge, although for a variety of reasons. But as needed as these sanctuaries are, supplying shelter and food, they cannot completely meet the needs of refugees and fugitives. That rest is found only in God. Those who walk with God find true shelter and the safest protection in Him. When ancient Israel was sent into exile, the Lord said, "I have been a sanctuary [safe haven] for them in the countries where they have gone" (EZEK. 11:16).

With the psalmist, we can say confidently to the Lord, "You are my hiding place; you will protect me from trouble and surround me with songs of deliverance" (32:7).   *LAWRENCE DARMANI*

Father, thank You for being a rock to which we can flee and that no matter where we are or in what circumstances we find ourselves, You are there with us. Help us to remember that even in the darkest of nights, You are our strong tower.

Nothing can shake those who are secure in God's hands.

⁶ You see, at just the right time, when we were still powerless, Christ died for the ungodly. ⁷ Very rarely will anyone die for a righteous person, though for a good person someone might possibly dare to die. ⁸ But God demonstrates his own love for us in this: While we were still sinners, Christ died for us.

⁹ Since we have now been justified by his blood, how much more shall we be saved from God's wrath through him! ¹⁰ For if, while we were God's enemies, we were reconciled to him through the death of his Son, how much more, having been reconciled, shall we be saved through his life! ¹¹ Not only is this so, but we also boast in God through our Lord Jesus Christ, through whom we have now received reconciliation.

You Have Value

After my mother-in-law died, my wife and I discovered a cache of US Indian Head pennies in a dresser drawer in her apartment. She wasn't a coin collector, as such, but she lived in the era when these pennies were in circulation and she had accumulated a few.

Some of these coins are in excellent condition; others are not. They are so worn and tarnished you can hardly see the imprint. All bear the stamp "One Cent" on the opposite side. Although a penny these days has little value and many consider them useless, this one-cent coin would have bought a newspaper in its day. And collectors still find value in them, even those that have been battered and abused.

TODAY'S READING
Romans 5:6–11

You were bought at a price.
1 Corinthians 6:20

Perhaps you feel tarnished, worn, old, or out of circulation. Even so, God finds value in you. The Creator of the universe wants you—not for your mind, your body, your clothes, your achievements, your intellect, or your personality, but because you are you! He would go any distance and pay any price to possess you (1 COR. 6:20).

In fact He did. He came down to earth from heaven and purchased you with His own blood (ROM. 5:6, 8–9). That's how much He wants you. You are valuable in His eyes, and He loves you. 🌼

DAVID ROPER

As I think about Your love for me, Father, I wonder with amazement how You could love someone like me—and I praise You.

Christ's death is the measure of God's love for you.

⁷ "To the angel of the church in Philadelphia write:
These are the words of him who is holy and true, who
holds the key of David. What he opens no one can shut,
and what he shuts no one can open. ⁸ I know your deeds.
See, I have placed before you an open door that no one can
shut. I know that you have little strength, yet you have kept
my word and have not denied my name. ⁹ I will make those
who are of the synagogue of Satan, who claim to be Jews
though they are not, but are liars—I will make them come and
fall down at your feet and acknowledge that I have loved you.
¹⁰ Since you have kept my command to endure patiently, I will
also keep you from the hour of trial that is going to come on
the whole world to test the inhabitants of the earth.

¹¹ I am coming soon. Hold on to what you have, so that
no one will take your crown. ¹² The one who is victorious I
will make a pillar in the temple of my God. Never again will
they leave it. I will write on them the name of my God and
the name of the city of my God, the new Jerusalem, which is
coming down out of heaven from my God; and I will also write
on them my new name. ¹³ Whoever has ears, let them hear
what the Spirit says to the churches.

Hold On!

A cowboy friend of mine who grew up on a ranch in Texas has a number of colorful sayings. One of my favorites is "It don't take much water to make good coffee." And when someone ropes a steer too big to handle or is in some kind of trouble, my friend will shout, "Hold everything you've got!" meaning "Help is on the way! Don't let go!"

In the book of Revelation we find letters to "the seven churches in the province of Asia" (CHS. 2–3). These messages from God are filled with encouragement, rebuke, and challenge, and they speak to

TODAY'S READING
Revelation 3:7–13

I am coming soon. Hold on to what you have. Revelation 3:11

us today just as they did to the first-century recipients.

Twice in these letters we find the phrase, "Hold on to what you have." The Lord told the church at Thyatira, "Hold on to what you have until I come" (2:25). And to the church in Philadelphia He said, "I am coming soon. Hold on to what you have, so that no one will take your crown" (3:11). In the midst of great trials and opposition, these believers clung to God's promises and persevered in faith.

When our circumstances are harsh and sorrows outnumber joys, Jesus shouts to us, "Hold everything you've got! Help is on the way!" And with that promise, we can hold on in faith and rejoice.

DAVID MCCASLAND

Lord, we cling to Your promise, expect Your return, and hold on
with confidence as we say, "Even so, come, Lord Jesus!"

The promise of Christ's return calls us to persevere in faith.

[1] "Very truly I tell you Pharisees, anyone who does not enter the sheep pen by the gate, but climbs in by some other way, is a thief and a robber. [2] The one who enters by the gate is the shepherd of the sheep. [3] The gatekeeper opens the gate for him, and the sheep listen to his voice. He calls his own sheep by name and leads them out. [4] When he has brought out all his own, he goes on ahead of them, and his sheep follow him because they know his voice. [5] But they will never follow a stranger; in fact, they will run away from him because they do not recognize a stranger's voice." [6] Jesus used this figure of speech, but the Pharisees did not understand what he was telling them.

[7] Therefore Jesus said again, "Very truly I tell you, I am the gate for the sheep. [8] All who have come before me are thieves and robbers, but the sheep have not listened to them. [9] I am the gate; whoever enters through me will be saved. They will come in and go out, and find pasture."

Gates of Paradise

talian artist **Lorenzo Ghiberti** (1378–1455) spent years skillfully crafting images of Jesus's life into the bronze doors of Italy's Florence Baptistery. These bronze reliefs were so moving that Michelangelo called them the Gates of Paradise.

As an artistic treasure, the doors greet visitors with echoes of the gospel story. It was Jesus who said, "I am the gate; whoever enters through me will be saved" (JOHN 10:9). On the night before His crucifixion, He told His disciples, "I am the way and the truth and the life. No one comes to the Father except through me" (14:6). Within a few hours Jesus would say to one of the criminals being crucified at His side, "Today you will be with me in paradise" (LUKE 23:43).

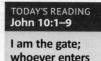

TODAY'S READING
John 10:1–9

I am the gate; whoever enters through me will be saved. John 10:9

The apostle Peter a few weeks later boldly proclaimed to those who had called for Jesus's death that "there is no other name under heaven . . . by which we must be saved" (ACTS 4:12). Years later, the apostle Paul wrote that there is only one mediator between God and humanity—the man Christ Jesus (1 TIM. 2:5).

The gates of paradise are found in the Savior who offers everlasting life to all who believe and come to Him. Enter into the joy of His salvation. 🌱

DENNIS FISHER

I needed a mediator because of my sin. Thank You, Jesus, for being the way to the Father by Your death and resurrection.
I will be forever grateful.

Jesus died in our place to give us His peace.

⁵⁷ As they were walking along the road, a man said to him, "I will follow you wherever you go."

⁵⁸ Jesus replied, "Foxes have dens and birds have nests, but the Son of Man has no place to lay his head."

⁵⁹ He said to another man, "Follow me."

But he replied, "Lord, first let me go and bury my father."

⁶⁰ Jesus said to him, "Let the dead bury their own dead, but you go and proclaim the kingdom of God."

⁶¹ Still another said, "I will follow you, Lord; but first let me go back and say goodbye to my family."

⁶² Jesus replied, "No one who puts a hand to the plow and looks back is fit for service in the kingdom of God."

Saying Goodbye

Saying goodbye is hard—to family and friends, to a favorite and familiar place, to an occupation or livelihood.

In Luke 9:57–62 our Lord describes the cost of being His disciple. A would-be follower says to Jesus, "I will follow you, Lord; but first let me go back and say goodbye to my family." Jesus responds, "No one who puts a hand to the plow and looks back is fit for service in the kingdom of God" (VV. 61–62). Is He asking His followers to say goodbye to everything and every relationship considered precious?

TODAY'S READING
Luke 9:57–62

> No one who puts a hand to the plow and looks back is fit for service in the kingdom of God. Luke 9:62

In the Chinese language there is no direct equivalent of the English word *goodbye*. The two Chinese characters used to translate this word really mean "see you again." Becoming a disciple of Christ may sometimes mean others will reject us, but it does not mean we say goodbye to people in the sense that we are to forget all our past relationships. Saying goodbye means that God wants us to follow Him on His terms—wholeheartedly. Then we will see people again from the right perspective.

God wants the best for us, but we must allow Him to take priority over everything else. 🌱

C. P. HIA

> **Dear Lord,** I want to follow You wholeheartedly.
> Help me not to place anything or anyone before You.

When we follow Jesus we get a new perspective.

¹⁶ So from now on we regard no one from a worldly point of view. Though we once regarded Christ in this way, we do so no longer. ¹⁷ Therefore, if anyone is in Christ, the new creation has come: The old has gone, the new is here! ¹⁸ All this is from God, who reconciled us to himself through Christ and gave us the ministry of reconciliation: ¹⁹ that God was reconciling the world to himself in Christ, not counting people's sins against them. And he has committed to us the message of reconciliation. ²⁰ We are therefore Christ's ambassadors, as though God were making his appeal through us. We implore you on Christ's behalf: Be reconciled to God. ²¹ God made him who had no sin to be sin for us, so that in him we might become the righteousness of God.

Minister of Reconciliation

A s Dr. Martin Luther King Jr. preached on a Sunday morning in 1957, he fought the temptation to retaliate against a society steeped in racism.

"How do you go about loving your enemies?" he asked the Dexter Avenue Baptist congregation in Montgomery, Alabama. "Begin with yourself. . . . When the opportunity presents itself for you to defeat your enemy, that is the time which you must not do it."

Quoting from the words of Jesus, King said: "Love your enemies, bless them that curse you, do good to them that hate you, and pray for them which despitefully use you . . . ; that ye may be the children of your Father which is in heaven" (MATT. 5:44–45 KJV).

> **TODAY'S READING**
> **2 Cor. 5:16–21**
>
> **While we were God's enemies, we were reconciled to him through the death of his Son.**
>
> Romans 5:10

As we consider those who harm us, we are wise to remember our former status as enemies of God (SEE ROM. 5:10). But "[God] reconciled us to himself through Christ and gave us the ministry of reconciliation," wrote Paul (2 COR. 5:18). Now we have a holy obligation. "He has committed to us the message of reconciliation" (V. 19). We are to take that message to the world.

Racial and political tensions are nothing new. But the business of the church is never to feed divisiveness. We should not attack those unlike us or those who hold different opinions or even those who seek our destruction. Ours is a "ministry of reconciliation" that imitates the selfless servant-heart of Jesus.

TIM GUSTAFSON

In Christ there is no east or west, in Him no south or north, but one great fellowship of love throughout the whole wide earth. JOHN OXENHAM

Hate destroys the hater as well as the hated. MARTIN LUTHER KING JR.

¹¹ We have much to say about this, but it is hard to make it clear to you because you no longer try to understand. ¹² In fact, though by this time you ought to be teachers, you need someone to teach you the elementary truths of God's word all over again. You need milk, not solid food! ¹³ Anyone who lives on milk, being still an infant, is not acquainted with the teaching about righteousness. ¹⁴ But solid food is for the mature, who by constant use have trained themselves to distinguish good from evil.

Desiring Growth

The axolotl (pronounced ACK suh LAH tuhl) is a biological enigma. Instead of maturing into adult form, this endangered Mexican salamander retains tadpole-like characteristics throughout its life. Writers and philosophers have used the axolotl as a symbol of someone who fears growth.

TODAY'S READING
Hebrews 5:11–14

Anyone who lives on milk . . . is not acquainted with the teaching about righteousness.

Herews 5:13

In Hebrews 5 we learn about Christians who were avoiding healthy growth, remaining content with spiritual "milk" intended for new believers. Perhaps because of fear of persecution, they weren't growing in the kind of faithfulness to Christ that would enable them to be strong enough to suffer with Him for the sake of others (VV. 7-10). Instead they were in danger of sliding backward from the Christlike attitudes they had already shown (6:9-11). They weren't ready for a solid diet of self-sacrifice (5:14). So the author wrote, "We have much to say about this, but it is hard to make it clear to you because you no longer try to understand" (v. 11).

Axolotls follow the natural pattern set for them by their Creator. But followers of Christ are designed to grow into spiritual maturity. As we do, we discover that growing up in Him involves more than our own peace and joy. Growth in His likeness honors God as we unselfishly encourage others.    *KEILA OCHOA*

Lord, I want to grow, so help me to go deeper into Your Word. Teach me more each day, so that I am better equipped to serve and worship You.

The more we live on a diet of God's Word, the more we grow.

⁶ Now, brothers and sisters, if I come to you and speak in tongues, what good will I be to you, unless I bring you some revelation or knowledge or prophecy or word of instruction? ⁷ Even in the case of lifeless things that make sounds, such as the pipe or harp, how will anyone know what tune is being played unless there is a distinction in the notes? ⁸ Again, if the trumpet does not sound a clear call, who will get ready for battle? ⁹ So it is with you. Unless you speak intelligible words with your tongue, how will anyone know what you are saying? You will just be speaking into the air.

¹⁰ Undoubtedly there are all sorts of languages in the world, yet none of them is without meaning. ¹¹ If then I do not grasp the meaning of what someone is saying, I am a foreigner to the speaker, and the speaker is a foreigner to me. ¹² So it is with you. Since you are eager for gifts of the Spirit, try to excel in those that build up the church.

²⁶ What then shall we say, brothers and sisters? When you come together, each of you has a hymn, or a word of instruction, a revelation, a tongue or an interpretation. Everything must be done so that the church may be built up.

A Hint of Heaven

The world-class botanical garden across the street from our church was the setting for an all-church community gathering. As I walked around the gardens greeting people I have known for years, catching up with those I hadn't seen recently, and enjoying the beautiful surroundings cared for by people who know and love plants, I realized that the evening was rich with symbols of how the church is supposed to function—a little hint of heaven on earth.

TODAY'S READING
1 Cor. 14:6–12,26

A garden is a place where each plant is placed in an environment in which it will thrive. Gardeners prepare the soil, protect the plants from pests, and make sure each one receives the food, water, and sunlight it needs. The result is a beautiful, colorful, and fragrant place for people to enjoy.

Since you are eager for gifts of the Spirit, try to excel in those that build up the church.

1 Corinthians 14:12

Like a garden, church is meant to be a place where everyone works together for the glory of God and the good of all; a place where everyone flourishes because we are living in a safe environment; a place where people are cared for according to their needs; where each of us does work we love—work that benefits others (1 COR. 14:26).

Like well-cared-for plants, people growing in a healthy environment have a sweet fragrance that draws people to God by displaying the beauty of His love. The church is not perfect, but it really is a hint of heaven.

JULIE ACKERMAN LINK

How can you promote the health of your church? Ask God to help you serve others as Christ serves us. Serve in a role that matches your skills and interests. Listen well to others and pray for them.

Hearts fragrant with the love of Christ display His beauty.

Ephesians 2:4-7

⁴ But because of his great love for us, God, who is rich in mercy, ⁵ made us alive with Christ even when we were dead in transgressions—it is by grace you have been saved. ⁶ And God raised us up with Christ and seated us with him in the heavenly realms in Christ Jesus, ⁷ in order that in the coming ages he might show the incomparable riches of his grace, expressed in his kindness to us in Christ Jesus.

What's in the Bank?

I n the winter of 2009, a large passenger plane made an emergency landing in New York's Hudson River. The pilot, Captain Chesley Sullenberger, who landed the plane safely with no casualties, was later asked about those moments in the air when he was faced with a life-or-death decision. "One way of looking at this," he said, "might be that for 42 years I've been making small, regular deposits in this bank of experience, education, and training. And on [that day] the balance was sufficient so that I could make a very large withdrawal."

Most of us will at some time face a crisis. Perhaps it will be a job termination or the results of a medical test, or the loss of a precious family member or friend. It is in those times that we must dig down deep into the reserves of our spiritual bank account.

TODAY'S READING
Ephesians 2:4–7

Let us then approach God's throne of grace with confidence, so that we may receive mercy and find grace to help us in our time of need. Hebrews 4:16

And what might we find there? If we have enjoyed a deepening relationship with God, we've been making regular "deposits" of faith. We have experienced His grace (2 COR. 8:9; EPH. 2:4–7). We trust the promise of Scripture that God is just and faithful (DEUT. 32:4; 2 THESS. 3:3).

God's love and grace are available when His children need to make a "withdrawal" (PS. 9:10; HEB. 4:16). 🌐   *CINDY HESS KASPER*

Great is Your faithfulness, O Lord God! Each day I see You provide
for me and show me mercy. Thank You.

Remembering God's faithfulness in the past strengthens us for the future.

¹ Therefore if you have any encouragement from being united with Christ, if any comfort from his love, if any common sharing in the Spirit, if any tenderness and compassion, ² then make my joy complete by being like-minded, having the same love, being one in spirit and of one mind. ³ Do nothing out of selfish ambition or vain conceit. Rather, in humility value others above yourselves, ⁴ not looking to your own interests but each of you to the interests of the others.

⁵ In your relationships with one another, have the same mindset as Christ Jesus:

⁶ Who, being in very nature God, did not consider equality with God something to be used to his own advantage;

⁷ rather, he made himself nothing by taking the very nature of a servant, being made in human likeness.

⁸ And being found in appearance as a man, he humbled himself by becoming obedient to death—even death on a cross!

⁹ Therefore God exalted him to the highest place and gave him the name that is above every name,

¹⁰ that at the name of Jesus every knee should bow, in heaven and on earth and under the earth,

¹¹ and every tongue acknowledge that Jesus Christ is Lord, to the glory of God the Father.

You First!

Tibetan-born Sherpa Nawang Gombu and American Jim Whittaker reached the top of Mount Everest on May 1, 1963. As they approached the peak, each considered the honor of being the first of the two to step to the summit. Whittaker motioned for Gombu to move ahead, but Gombu declined with a smile, saying, "You first, Big Jim!" Finally, they decided to step to the summit at the same time.

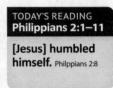

TODAY'S READING
Philippians 2:1–11

[Jesus] humbled himself. Philippians 2:8

Paul encouraged the Philippian believers to demonstrate this kind of humility. He said, "Let each of you look out not only for his own interests, but also for the interests of others" (PHIL. 2:4 NKJV). Selfishness and superiority can divide people, but humility unites us, since it is the quality of "being one in spirit and of one mind" (V. 2).

When quarrels and disagreements occur, we can often diffuse them by giving up our right to be right. Humility calls us to show grace and gentleness when we would rather insist on our own way. "In humility value others above yourselves" (V. 3).

Practicing humility helps us to become more like Jesus who, for our sake, "humbled himself by becoming obedient to death" (VV. 7–8). Following in Jesus's footsteps means backing away from what is best for us and doing what is best for others. 🍂

JENNIFER BENSON SCHULDT

Jesus, You gave up Your life for me.
Help me to see each sacrifice I make as a reflection of Your humility.
In putting others first, let me honor You.

Humility promotes unity.

¹⁷ Join together in following my example, brothers and sisters, and just as you have us as a model, keep your eyes on those who live as we do. ¹⁸ For, as I have often told you before and now tell you again even with tears, many live as enemies of the cross of Christ. ¹⁹ Their destiny is destruction, their god is their stomach, and their glory is in their shame. Their mind is set on earthly things. ²⁰ But our citizenship is in heaven. And we eagerly await a Savior from there, the Lord Jesus Christ, ²¹ who, by the power that enables him to bring everything under his control, will transform our lowly bodies so that they will be like his glorious body.

Real People, Real God

Several years ago I received a letter from an *Our Daily Bread* reader after I had written about a family tragedy. "When you told about your tragedy," this person wrote, "I realized that the writers were real people with real problems." How true that is! I look across the list of men and women who pen these articles, and I see cancer and wayward children and unfulfilled dreams and many other kinds of loss. We are indeed just regular, real people writing about a real God who understands our real problems.

TODAY'S READING
Philippians 3:17–21

Join together in following my example. Philippians 3:17

The apostle Paul stands out in the Real People Hall of Fame. He had physical problems. He had legal issues. He had interpersonal relationship struggles to deal with. And in all of this messy reality, he was setting an example for us. In Philippians 3:17, he said, "Join together in following my example, brothers and sisters, and just as you have us as a model, keep your eyes on those who live as we do."

Those around us who need the gospel—who need Jesus— are looking for believable people who can point them to our perfect Savior. And that means we must be real. 🌱 *DAVE BRANON*

> **You, Lord,** are perfection. Yet You welcome us imperfect people to come to You for salvation. You sent Your perfect Son to earth to die for us. Help us to be real and genuine as we seek to point people to You.

If we are true to God, we will not be false to people.

¹¹ Jesus continued: "There was a man who had two sons. ¹² The younger one said to his father, 'Father, give me my share of the estate.' So he divided his property between them.

¹³ "Not long after that, the younger son got together all he had, set off for a distant country and there squandered his wealth in wild living. ¹⁴ After he had spent everything, there was a severe famine in that whole country, and he began to be in need. ¹⁵ So he went and hired himself out to a citizen of that country, who sent him to his fields to feed pigs. ¹⁶ He longed to fill his stomach with the pods that the pigs were eating, but no one gave him anything.

¹⁷ "When he came to his senses, he said, 'How many of my father's hired servants have food to spare, and here I am starving to death! ¹⁸ I will set out and go back to my father and say to him: Father, I have sinned against heaven and against you. ¹⁹ I am no longer worthy to be called your son; make me like one of your hired servants.' ²⁰ So he got up and went to his father.

"But while he was still a long way off, his father saw him and was filled with compassion for him; he ran to his son, threw his arms around him and kissed him.

²¹ "The son said to him, 'Father, I have sinned against heaven and against you. I am no longer worthy to be called your son.'

²² "But the father said to his servants, 'Quick! Bring the best robe and put it on him. Put a ring on his finger and sandals on his feet. ²³ Bring the fattened calf and kill it. Let's have a feast and celebrate. ²⁴ For this son of mine was dead and is alive again; he was lost and is found.' So they began to celebrate.

Welcome Home!

When we were going through a particularly challenging time with our son, a friend pulled me aside after a church meeting. "I want you to know that I pray for you and your son every day," he said. Then he added: "I feel so guilty."

"Why?" I asked.

"Because I've never had to deal with prodigal children," he said. "My kids pretty much played by the rules. But it wasn't because of anything I did or didn't do. Kids," he shrugged, "make their own choices."

I wanted to hug him. His compassion was a reminder, a gift from God, communicating to me the Father's understanding for my struggle with my son.

No one understands the struggle with prodigals better than our heavenly Father. The story of the prodigal son in Luke 15 is our story and God's. Jesus told it on behalf of all sinners who so desperately need to come home to their Creator and discover the warmth of a loving relationship with Him.

Jesus is God in the flesh seeing us in the distance and looking on us with compassion. He is God running to us and throwing His arms around us. He is heaven's kiss welcoming the repentant sinner home (V. 20).

God hasn't just left the porch light on for us. He's out on the front porch watching, waiting, calling us home. ✤ *JAMES BANKS*

> TODAY'S READING
> **Luke 15:11–24**
>
> **While he was still a long way off, his father saw him and was filled with compassion for him.** Luke 15:20

We ask again today, Lord, that our prodigals would come home.

James Banks is author of *Prayers for Prodigals* from Discovery House.

Our loved ones may spurn our appeals, reject our message, oppose our arguments, despise our persons—but they are helpless against our prayers.
J. SIDLOW BAXTER

¹⁵ I do not understand what I do. For what I want to do I do not do, but what I hate I do. ¹⁶ And if I do what I do not want to do, I agree that the law is good. ¹⁷ As it is, it is no longer I myself who do it, but it is sin living in me. ¹⁸ For I know that good itself does not dwell in me, that is, in my sinful nature. For I have the desire to do what is good, but I cannot carry it out. ¹⁹ For I do not do the good I want to do, but the evil I do not want to do—this I keep on doing. ²⁰ Now if I do what I do not want to do, it is no longer I who do it, but it is sin living in me that does it.

²¹ So I find this law at work: Although I want to do good, evil is right there with me. ²² For in my inner being I delight in God's law; ²³ but I see another law at work in me, waging war against the law of my mind and making me a prisoner of the law of sin at work within me. ²⁴ What a wretched man I am! Who will rescue me from this body that is subject to death? ²⁵ Thanks be to God, who delivers me through Jesus Christ our Lord!

So then, I myself in my mind am a slave to God's law, but in my sinful nature a slave to the law of sin.

A Prisoner No More

A **middle-aged man approached** me after I led a workshop at his place of employment and asked this question: "I've been a Christian nearly my whole life, but I'm constantly disappointed in myself. Why is it that I always seem to keep doing the things I wish I didn't do and never seem to do the things I know I should? Isn't God getting tired of me?" Two men standing next to me also seemed eager to hear the response.

> TODAY'S READING
> **Romans 7:15–25**

That's a common struggle that even the apostle Paul experienced. "I do not understand what I do," he said, "For what I want to do I do not do, but what I hate I do" (ROM. 7:15). But here's some good

> **I do not understand what I do. For what I want to do I do not do, but what I hate I do.** Romans 7:15

news: We don't have to stay in that trap of discouragement. To paraphrase Paul as he writes in Romans 8, the key is to stop focusing on the law and start focusing on Jesus. We can't do anything about our sinfulness in our own strength. The answer is not "try harder to be good at keeping the rules." Instead, we must focus on the One who shows us mercy and cooperate with the Spirit who changes us.

When we focus on the law, we are constantly reminded that we'll never be good enough to deserve God's grace. But when we focus on Jesus, we become more like Him. *RANDY KILGORE*

I sometimes get caught in the cycle of trying harder to be good, failing, getting discouraged, and giving up.
Help me, Lord, to depend on Your grace and to draw near to You so that You can change my heart.

Focus on Jesus.

¹ A good name is more desirable than great riches;
  to be esteemed is better than silver or gold.
² Rich and poor have this in common:
  The LORD is the Maker of them all.
³ The prudent see danger and take refuge,
  but the simple keep going and pay the penalty.
⁴ Humility is the fear of the LORD;
  its wages are riches and honor and life.
⁵ In the paths of the wicked are snares and pitfalls,
  but those who would preserve their life stay far from
them.
⁶ Start children off on the way they should go,
  and even when they are old they will not turn from it.
⁷ The rich rule over the poor,
  and the borrower is slave to the lender.
⁸ Whoever sows injustice reaps calamity,
  and the rod they wield in fury will be broken.
⁹ The generous will themselves be blessed,
  for they share their food with the poor.
¹⁰ Drive out the mocker, and out goes strife;
  quarrels and insults are ended.
¹¹ One who loves a pure heart and who speaks with grace
  will have the king for a friend.
¹² The eyes of the LORD keep watch over knowledge,
  but he frustrates the words of the unfaithful.
¹³ The sluggard says, "There's a lion outside!
  I'll be killed in the public square!"
¹⁴ The mouth of an adulterous woman is a deep pit;
  a man who is under the LORD's wrath falls into it.
¹⁵ Folly is bound up in the heart of a child,
  but the rod of discipline will drive it far away.
¹⁶ One who oppresses the poor to increase his wealth
  and one who gives gifts to the rich—both come to poverty.

Lessons for Little Ones

When my daughter described a problem she was having in the school lunchroom, I immediately wondered how I could fix the issue for her. But then another thought occurred. Maybe God had allowed the problem so she could see Him at work and get to know Him better. Instead of running to the rescue, I decided to pray with her. The trouble cleared up without any help from me!

TODAY'S READING
Proverbs 22:1–16

Start children off on the way they should go. Proverbs 22:6

This situation showed my little one that God cares for her, that He listens when she prays, and that He answers prayers. The Bible says there's something significant about learning these lessons early in life. If we "start children off on the way they should go, . . . when they are old they will not turn from it" (PROV. 22:6). When we start kids off with an awareness of Jesus and His power, we are giving them a place to return to if they wander and a foundation for spiritual growth throughout their lives.

Consider how you might foster faith in a child. Point out God's design in nature, tell a story about how He has helped you, or invite a little one to thank God with you when things go right. God can work through you to tell of His goodness throughout all generations. 🕊   *JENNIFER BENSON SCHULDT*

Dear God, I pray that You will raise up believers in the next generation. Show me how I can encourage young people to trust in You.

We influence future generations by living for Christ today.

¹ "I am the true vine, and my Father is the gardener. ² He cuts off every branch in me that bears no fruit, while every branch that does bear fruit he prunes so that it will be even more fruitful. ³ You are already clean because of the word I have spoken to you. ⁴ Remain in me, as I also remain in you. No branch can bear fruit by itself; it must remain in the vine. Neither can you bear fruit unless you remain in me.

⁵ "I am the vine; you are the branches. If you remain in me and I in you, you will bear much fruit; apart from me you can do nothing.

Honoring God

The church service was still in progress, and we had some visitors there that morning. The speaker was only halfway through his sermon when I noticed one of our visitors walking out. I was curious and concerned, so I walked out to talk with her.

"You're leaving so soon," I said, approaching her. "Is there a problem I can help with?" She was frank and forthright. "Yes," she said, "my problem is that sermon! I don't accept what the preacher is saying." He had said that no matter what we accomplish in life, the credit and praise belong to God. "At least," the woman moaned, "I deserve *some* credit for my achievements!"

TODAY'S READING
John 15:1–5

[Jesus said,] "If you remain in me and I in you, you will bear much fruit."

John 15:5

I explained to her what the pastor meant. People do deserve recognition and appreciation for what they do. Yet even our gifts and talents are from God, so He gets the glory. Even Jesus, the Son of God, said, "The Son can do nothing by himself; he can do only what he sees his Father doing" (JOHN 5:19). He told His followers, "Apart from me you can do nothing" (15:5).

We acknowledge the Lord as the one who helps us to accomplish everything. ❧
LAWRENCE DARMANI

> **Lord, let me not** forget to acknowledge You
> for all that You do for me and enable me to do.

God's children do His will for His glory.

¹ Not many of you should become teachers, my fellow believers, because you know that we who teach will be judged more strictly. ² We all stumble in many ways. Anyone who is never at fault in what they say is perfect, able to keep their whole body in check.

³ When we put bits into the mouths of horses to make them obey us, we can turn the whole animal. ⁴ Or take ships as an example. Although they are so large and are driven by strong winds, they are steered by a very small rudder wherever the pilot wants to go. ⁵ Likewise, the tongue is a small part of the body, but it makes great boasts. Consider what a great forest is set on fire by a small spark. ⁶ The tongue also is a fire, a world of evil among the parts of the body. It corrupts the whole body, sets the whole course of one's life on fire, and is itself set on fire by hell.

⁷ All kinds of animals, birds, reptiles and sea creatures are being tamed and have been tamed by mankind, ⁸ but no human being can tame the tongue. It is a restless evil, full of deadly poison.

⁹ With the tongue we praise our Lord and Father, and with it we curse human beings, who have been made in God's likeness. ¹⁰ Out of the same mouth come praise and cursing. My brothers and sisters, this should not be. ¹¹ Can both fresh water and salt water flow from the same spring? ¹² My brothers and sisters, can a fig tree bear olives, or a grapevine bear figs? Neither can a salt spring produce fresh water.

Careless Words

My daughter has had a lot of ill health recently, and her husband has been wonderfully caring and supportive. "You have a real treasure there!" I said.

"You didn't think that when I first knew him," she said with a grin.

She was quite right. When Icilda and Philip got engaged, I was concerned. They were such different personalities. We have a large and noisy family, and Philip is more reserved. And I had shared my misgivings with my daughter quite bluntly.

> TODAY'S READING
> **James 3:1–12**
>
> **The tongue is a small part of the body, but it makes great boasts.** James 3:5

I was horrified to realize that the critical things I said so casually 15 years ago had stayed in her memory and could possibly have destroyed a relationship that has proved to be so right and happy. It reminded me how much we need to guard what we say to others. So many of us are quick to point out what we consider to be weaknesses in family, friends, or work colleagues, or to focus on their mistakes rather than their successes. "The tongue is a small part of the body," says James (3:5), yet the words it shapes can either destroy relationships or bring peace and harmony to a situation in the workplace, the church, or the family.

Perhaps we should make David's prayer our own as we start each day: "Set a guard over my mouth, LORD; keep watch over the door of my lips" (PS. 141:3).

MARION STROUD

Father, please curb my careless speech
and put a guard on my tongue today and every day.

A word fitly spoken is like apples of gold in settings of silver.

PROVERBS 25:11 NKJV

¹ Then Job replied:
² "Even today my complaint is bitter;
   his hand is heavy in spite of my groaning.
³ If only I knew where to find him;
 if only I could go to his dwelling!
⁴ I would state my case before him
 and fill my mouth with arguments.
⁵ I would find out what he would answer me,
 and consider what he would say to me.
⁶ Would he vigorously oppose me?
 No, he would not press charges against me.
⁷ There the upright can establish their innocence before
him,
 and there I would be delivered forever from my judge.
⁸ "But if I go to the east, he is not there;
 if I go to the west, I do not find him.
⁹ When he is at work in the north, I do not see him;
 when he turns to the south, I catch no glimpse of him.
¹⁰ But he knows the way that I take;
 when he has tested me, I will come forth as gold.
¹¹ My feet have closely followed his steps;
 I have kept to his way without turning aside.
¹² I have not departed from the commands of his lips;
 I have treasured the words of his mouth more than my
daily bread.

When Questions Remain

O n October 31, 2014, an experimental spacecraft broke apart during a test flight and crashed into the Mojave Desert. The copilot died while the pilot miraculously survived. Investigators soon determined what had happened, but not why. The title of a newspaper article about the crash began with the words "Questions remain."

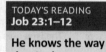

TODAY'S READING
Job 23:1–12

He knows the way that I take. Job 23:10

Throughout life we may experience sorrows for which there are no adequate explanation. Some are catastrophic events with far-reaching effects while others are personal, private tragedies that alter our individual lives and families. We want to know why, but we seem to find more questions than answers. Yet even as we struggle with "Why?" God extends His unfailing love to us.

When Job lost his children and his wealth in a single day (JOB 1:13–19), he sank into an angry depression and resisted any attempted explanations by his friends. Yet he held out hope that someday there would be an answer from God. Even in the darkness Job could say, "[God] knows the way that I take; when he has tested me, I will come forth as gold" (23:10).

Oswald Chambers said, "There will come one day a personal and direct touch from God when every tear and perplexity, every oppression and distress, every suffering and pain, and wrong and injustice will have a complete and ample and overwhelming explanation."

Today, as we face life's unanswered questions, we can find help and hope in God's love and promises. 🟊   *DAVID MCCASLAND*

When we face unanswered questions, we find help and hope in God's love.

[11] The Lord said to Moses, [12] "I have heard the grumbling of the Israelites. Tell them, 'At twilight you will eat meat, and in the morning you will be filled with bread. Then you will know that I am the Lord your God.'" [13] That evening quail came and covered the camp, and in the morning there was a layer of dew around the camp. [14] When the dew was gone, thin flakes like frost on the ground appeared on the desert floor. [15] When the Israelites saw it, they said to each other, "What is it?" For they did not know what it was. Moses said to them, "It is the bread the Lord has given you to eat. [16] This is what the Lord has commanded: 'Everyone is to gather as much as they need. Take an omer for each person you have in your tent.'" [17] The Israelites did as they were told; some gathered much, some little. [18] And when they measured it by the omer, the one who gathered much did not have too much, and the one who gathered little did not have too little. Everyone had gathered just as much as they needed. [19] Then Moses said to them, "No one is to keep any of it until morning." [20] However, some of them paid no attention to Moses; they kept part of it until morning, but it was full of maggots and began to smell. So Moses was angry with them. [21] Each morning everyone gathered as much as they needed, and when the sun grew hot, it melted away. [22] On the sixth day, they gathered twice as much— two omers for each person—and the leaders of the community came and reported this to Moses. [23] He said to them, "This is what the Lord commanded: 'Tomorrow is to be a day of sabbath rest, a holy sabbath to the Lord. So bake what you want to bake and boil what you want to boil. Save whatever is left and keep it until morning.'" [24] So they saved it until morning, as Moses commanded, and it did not stink or get maggots in it. [25] "Eat it today," Moses said, "because today is a sabbath to the Lord. You will not find any of it on the ground today. [26] Six days you are to gather it, but on the seventh day, the Sabbath, there will not be any." [27] Nevertheless, some of the people went out on the seventh day to gather it, but they found none. [28] Then the Lord said to Moses, "How long will you refuse to keep my commands and my instructions? [29] Bear in mind that the Lord has given you the Sabbath; that is why on the sixth day he gives you bread for two days. Everyone is to stay where they are on the seventh day; no one is to go out." [30] So the people rested on the seventh day. [31] The people of Israel called the bread manna. It was white like coriander seed and tasted like wafers made with honey.

What Is It?

My mother taught Sunday school for decades. One week she wanted to explain how God supplied food for the Israelites in the wilderness. To make the story come alive, she created something to represent "manna" for the kids in her class. She cut bread into small pieces and topped them with honey. Her recipe was inspired by the Bible's description of manna that says it "tasted like wafers made with honey" (EX. 16:31).

TODAY'S READING
Exodus 16:11–31

When the Israelites saw it, they said to each other, "What is it?" Exodus 16:15

When the Israelites first encountered God's bread from heaven, it appeared on the ground outside their tents like frost. "When [they] saw it, they said to each other, 'What is it?' " (V. 15). The Hebrew word *man* means "what," so they called it *manna.* They discovered they could grind it and form it into loaves or cook it in a pot (NUM. 11:7–8). Whatever it was, it had a baffling arrival (EX. 16:4,14), a unique consistency (V. 14), and a short expiration date (VV. 19–20).

Sometimes God provides for us in surprising ways. This reminds us that He is not bound by our expectations, and we can't predict what He will choose to do. While we wait, focusing on who He is rather than what we think He should do will help us find joy and satisfaction in our relationship with Him. 🌿
JENNIFER BENSON SCHULDT

Dear God, please help me to freely accept Your provision and the way You choose to deliver it. Thank You for caring for me and meeting my needs.

Those who let God provide will always be satisfied.

¹ I love you, LORD, my strength.
² The LORD is my rock, my fortress and my deliverer;
   my God is my rock, in whom I take refuge,
   my shield and the horn of my salvation, my stronghold.
³ I called to the LORD, who is worthy of praise,
   and I have been saved from my enemies.
⁴ The cords of death entangled me;
   the torrents of destruction overwhelmed me.
⁵ The cords of the grave coiled around me;
   the snares of death confronted me.
⁶ In my distress I called to the LORD;
   I cried to my God for help.
From his temple he heard my voice;
   my cry came before him, into his ears.

Before the Phone

As a mom of young children I'm sometimes susceptible to panic. My first reaction is to call my mom on the phone and ask her what to do with my son's allergy or my daughter's sudden cough.

Mom is a great resource, but when I read the Psalms, I'm reminded of how often we need the kind of help that no mortal can give. In Psalm 18 David was in great danger. Afraid, close to death, and in anguish, he called on the Lord.

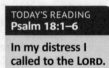

TODAY'S READING
Psalm 18:1–6

In my distress I called to the LORD.

Pslam 18:6

David could say, "I love you, LORD" because he understood God was a fortress, a rock, and a deliverer (VV. 1–2). God was his shield, his salvation, and his stronghold. Maybe we cannot understand David's praise because we have not experienced God's help. It may be that we reach for the phone before going to God for advice and help.

Surely God puts people in our lives to give us help and comfort. But let's also remember to pray. God will hear us. As David sang, "From his temple he heard my voice; my cry came before him, into his ears" (V. 6). When we go to God, we join David's song and enjoy Him as our rock, our fortress, and our deliverer.

Next time you reach for the phone, remember also to pray. 🍂

KEILA OCHOA

Dear Lord, help me to remember You are my deliverer,
and You always hear my cry.

Prayer is the bridge between panic and peace.

²⁹ God gave Solomon wisdom and very great insight, and a breadth of understanding as measureless as the sand on the seashore. ³⁰ Solomon's wisdom was greater than the wisdom of all the people of the East, and greater than all the wisdom of Egypt. ³¹ He was wiser than anyone else, including Ethan the Ezrahite—wiser than Heman, Kalkol and Darda, the sons of Mahol. And his fame spread to all the surrounding nations. ³² He spoke three thousand proverbs and his songs numbered a thousand and five.

³³ He spoke about plant life, from the cedar of Lebanon to the hyssop that grows out of walls. He also spoke about animals and birds, reptiles and fish. ³⁴ From all nations people came to listen to Solomon's wisdom, sent by all the kings of the world, who had heard of his wisdom.

Her Father's Zoo

June Williams was only 4 when her father bought 7 acres of land to build a zoo without bars or cages. Growing up she remembers how creative her father was in trying to help wild animals feel free in confinement. Today Chester Zoo is one of England's most popular wildlife attractions. Home to 11,000 animals on 110 acres of land, the zoo reflects her father's concern for animal welfare, education, and conservation.

TODAY'S READING
1 Kings 4:29–34

Solomon had a similar interest in all creatures great and small. In addition to studying the wildlife of the Middle East, he imported exotic animals like apes and monkeys from far-off lands (1 KINGS 10:22). But one of his proverbs shows us that Solomon's knowledge of nature went

The righteous care for the needs of their animals, but the kindest acts of the wicked are cruel. Proverbs 12:10

beyond intellectual curiosity. When he expressed the spiritual implications of how we treat our animals, he mirrored something of the heart of our Creator: "The righteous care for the needs of their animals, but the kindest acts of the wicked are cruel" (PROV. 12:10).

With God-given wisdom, Solomon saw that our relationship to our Creator affects not only how we treat people but also how much thoughtful consideration we give to the creatures in our care. *MART DEHAAN*

Father in heaven, when we think about the wonder and diversity of Your animal kingdom, please help us not only to worship You, but to care for what You've entrusted to us.

God is the real Owner of all of us.

¹⁷ At this, some of his disciples said to one another, "What does he mean by saying, 'In a little while you will see me no more, and then after a little while you will see me,' and 'Because I am going to the Father'?" ¹⁸ They kept asking, "What does he mean by 'a little while'? We don't understand what he is saying."

¹⁹ Jesus saw that they wanted to ask him about this, so he said to them, "Are you asking one another what I meant when I said, 'In a little while you will see me no more, and then after a little while you will see me'? ²⁰ Very truly I tell you, you will weep and mourn while the world rejoices. You will grieve, but your grief will turn to joy. ²¹ A woman giving birth to a child has pain because her time has come; but when her baby is born she forgets the anguish because of her joy that a child is born into the world. ²² So with you: Now is your time of grief, but I will see you again and you will rejoice, and no one will take away your joy. ²³ In that day you will no longer ask me anything. Very truly I tell you, my Father will give you whatever you ask in my name. ²⁴ Until now you have not asked for anything in my name. Ask and you will receive, and your joy will be complete.

The Mention of His Name

When the soloist began to sing during our Sunday service, the congregation gave him full, hushed attention. His mellow bass-baritone voice brought them the soul-touching words of an old song by Gordon Jensen. The song's title expresses a truth that grows more precious the older we become: "He's as Close as the Mention of His Name."

We've all experienced times of separation from our loved ones. A child marries and moves far away. Parents are separated from us because of career or health. A child goes off to school in another state or country. True, we have texting and Skype. But we are *here* and they are *there*. And then there is the separation of death.

TODAY'S READING
John 16:17–24

I will see you again and you will rejoice, and no one will take away your joy.
John 16:22

But as believers in Christ, we have His promise that we are never alone. Though we may feel alone, He hasn't gone anywhere. He's right here, right now, always and forever. When He left this earth, He told His followers, "Surely I am with you always, to the very end of the age" (MATT. 28:20). He also promised us, "Never will I leave you; never will I forsake you" (HEB. 13:5).

The silent plea, the whispered mention of His name, even the very thought of Him brings us solace and reassurance. "He's as close as the mention of his name." ❧ 　　　*DAVE EGNER*

Jesus, thank You that You are near.
I need You.

Jesus never abandons or forgets His own.

¹⁴ Jesus returned to Galilee in the power of the Spirit, and news about him spread through the whole countryside. ¹⁵ He was teaching in their synagogues, and everyone praised him.

¹⁶ He went to Nazareth, where he had been brought up, and on the Sabbath day he went into the synagogue, as was his custom. He stood up to read, ¹⁷ and the scroll of the prophet Isaiah was handed to him. Unrolling it, he found the place where it is written:

¹⁸ "The Spirit of the Lord is on me,
   because he has anointed me
   to proclaim good news to the poor.
He has sent me to proclaim freedom for the prisoners
   and recovery of sight for the blind,
to set the oppressed free,
¹⁹ to proclaim the year of the Lord's favor."

²⁰ Then he rolled up the scroll, gave it back to the attendant and sat down. The eyes of everyone in the synagogue were fastened on him. ²¹ He began by saying to them, "Today this scripture is fulfilled in your hearing."

He Came for You

In his novels *The Trial* and *The Castle,* Franz Kafka (1883–1924) portrays life as a dehumanizing existence that turns people into a sea of empty faces without identity or worth. Kafka said, "The conveyer belt of life carries you on, no one knows where. One is more of an object, a thing, than a living creature."

Early in His ministry, Jesus went to a synagogue in Nazareth, stood up in front of the crowd, and read from Isaiah: "The Spirit of the Lord is on me because he has anointed me to proclaim good news to the poor. He has sent me to proclaim freedom for the prisoners and recovery of sight for the blind, to set the oppressed free, to proclaim the year of the Lord's favor" (LUKE 4:18–19).

TODAY'S READING
Luke 4:14–21

The Spirit of the Lord is on me, because he has anointed me to proclaim good news to the poor. Luke 4:18

Then Christ sat down and declared, "Today this scripture is fulfilled in your hearing" (V. 21). Centuries earlier, the prophet Isaiah had proclaimed these words (ISA. 61:1–2). Now Jesus announced that He was the fulfillment of that promise.

Notice who Jesus came to rescue—the poor, broken-hearted, captive, blind, and oppressed. He came for people dehumanized by sin and suffering, by brokenness and sorrow. He came for us!

BILL CROWDER

For those who sin and those who suffer. For those who suffer because of sin. For those who sin to alleviate suffering.
Lord, have mercy on us.
ROBERT GELINAS, *THE MERCY PRAYER*

No matter how impersonal the world may seem, Jesus loves each of us as if we were His only child.

¹ Then Jesus told his disciples a parable to show them that they should always pray and not give up. ² He said: "In a certain town there was a judge who neither feared God nor cared what people thought. ³ And there was a widow in that town who kept coming to him with the plea, 'Grant me justice against my adversary.'

⁴ "For some time he refused. But finally he said to himself, 'Even though I don't fear God or care what people think, ⁵ yet because this widow keeps bothering me, I will see that she gets justice, so that she won't eventually come and attack me!'"

⁶ And the Lord said, "Listen to what the unjust judge says. ⁷ And will not God bring about justice for his chosen ones, who cry out to him day and night? Will he keep putting them off? ⁸ I tell you, he will see that they get justice, and quickly. However, when the Son of Man comes, will he find faith on the earth?"

Always Pray and Don't Give Up

Are you going through one of those times when it seems every attempt to resolve a problem is met with a new difficulty? You thank the Lord at night that it's taken care of but awake to find that something else has gone wrong and the problem remains.

During an experience like that, I was reading the gospel of Luke and was astounded by the opening words of chapter 18: "Then Jesus told his disciples a parable to show them that they should always pray and not give up" (v. 1). I had read the story of the persistent widow many times but never grasped why Jesus told it (vv. 2–8). Now I connected those opening words with the story. The lesson to His followers was very clear: "Always pray and never give up."

TODAY'S READING
Luke 18:1–8

Jesus told his disciples a parable to show them that they should always pray and not give up. Luke 18:1

Prayer is not a means of coercing God to do what we want. It is a process of recognizing His power and plan for our lives. In prayer we yield our lives and circumstances to the Lord and trust Him to act in His time and in His way.

As we rely on God's grace not only for the outcome of our requests but for the process as well, we can keep coming to the Lord in prayer, trusting His wisdom and care for us.

Our Lord's encouragement to us is clear: Always pray and don't give up! ❧

DAVID MCCASLAND

Lord, in the difficulty I face today, guard my heart, guide my words, and show Your grace. May I always turn to You in prayer.

Prayer changes everything.

⁴ When Jehoram established himself firmly over his father's kingdom, he put all his brothers to the sword along with some of the officials of Israel. ⁵ Jehoram was thirty-two years old when he became king, and he reigned in Jerusalem eight years. ⁶ He followed the ways of the kings of Israel, as the house of Ahab had done, for he married a daughter of Ahab. He did evil in the eyes of the Lord. ⁷ Nevertheless, because of the covenant the Lord had made with David, the Lord was not willing to destroy the house of David. He had promised to maintain a lamp for him and his descendants forever. ⁸ In the time of Jehoram, Edom rebelled against Judah and set up its own king. ⁹ So Jehoram went there with his officers and all his chariots. The Edomites surrounded him and his chariot commanders, but he rose up and broke through by night. ¹⁰ To this day Edom has been in rebellion against Judah. Libnah revolted at the same time, because Jehoram had forsaken the Lord, the God of his ancestors. ¹¹ He had also built high places on the hills of Judah and had caused the people of Jerusalem to prostitute themselves and had led Judah astray. ¹² Jehoram received a letter from Elijah the prophet, which said: "This is what the Lord, the God of your father David, says: 'You have not followed the ways of your father Jehoshaphat or of Asa king of Judah. ¹³ But you have followed the ways of the kings of Israel, and you have led Judah and the people of Jerusalem to prostitute themselves, just as the house of Ahab did. You have also murdered your own brothers, members of your own family, men who were better than you. ¹⁴ So now the Lord is about to strike your people, your sons, your wives and everything that is yours, with a heavy blow. ¹⁵ You yourself will be very ill with a lingering disease of the bowels, until the disease causes your bowels to come out.'" ¹⁶ The Lord aroused against Jehoram the hostility of the Philistines and of the Arabs who lived near the Cushites. ¹⁷ They attacked Judah, invaded it and carried off all the goods found in the king's palace, together with his sons and wives. Not a son was left to him except Ahaziah, the youngest. ¹⁸ After all this, the Lord afflicted Jehoram with an incurable disease of the bowels. ¹⁹ In the course of time, at the end of the second year, his bowels came out because of the disease, and he died in great pain. His people made no funeral fire in his honor, as they had for his predecessors. ²⁰ Jehoram was thirty-two years old when he became king, and he reigned in Jerusalem eight years. He passed away, to no one's regret, and was buried in the City of David, but not in the tombs of the kings.

Leave a Legacy

When a road-construction foreman was killed in an accident, the love of this man for his family, co-workers, and community resulted in an overwhelming sense of loss. His country church couldn't accommodate all the mourners, so planners moved the service to a much larger building. Friends and family packed the auditorium! The message was clear: Tim touched many lives in a way uniquely his. So many would miss his kindness, sense of humor, and enthusiasm for life.

As I returned from the funeral, I thought about the life of King Jehoram. What a contrast! His brief reign of terror is traced in 2 Chronicles 21. To solidify his power, Jehoram killed his own brothers and other leaders (v. 4). Then he led Judah into idol worship. The record tells us, "He passed away, to no one's regret" (v. 20). Jehoram thought that brute force would ensure his legacy. It did. He is forever commemorated in Scripture as an evil man and a self-centered leader.

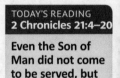

TODAY'S READING
2 Chronicles 21:4–20

Even the Son of Man did not come to be served, but to serve. Mark 10:45

Although Jesus also was a king, He came to Earth to be a servant. As He went about doing good, He endured the hatred of those who grasped for power. In the process, this Servant-King gave His life away.

Today, Jesus lives along with His legacy. That legacy includes those who understand that life isn't just about themselves. It's about Jesus—the One who longs to wrap His strong, forgiving arms around anyone who turns to Him. ✿ *TIM GUSTAFSON*

Lord, in Your death as well as in Your life, You served others.
In some small way, help us to serve others with our lives today.

A life lived for God leaves a lasting legacy.

²⁴ Do you not know that in a race all the runners run, but only one gets the prize? Run in such a way as to get the prize. ²⁵ Everyone who competes in the games goes into strict training. They do it to get a crown that will not last, but we do it to get a crown that will last forever. ²⁶ Therefore I do not run like someone running aimlessly; I do not fight like a boxer beating the air. ²⁷ No, I strike a blow to my body and make it my slave so that after I have preached to others, I myself will not be disqualified for the prize.

Training for Life

recently met a woman who has pushed her body and mind to the limit. She climbed mountains, faced death, and even broke a Guinness world record. Now she's engaged in a different challenge—that of raising her special-needs child. The courage and faith she employed while ascending the mountains she now pours into motherhood.

In 1 Corinthians, the apostle Paul speaks of a runner competing in a race. After urging a church enamored with their rights to give consideration to one another (CH. 8), he explains how he sees the challenges of love and self-sacrifice to be like a marathon of endurance (CH. 9). As followers of Jesus, they are to relinquish their rights in obedience to Him.

> **TODAY'S READING**
> 1 Cor. 9:24–27
>
> I discipline my body and bring it into subjection, lest... I myself should become disqualified.
>
> 1 Corinthians 9:27 NKJV

As athletes train their bodies that they might win the crown, we too train our bodies and minds for our souls to flourish. As we ask the Holy Spirit to transform us, moment by moment, we leave our old selves behind. Empowered by God, we stop ourselves from uttering that cruel word. We put away our electronic device and remain present with our friends. We don't have to speak the last word in a disagreement.

As we train to run in the Spirit of Christ, how might God want to mold us today? ❂

AMY BOUCHER PYE

Lord, let me not demand my rights, but train to win the prize that lasts forever.

Amy Boucher Pye is a writer, editor, and speaker. The author of *Finding Myself in Britain: Our Search for Faith, Home, and True Identity,* she runs the Woman Alive book club in the UK and enjoys life with her family in their English vicarage.

Training leads to transformation.

¹ My son, if you accept my words
   and store up my commands within you,
² turning your ear to wisdom
   and applying your heart to understanding—
³ indeed, if you call out for insight
   and cry aloud for understanding,
⁴ and if you look for it as for silver
   and search for it as for hidden treasure,
⁵ then you will understand the fear of the LORD
   and find the knowledge of God.

Hidden Treasure

My husband and I read in different ways. Since English is a second language for Tom, he has a tendency to read slowly, word-for-word. I often speed-read by skimming. But Tom retains more than I do. He can easily quote something he read a week ago, while my retention can evaporate seconds after I turn away from the screen or book.

Skimming is also a problem when I'm reading the Bible—and not just the genealogies. I'm tempted to skim familiar passages, stories I've heard since I was a child, or a psalm that is part of a familiar chorus.

TODAY'S READING
Proverbs 2:1–5

Search for [insight and understanding] as for hidden treasure. Proverbs 2:4

Proverbs 2 encourages us to make the effort to know God better by carefully seeking a heart of understanding. When we read the Bible carefully and invest time memorizing Scripture, we absorb its truths more deeply (VV. 1–2). Sometimes reading the Word aloud helps us to hear and understand the wisdom of God more fully. And when we pray the words of Scripture back to God and ask Him for "insight and understanding" (V. 3), we enjoy a conversation with the Author.

We come to know God and His wisdom when we search for it with our whole heart. We find understanding when we seek it like silver and search for it like hidden treasure. 🖊 *CINDY HESS KASPER*

Dear Lord, help me to slow down and listen to what You want to teach me through Your Word so I can be the person You want me to be.

Read the Bible carefully and study it prayerfully.

¹ Rehoboam went to Shechem, for all Israel had gone there to make him king. ² When Jeroboam son of Nebat heard this (he was still in Egypt, where he had fled from King Solomon), he returned from Egypt. ³ So they sent for Jeroboam, and he and the whole assembly of Israel went to Rehoboam and said to him: ⁴ "Your father put a heavy yoke on us, but now lighten the harsh labor and the heavy yoke he put on us, and we will serve you."

⁵ Rehoboam answered, "Go away for three days and then come back to me." So the people went away.

⁶ Then King Rehoboam consulted the elders who had served his father Solomon during his lifetime. "How would you advise me to answer these people?" he asked.

⁷ They replied, "If today you will be a servant to these people and serve them and give them a favorable answer, they will always be your servants."

⁸ But Rehoboam rejected the advice the elders gave him and consulted the young men who had grown up with him and were serving him. ⁹ He asked them, "What is your advice? How should we answer these people who say to me, 'Lighten the yoke your father put on us'?"

¹⁰ The young men who had grown up with him replied, "These people have said to you, 'Your father put a heavy yoke on us, but make our yoke lighter.' Now tell them, 'My little finger is thicker than my father's waist. ¹¹ My father laid on you a heavy yoke; I will make it even heavier. My father scourged you with whips; I will scourge you with scorpions.'"

¹² Three days later Jeroboam and all the people returned to Rehoboam, as the king had said, "Come back to me in three days." ¹³ The king answered the people harshly. Rejecting the advice given him by the elders, ¹⁴ he followed the advice of the young men and said, "My father made your yoke heavy; I will make it even heavier. My father scourged you with whips; I will scourge you with scorpions." ¹⁵ So the king did not listen to the people, for this turn of events was from the LORD, to fulfill the word the LORD had spoken to Jeroboam son of Nebat through Ahijah the Shilonite.

A Serving Leader

In traditional African societies, leadership succession is a serious decision. After a king's demise, great care is taken selecting the next ruler. Besides being from a royal family, the successor must be strong, fearless, and sensible. Candidates are questioned to determine if they will serve the people or rule with a heavy hand. The king's successor needs to be someone who leads but also serves.

TODAY'S READING
1 Kings 12:1–15

Whoever wants to become great among you must be your servant.

Matthew 20:26

Even though Solomon made his own bad choices, he worried over his successor. "Who knows whether that person will be wise or foolish? Yet they will have control over all the fruit of my toil into which I have poured my effort and skill" (ECCL. 2:19). His son Rehoboam was that successor. He demonstrated a lack of sound judgment and ended up fulfilling his father's worst fear.

When the people requested more humane working conditions, it was an opportunity for Rehoboam to show servant leadership. "If today you will be a servant to these people and serve them . . . ," the elders advised, "they will always be your servants" (1 KINGS 12:7). But he rejected their counsel. Rehoboam failed to seek God. His harsh response to the people divided the kingdom and accelerated the spiritual decline of God's people (12:14–19).

In the family, the workplace, at church, or in our neighborhood—we need His wisdom for the humility to serve rather than be served. 🌿

LAWRENCE DARMANI

Dear Lord, please give me a humble servant's heart.
Help me to lead and follow with humility and compassion.
A good leader is a good servant.

¹ Then the angel showed me the river of the water of life, as clear as crystal, flowing from the throne of God and of the Lamb ² down the middle of the great street of the city. On each side of the river stood the tree of life, bearing twelve crops of fruit, yielding its fruit every month. And the leaves of the tree are for the healing of the nations. ³ No longer will there be any curse. The throne of God and of the Lamb will be in the city, and his servants will serve him. ⁴ They will see his face, and his name will be on their foreheads. ⁵ There will be no more night. They will not need the light of a lamp or the light of the sun, for the Lord God will give them light. And they will reign for ever and ever.

What Will Be

You and I have something in common. We live in a mixed-up, tarnished world and we have never known anything different. Adam and Eve, however, could remember what life was like before the curse. They could recall the world as God intended it to be—free of death, hardship, and pain (GEN. 3:16–19). In pre-fall Eden, hunger, unemployment, and illness did not exist. No one questioned God's creative power or His plan for human relationships.

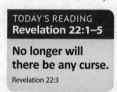

TODAY'S READING
Revelation 22:1–5

No longer will there be any curse.
Revelation 22:3

The world we have inherited resembles God's perfect garden only slightly. To quote C. S. Lewis, "This is a good world gone wrong, but [it] still retains the memory of what ought to have been." Fortunately, the cloudy memory of what the earth should have been is also a prophetic glimpse into eternity. There, just as Adam and Eve walked and talked with God, believers will see His face and serve Him directly. There will be nothing between God and us. "No longer will there be any curse" (REV. 22:3). There will be no sin, no fear, and no shame.

The past and its consequences may cast a shadow on today, but a believer's destiny carries the promise of something better—life in a place as perfect as Eden. ❧ *JENNIFER BENSON SCHULDT*

Dear God, help me to remember that even though this world does not measure up to Your original design there is much to enjoy and much to do for You and others. Thank You for the promise of life with You in a perfect setting.

One day God will put everything right.

²⁸ I came from the Father and entered the world; now I am leaving the world and going back to the Father."

²⁹ Then Jesus' disciples said, "Now you are speaking clearly and without figures of speech. ³⁰ Now we can see that you know all things and that you do not even need to have anyone ask you questions. This makes us believe that you came from God."

³¹ "Do you now believe?" Jesus replied. ³² "A time is coming and in fact has come when you will be scattered, each to your own home. You will leave me all alone. Yet I am not alone, for my Father is with me.

³³ "I have told you these things, so that in me you may have peace. In this world you will have trouble. But take heart! I have overcome the world."

The Factory of Sadness

As a lifelong Cleveland Browns football fan, I grew up knowing my share of disappointment. Despite being one of only four teams to have never appeared in a Super Bowl championship game, the Browns have a loyal fan base that sticks with the team year in and year out. But because the fans usually end up disappointed, many of them now refer to the home stadium as the "Factory of Sadness."

The broken world we live in can be a "factory of sadness" too. There seems to be an endless supply of heartache and disappointment, whether from our own choices or things beyond our control.

TODAY'S READING
John 16:28–33

[God] will wipe every tear from their eyes.

Revelation 21:4

Yet the follower of Christ has hope—not only in the life to come but for this very day. Jesus said, "I have told you these things, so that in me you may have peace. In this world you will have trouble. But take heart! I have overcome the world" (JOHN 16:33). Notice that without minimizing the struggles or sadness we may experience, Christ counters them with His promises of peace, joy, and ultimate victory.

Great peace is available in Christ, and it's more than enough to help us navigate whatever life throws at us. 🕊   *BILL CROWDER*

> **When peace,** like a river, attendeth my way,
> when sorrows like sea billows roll; whatever my lot,
> Thou hast taught me to say, It is well, it is well, with my soul.
> HORATIO G. SPAFFORD

Our hope and peace are found in Jesus.

¹³ You, my brothers and sisters, were called to be free. But do not use your freedom to indulge the flesh; rather, serve one another humbly in love. ¹⁴ For the entire law is fulfilled in keeping this one command: "Love your neighbor as yourself." ¹⁵ If you bite and devour each other, watch out or you will be destroyed by each other.

¹⁶ So I say, walk by the Spirit, and you will not gratify the desires of the flesh. ¹⁷ For the flesh desires what is contrary to the Spirit, and the Spirit what is contrary to the flesh. They are in conflict with each other, so that you are not to do whatever you want. ¹⁸ But if you are led by the Spirit, you are not under the law.

¹⁹ The acts of the flesh are obvious: sexual immorality, impurity and debauchery; ²⁰ idolatry and witchcraft; hatred, discord, jealousy, fits of rage, selfish ambition, dissensions, factions ²¹ and envy; drunkenness, orgies, and the like. I warn you, as I did before, that those who live like this will not inherit the kingdom of God.

²² But the fruit of the Spirit is love, joy, peace, forbearance, kindness, goodness, faithfulness, ²³ gentleness and self-control. Against such things there is no law. ²⁴ Those who belong to Christ Jesus have crucified the flesh with its passions and desires. ²⁵ Since we live by the Spirit, let us keep in step with the Spirit. ²⁶ Let us not become conceited, provoking and envying each other.

Can't Take It Back

I couldn't take my actions back. A woman had parked her car and blocked my way of getting to the gas pump. She hopped out to drop off some recycling items, and I didn't feel like waiting, so I honked my horn at her. Irritated, I put my car in reverse and drove around another way. I immediately felt bad about being impatient and unwilling to wait 30 seconds (at the most) for her to move. I apologized to God. Yes, she should have parked in the designated area, but I could have spread kindness and patience instead of harshness. Unfortunately it was too late to apologize to her—she was gone.

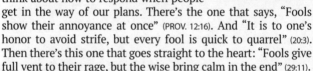

TODAY'S READING
Galatians 5:13–26

The fruit of the Spirit is . . . gentleness and self-control.

Galatians 5:22–23

Many of the Proverbs challenge us to think about how to respond when people get in the way of our plans. There's the one that says, "Fools show their annoyance at once" (PROV. 12:16). And "It is to one's honor to avoid strife, but every fool is quick to quarrel" (20:3). Then there's this one that goes straight to the heart: "Fools give full vent to their rage, but the wise bring calm in the end" (29:11).

Growing in patience and kindness seems pretty difficult sometimes. But the apostle Paul says it is the work of God, the "fruit of the Spirit" (GAL. 5:22–23). As we cooperate with Him and depend on Him, He produces that fruit in us. Please change us, Lord. 🌱
ANNE CETAS

Make me a gentle person, Lord. One who doesn't quickly react in frustration to every annoyance that comes my way. Give me a spirit of self-control and patience.

God tests our patience to enlarge our hearts.

³¹ Meanwhile his disciples urged him, "Rabbi, eat something."

³² But he said to them, "I have food to eat that you know nothing about."

³³ Then his disciples said to each other, "Could someone have brought him food?"

³⁴ "My food," said Jesus, "is to do the will of him who sent me and to finish his work.

Secret Menu

Meat Mountain is a super-sandwich layered with six kinds of meat. Stacked with chicken tenders, three strips of bacon, two cheeses, and much more, it looks like it should be a restaurant's featured item.

But Meat Mountain isn't on any restaurant's published menu. The sandwich represents a trend in off-menu items known only by social media or word of mouth. It seems that competition is driving fast-food restaurants to offer a secret menu to in-the-know customers.

TODAY'S READING
John 4:31–34

I have food to eat that you know nothing about.

John 4:32

When Jesus told His disciples that He had "food" they knew nothing about, it must have seemed like a secret menu to them (JOHN 4:32). He sensed their confusion and explained that His food was to do the will of His Father and to finish the work given to Him (V. 34).

Jesus had just spoken to a Samaritan woman at Jacob's well about living water she had never heard of. As they talked, He revealed a supernatural understanding of her unquenched thirst for life. When He disclosed who He was, she left her water pot behind and ran to ask her neighbors, "Could this be the Messiah?" (V. 29).

What was once a secret can now be offered to everyone. Jesus invites all of us to trust His ability to satisfy the deepest needs of our hearts. As we do, we discover how to live not just by our physical appetites but by the soul-satisfying Spirit of our God. ❂

MART DEHAAN

Father, we praise You for revealing Your truth to us.
Help us live each day in the power of Your Spirit.

Only Christ the Living Bread can satisfy the world's spiritual hunger.

¹⁵ The Son is the image of the invisible God, the firstborn over all creation. ¹⁶ For in him all things were created: things in heaven and on earth, visible and invisible, whether thrones or powers or rulers or authorities; all things have been created through him and for him. ¹⁷ He is before all things, and in him all things hold together. ¹⁸ And he is the head of the body, the church; he is the beginning and the firstborn from among the dead, so that in everything he might have the supremacy. ¹⁹ For God was pleased to have all his fullness dwell in him, ²⁰ and through him to reconcile to himself all things, whether things on earth or things in heaven, by making peace through his blood, shed on the cross.

Jesus Over Everything

My friend's son decided to wear a sports jersey over his school clothing one day. He wanted to show support for his favorite team that would be playing an important game later that night. Before leaving home, he put something on over his sports jersey—it was a chain with a pendant that read, "Jesus." His simple action illustrated a deeper truth: Jesus deserves first place over everything in our lives.

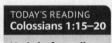

TODAY'S READING
Colossians 1:15–20

He is before all things. Colossians 1:17

Jesus is above and over all. "He is before all things, and in him all things hold together" (COL. 1:17). Jesus is supreme over all creation (VV. 15-16). He is "the head of the body, the church" (V. 18). Because of this, He should have first place in all things.

When we give Jesus the highest place of honor in each area of our lives, this truth becomes visible to those around us. At work, are we laboring first for God or only to please our employer? (3:23). How do God's standards show up in the way we treat others? (VV. 12-14). Do we put Him first as we live our lives and pursue our favorite pastimes?

When Jesus is our greatest influence in all of life, He will have His rightful place in our hearts. 🕊 *JENNIFER BENSON SCHULDT*

Dear Jesus, You deserve the best of my time, energy, and affection.
I crown You King of my heart and Lord over everything I do.

Put Jesus first.

²⁵ Therefore each of you must put off falsehood and speak truthfully to your neighbor, for we are all members of one body. ²⁶ "In your anger do not sin": Do not let the sun go down while you are still angry, ²⁷ and do not give the devil a foothold. ²⁸ Anyone who has been stealing must steal no longer, but must work, doing something useful with their own hands, that they may have something to share with those in need.

²⁹ Do not let any unwholesome talk come out of your mouths, but only what is helpful for building others up according to their needs, that it may benefit those who listen. ³⁰ And do not grieve the Holy Spirit of God, with whom you were sealed for the day of redemption. ³¹ Get rid of all bitterness, rage and anger, brawling and slander, along with every form of malice. ³² Be kind and compassionate to one another, forgiving each other, just as in Christ God forgave you.

Turn Off the Scoreboard

At his son's wedding reception, my friend Bob offered advice and encouragement to the newlyweds. In his speech he told of a football coach in a nearby town who, when his team lost a game, kept the losing score on the scoreboard all week to remind the team of their failure. While that may be a good football strat-egy, Bob wisely advised, it's a terrible strategy in marriage. When your spouse upsets you or fails you in some way, don't keep drawing attention to the fail-ure. Turn off the scoreboard.

TODAY'S READING
Ephesians 4:25–32

Forgiving each other, just as in Christ God forgave you. Ephesians 4:32

What great advice! Scripture is full of commands for us to love each other and overlook faults. We are reminded that love "keeps no record of wrongs" (1 COR. 13:5) and that we should be ready to forgive one another "just as in Christ God forgave you" (EPH. 4:32).

I am deeply grateful that God turns off the scoreboard when I fail. He doesn't simply forgive when we repent; He removes our sin as far as the east is from the west (PS. 103:12). With God, forgiveness means that our sin is out of sight *and* out of mind. May He give us grace to extend forgiveness to those around us. ❧   *JOE STOWELL*

Lord, thank You for not holding my sins against me and for granting me a second chance. Help me today to forgive others just as You have so freely forgiven me.

Forgive as God forgives you—don't keep score.

³⁹ "Abraham is our father," they answered.

"If you were Abraham's children," said Jesus, "then you would do what Abraham did. ⁴⁰ As it is, you are looking for a way to kill me, a man who has told you the truth that I heard from God. Abraham did not do such things. ⁴¹ You are doing the works of your own father."

"We are not illegitimate children," they protested. "The only Father we have is God himself."

⁴² Jesus said to them, "If God were your Father, you would love me, for I have come here from God. I have not come on my own; God sent me. ⁴³ Why is my language not clear to you? Because you are unable to hear what I say. ⁴⁴ You belong to your father, the devil, and you want to carry out your father's desires. He was a murderer from the beginning, not holding to the truth, for there is no truth in him. When he lies, he speaks his native language, for he is a liar and the father of lies. ⁴⁵ Yet because I tell the truth, you do not believe me! ⁴⁶ Can any of you prove me guilty of sin? If I am telling the truth, why don't you believe me? ⁴⁷ Whoever belongs to God hears what God says. The reason you do not hear is that you do not belong to God."

Undigested Knowledge

I **n his book** on language, British diplomat Lancelot Oliphant (1881–1965) observed that many students give correct answers on tests but fail to put those lessons into practice. "Such undigested knowledge is of little use," declared Oliphant.

Author Barnabas Piper noticed a parallel in his own life: "I thought I was close to God because I knew all the answers," he said, "but I had fooled myself into thinking that was the same as *relationship* with Jesus."

At the temple one day, Jesus encountered people who thought they had all the right answers. They were proudly proclaiming their status as Abraham's descendants yet refused to believe in God's Son.

TODAY'S READING
John 8:39–47

If you hold to my teaching, you are really my disciples.
John 8:31

"If you were Abraham's children," said Jesus, "then you would do what Abraham did" (JOHN 8:39). And what was that? Abraham "believed the LORD, and he credited it to him as righteousness" (GEN. 15:6). Still, Jesus's hearers refused to believe. "The only Father we have is God himself," they said (JOHN 8:41). Jesus replied, "Whoever belongs to God hears what God says. The reason you do not hear is that you do not belong to God" (V. 47).

Piper recalls how things "fell apart" for him before he "encountered God's grace and the person of Jesus in a profound way." When we allow God's truth to transform our lives, we gain much more than the right answer. We introduce the world to Jesus. ✒   *TIM GUSTAFSON*

Father, thank You that You receive anyone who turns to You in faith.

Faith is not accepting the fact of God but of receiving the life of God.

⁴ There are different kinds of gifts, but the same Spirit distributes them. ⁵ There are different kinds of service, but the same Lord. ⁶ There are different kinds of working, but in all of them and in everyone it is the same God at work.

⁷ Now to each one the manifestation of the Spirit is given for the common good. ⁸ To one there is given through the Spirit a message of wisdom, to another a message of knowledge by means of the same Spirit, ⁹ to another faith by the same Spirit, to another gifts of healing by that one Spirit, ¹⁰ to another miraculous powers, to another prophecy, to another distinguishing between spirits, to another speaking in different kinds of tongues, and to still another the interpretation of tongues. ¹¹ All these are the work of one and the same Spirit, and he distributes them to each one, just as he determines.

¹² Just as a body, though one, has many parts, but all its many parts form one body, so it is with Christ. ¹³ For we were all baptized by one Spirit so as to form one body—whether Jews or Gentiles, slave or free—and we were all given the one Spirit to drink. ¹⁴ Even so the body is not made up of one part but of many.

Ice Flowers

Fifteen-year-old Wilson Bentley was captivated by the intricate beauty of snowflakes. He looked with fascination through an old microscope his mother had given him and made hundreds of sketches of their remarkable designs, but they melted too quickly to adequately capture their detail. Several years later, in 1885, he had an idea. He attached a bellows camera to the microscope and, after much trial and error, took his first picture of a snowflake. During his lifetime Bentley would capture 5,000 snowflake images and each one was a unique design. He described them as "tiny miracles of beauty" and "ice flowers."

TODAY'S READING
1 Cor. 12:4–14

There are different kinds of gifts, but the same Spirit distributes them. 1 Corinthians 12:4

No two snowflakes are alike, yet all come from the same source. So it is with followers of Christ. We all come from the same Creator and Redeemer, yet we are all different. In God's glorious plan He has chosen to bring a variety of people together into a unified whole, and He has gifted us in various ways. In describing the diversity of gifts to believers, Paul writes: "There are different kinds of gifts, but the same Spirit distributes them. There are different kinds of service, but the same Lord. There are different kinds of working, but in all of them and in everyone it is the same God at work" (1 COR. 12:4–6).

Thank God for the unique contribution you can offer as you help and serve others. ❧

DENNIS FISHER

Dear Lord, thank You for the unique way that You have gifted me.
Help me to use my gifts faithfully to serve You and others.

Each person is a unique expression of God's loving design.

¹⁸ You have not come to a mountain that can be touched and that is burning with fire; to darkness, gloom and storm; ¹⁹ to a trumpet blast or to such a voice speaking words that those who heard it begged that no further word be spoken to them, ²⁰ because they could not bear what was commanded: "If even an animal touches the mountain, it must be stoned to death." ²¹ The sight was so terrifying that Moses said, "I am trembling with fear."

²² But you have come to Mount Zion, to the city of the living God, the heavenly Jerusalem. You have come to thousands upon thousands of angels in joyful assembly, ²³ to the church of the firstborn, whose names are written in heaven. You have come to God, the Judge of all, to the spirits of the righteous made perfect, ²⁴ to Jesus the mediator of a new covenant, and to the sprinkled blood that speaks a better word than the blood of Abel.

²⁵ See to it that you do not refuse him who speaks. If they did not escape when they refused him who warned them on earth, how much less will we, if we turn away from him who warns us from heaven? ²⁶ At that time his voice shook the earth, but now he has promised, "Once more I will shake not only the earth but also the heavens." ²⁷ The words "once more" indicate the removing of what can be shaken—that is, created things—so that what cannot be shaken may remain.

²⁸ Therefore, since we are receiving a kingdom that cannot be shaken, let us be thankful, and so worship God acceptably with reverence and awe, ²⁹ for our "God is a consuming fire."

The Ease of Ingratitude

Thwip, thwap. Thwip, thwap.

The windshield wipers slamming back and forth trying to keep up with the pelting rain only added to my irritation as I adjusted to driving the used car I had just purchased—an old station wagon with 80,000+ miles and no side-impact airbag protection for the kids.

TODAY'S READING
Hebrews 12:18–29

To get this station wagon, and some badly needed cash for groceries, I had sold the last "treasure" we owned: a 1992 Volvo station wagon *with* side-impact air-bag protection for the kids. By then, everything else was gone. Our house and our savings had all disappeared under the weight of uncovered medical expenses from life-threatening illnesses.

Since we are receiving a kingdom that cannot be shaken, let us be thankful. Hebrews 12:28

"Okay, God," I actually said out loud, "now I can't even protect my kids from side-impact crashes. If anything happens to them, let me tell You what I'm going to do . . ."

Thwip, thwap. Thwip, thwap. (Gulp.)

I was instantly ashamed. In the previous 2 years God had spared both my wife and my son from almost certain death, and yet here I was whining about "things" I had lost. Just like that I'd learned how quickly I could grow ungrateful to God. The loving Father, who did not spare *His* own Son so I could be saved, had actually spared *my* son in a miraculous fashion.

"Forgive me, Father," I prayed. *Already done, My child.* 🌱

RANDY KILGORE

How easy it is, Lord, to let the trials of the moment strip us of the memory of Your protection and provision. Praise You, Father, for Your patience and Your unending, unconditional love.

Thankfulness is the soil in which joy thrives.

¹⁵ The eyes of the LORD are on the righteous,
and his ears are attentive to their cry;
¹⁶ but the face of the LORD is against those who do evil,
to blot out their name from the earth.
¹⁷ The righteous cry out, and the LORD hears them;
he delivers them from all their troubles.
¹⁸ The LORD is close to the brokenhearted
and saves those who are crushed in spirit.
¹⁹ The righteous person may have many troubles,
but the LORD delivers him from them all;
²⁰ he protects all his bones,
not one of them will be broken.
²¹ Evil will slay the wicked;
the foes of the righteous will be condemned.
²² The LORD will rescue his servants;
no one who takes refuge in him will be condemned.

A Widow's Choice

When a good friend suddenly lost her husband to a heart attack, we grieved with her. As a counselor, she had comforted many others. Now, after 40 years of marriage, she faced the unwelcome prospect of returning to an empty house at the end of each day.

In the midst of her grief, our friend leaned on the One who "is close to the brokenhearted." As God walked with her through her pain, she told us she would choose to "wear the label *widow* proudly," because she felt it was the label God had given her.

TODAY'S READING
Psalm 34:15–22

The LORD is close to the brokenhearted.

Psalm 34:18

All grief is personal, and others may grieve differently than she does. Her response doesn't diminish her grief or make her home less empty. Yet it reminds us that even in the midst of our worst sorrows, our sovereign and loving God can be trusted.

Our heavenly Father suffered a profound separation of His own. As Jesus hung on the cross He cried out, "My God, my God, why have you forsaken me?" (MATT. 27:46). Yet He endured the pain and separation of crucifixion for our sins out of love for us!

He understands! And because "the LORD is close to the brokenhearted" (PS. 34:18), we find the comfort we need. He is near. 🌣

DAVE BRANON

Dear heavenly Father, as we think about the sadness that comes from the death of a loved one, help us to cling to You and trust Your love and goodness. Thank You for being close to our broken hearts.

God shares in our sorrow.

¹ I will exalt you, my God the King;
    I will praise your name for ever and ever.
² Every day I will praise you
    and extol your name for ever and ever.
³ Great is the LORD and most worthy of praise;
    his greatness no one can fathom.
⁴ One generation commends your works to another;
    they tell of your mighty acts.
⁵ They speak of the glorious splendor of your majesty—
    and I will meditate on your wonderful works.
⁶ They tell of the power of your awesome works—
    and I will proclaim your great deeds.
⁷ They celebrate your abundant goodness
    and joyfully sing of your righteousness.
⁸ The LORD is gracious and compassionate,
    slow to anger and rich in love.
⁹ The LORD is good to all;
    he has compassion on all he has made.
¹⁰ All your works praise you, LORD;
    your faithful people extol you.
¹¹ They tell of the glory of your kingdom
    and speak of your might,
¹² so that all people may know of your mighty acts
    and the glorious splendor of your kingdom.
¹³ Your kingdom is an everlasting kingdom,
    and your dominion endures through all generations.
The LORD is trustworthy in all he promises
    and faithful in all he does.

Grandma's Recipe

Many families have a secret recipe, a special way of cooking a dish that makes it especially savory. For us Hakkas (my Chinese ethnic group), we have a traditional dish called abacus beads, named for its beadlike appearance. Really, you have to try it!

Of course Grandma had the best recipe. Each Chinese New Year at the family reunion dinner we would tell ourselves, "We should really learn how to cook this." But we never got around to asking Grandma. Now she is no longer with us, and her secret recipe is gone with her.

We miss Grandma, and it's sad to lose her recipe. It would be far more tragic if we were to fail to preserve the legacy of faith entrusted to us. God intends that every generation share with the next generation about the mighty acts of God. "One

> TODAY'S READING
> **Psalm 145:1–13**
>
> **Remember the days of old; consider the generations long past. Ask your father and he will tell you, your elders, and they will explain to you.**
>
> Deuteronomy 32:7

generation commends [God's] works to another," said the psalmist (PS. 145:4), echoing Moses's earlier instructions to "remember the days of old . . . . Ask your father and he will tell you, your elders, and they will explain to you" (DEUT. 32:7).

As we share our stories of how we received salvation and the ways the Lord has helped us face challenges, we encourage each other and honor Him. He designed us to enjoy family and community and to benefit from each other. ✿ *POH FANG CHIA*

Is there someone from a different age group with whom you can share your own faith journey? How about asking someone from an older generation to share their story with you. What might you learn?

What we teach our children today will influence tomorrow's world.

16 Then the eleven disciples went to Galilee, to the mountain where Jesus had told them to go. 17 When they saw him, they worshiped him; but some doubted. 18 Then Jesus came to them and said, "All authority in heaven and on earth has been given to me. 19 Therefore go and make disciples of all nations, baptizing them in the name of the Father and of the Son and of the Holy Spirit, 20 and teaching them to obey everything I have commanded you. And surely I am with you always, to the very end of the age."

Opening Doors

Charlie Sifford is an important name in American sports. He became the first African-American playing member of the Professional Golfers Association (PGA) Tour, joining a sport that, until 1961, had a "whites only" clause in its by-laws. Enduring racial injustice and harassment, Sifford earned his place at the game's highest level, won two tournaments, and in 2004 was the first African-American inducted into the World Golf Hall of Fame. Charlie Sifford opened the doors of professional golf for players of all ethnicities.

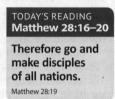

TODAY'S READING
Matthew 28:16–20

Therefore go and make disciples of all nations.

Matthew 28:19

Opening doors is also a theme at the heart of the gospel mission. Jesus said, "Therefore go and make disciples of all nations, baptizing them in the name of the Father and of the Son and of the Holy Spirit, and teaching them to obey everything I have commanded you. And surely I am with you always, to the very end of the age" (MATT. 28:19–20).

The word *nations* (V. 19) is from the Greek word *ethnos*, which is also the source of the word *ethnic*. In other words, "Go and make disciples of all ethnicities." Jesus's work on the cross opened the way to the Father for everyone.

Now we have the privilege of caring for others as God has cared for us. We can open the door for someone who never dreamed they'd be welcomed personally into the house and family of God. ❧

BILL CROWDER

> **Lord, help me** to be sensitive to others I meet today.
> Give me the words to tell others about You.

Jesus opened the doors of salvation to all who will believe.

¹ When Jesus had called the Twelve together, he gave them power and authority to drive out all demons and to cure diseases, ² and he sent them out to proclaim the kingdom of God and to heal the sick.

¹⁰ When the apostles returned, they reported to Jesus what they had done. Then he took them with him and they withdrew by themselves to a town called Bethsaida, ¹¹ but the crowds learned about it and followed him. He welcomed them and spoke to them about the kingdom of God, and healed those who needed healing.

¹² Late in the afternoon the Twelve came to him and said, "Send the crowd away so they can go to the surrounding villages and countryside and find food and lodging, because we are in a remote place here."

¹³ He replied, "You give them something to eat."

They answered, "We have only five loaves of bread and two fish—unless we go and buy food for all this crowd." ¹⁴ (About five thousand men were there.)

¹⁴ But he said to his disciples, "Have them sit down in groups of about fifty each." ¹⁵ The disciples did so, and everyone sat down. ¹⁶ Taking the five loaves and the two fish and looking up to heaven, he gave thanks and broke them. Then he gave them to the disciples to distribute to the people. ¹⁷ They all ate and were satisfied, and the disciples picked up twelve basketfuls of broken pieces that were left over.

Solitude and Service

Comedian **Fred Allen** said, "A celebrity is a person who works hard all his life to become well-known, then wears dark glasses to avoid being recognized." Fame often brings loss of privacy along with a relentless frenzy of attention.

When Jesus began His public ministry of teaching and healing, He was catapulted into the public eye and thronged by people seeking help. Crowds followed Him wherever He went. But Jesus knew that having regular time alone with God was essential to maintaining strength and perspective.

> TODAY'S READING
> **Luke 9:1–2, 10–17**
>
> **He welcomed them and spoke to them about the kingdom of God, and healed those who needed healing.** Luke 9:11

After Jesus's twelve disciples returned from their successful mission "to proclaim the kingdom of God and to heal the sick," He took them to a quiet place to rest (LUKE 9:2,10). Soon, however, crowds of people found them and Jesus welcomed them. He "spoke to them about the kingdom of God, and healed those who needed healing" (V. 11). Instead of sending them away to find food, the Lord provided an outdoor picnic for 5,000! (VV. 12–17).

Jesus was not immune to the pressure of curious and hurting people, but He maintained the balance of public service and private solitude by taking time for rest and for prayer alone with His Father (LUKE 5:16).

May we follow our Lord's example as we serve others in His name.   *DAVID MCCASLAND*

Dear Father, as Jesus Your Son and our Savior honored You in solitude and service to others, may we follow His example in our lives.

Turning down the volume of life allows you to listen to God.

¹⁶ I heard and my heart pounded,
   my lips quivered at the sound;
decay crept into my bones,
   and my legs trembled.
Yet I will wait patiently for the day of calamity
   to come on the nation invading us.
¹⁷ Though the fig tree does not bud
   and there are no grapes on the vines,
though the olive crop fails
   and the fields produce no food,
though there are no sheep in the pen
   and no cattle in the stalls,
¹⁸ yet I will rejoice in the LORD,
   I will be joyful in God my Savior.
¹⁹ The Sovereign LORD is my strength;
   he makes my feet like the feet of a deer,
   he enables me to tread on the heights.

The Voice of Faith

The news was numbing. The tears came so quickly that she couldn't fight them. Her mind raced with questions, and fear threatened to overwhelm her. Life had been going along so well, when it was abruptly interrupted and forever changed without warning.

Tragedy can come in many forms— the loss of a loved one, an illness, the loss of wealth or our livelihood. And it can happen to anyone at any time.

Although the prophet Habakkuk knew that tragedy was coming, it still struck fear in his heart. As he waited for the day when Babylon would invade the kingdom of Judah, his heart pounded, his lips quivered, and his legs trembled (HAB. 3:16).

TODAY'S READING
Habakkuk 3:16–19

Though the fig tree does not bud . . . yet I will rejoice in the LORD.

Habakkuk 3:17–18

Fear is a legitimate emotion in the face of tragedy, but it doesn't have to immobilize us. When we don't understand the trials we are going through, we can recount how God has worked in history (VV. 3-15). That's what Habakkuk did. It didn't dispel his fear, but it gave him the courage to move on by choosing to praise the Lord (V. 18).

Our God who has proven Himself faithful throughout the years is always with us. Because His character doesn't change, in our fear we can say with a confident voice of faith, "The Sovereign LORD is my strength!" (V. 19). 🦋   *POH FANG CHIA*

Dear Lord, when my world is turned upside down,
help me to trust You. You have always been faithful to me.

We can learn the lesson of trust in the school of trial.

¹ I cried out to God for help;
  I cried out to God to hear me.
² When I was in distress, I sought the LORD;
  at night I stretched out untiring hands,
and I would not be comforted.
³ I remembered you, God, and I groaned;
  I meditated, and my spirit grew faint.
⁴ You kept my eyes from closing;
  I was too troubled to speak.
⁵ I thought about the former days,
  the years of long ago;
⁶ I remembered my songs in the night.
  My heart meditated and my spirit asked:
⁷ "Will the LORD reject forever?
  Will he never show his favor again?
⁸ Has his unfailing love vanished forever?
  Has his promise failed for all time?
⁹ Has God forgotten to be merciful?
  Has he in anger withheld his compassion?"
¹⁰ Then I thought, "To this I will appeal:
  the years when the Most High stretched out his right
hand.
¹¹ I will remember the deeds of the LORD;
  yes, I will remember your miracles of long ago.
¹² I will consider all your works
  and meditate on all your mighty deeds."
¹³ Your ways, God, are holy.
  What god is as great as our God?
¹⁴ You are the God who performs miracles;
  you display your power among the peoples.
¹⁵ With your mighty arm you redeemed your people,
  the descendants of Jacob and Joseph.

Four Ways to Look

Joan was struggling with some difficult issues with her children when she sat down for a worship service. Exhausted, she wanted to "resign" from motherhood. Then the speaker began to share encouragement for those who feel like quitting. These four thoughts that Joan heard that morning helped her to keep going:

Look up and pray. Asaph prayed all night long and even expressed feelings that God had forgotten and rejected him (PS. 77:9–10). We can tell God everything and be honest about our feelings. We can ask Him anything. His answer may not come right away or in the form we want or expect, but He won't criticize us for asking.

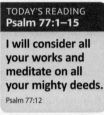

TODAY'S READING
Psalm 77:1–15

I will consider all your works and meditate on all your mighty deeds.

Psalm 77:12

Look back and remember what God has done in the past for you and others. Asaph didn't talk to God only about the pain; he also recalled God's power and mighty works for him and God's people. He wrote, "I will remember the deeds of the LORD; yes, I will remember your miracles of long ago" (V. 11).

Look forward. Think about the good that might come out of the situation. What might you learn? What might God want to do? What do you know He will do because His ways are perfect? (V.13).

Look again. This time look at your circumstances with eyes of faith. Remind yourself that He is the God of great wonders and can be trusted (V. 14).

May these ideas help us gain perspective and keep moving in our faith journey with Jesus. 🌿 ANNE CETAS

Lord, I can't help but see my problems. Help me not to be discouraged and weary, but to see You in the midst of them.

Our problems are opportunities to discover God's solutions.

⁸ Finally, brothers and sisters, whatever is true, whatever is noble, whatever is right, whatever is pure, whatever is lovely, whatever is admirable—if anything is excellent or praiseworthy—think about such things.

⁹ Whatever you have learned or received or heard from me, or seen in me—put it into practice. And the God of peace will be with you.

¹⁰ I rejoiced greatly in the Lord that at last you renewed your concern for me. Indeed, you were concerned, but you had no opportunity to show it. ¹¹ I am not saying this because I am in need, for I have learned to be content whatever the circumstances. ¹² I know what it is to be in need, and I know what it is to have plenty. I have learned the secret of being content in any and every situation, whether well fed or hungry, whether living in plenty or in want. ¹³ I can do all this through him who gives me strength.

The View from the Mountain

Our valley in Idaho can be very cold in the winter. Clouds and fog roll in and blanket the ground, trapping frigid air under warmer layers above. But you can get above the valley. There's a road nearby that winds up the flank of Shafer Butte, a 7,500-foot mountain that rises out of our valley. A few minutes of driving and you break out of the fog and emerge into the warmth and brilliance of a sunlit day. You can look down on the clouds that shroud the valley below and see it from a different point of view.

> TODAY'S READING
> **Philippians 4:8–13**
>
> **Since, then, you have been raised with Christ, set your hearts on things above.**
> Colossians 3:1

Life is like that at times. Circumstances seem to surround us with a fog that sunlight cannot penetrate. Yet *faith* is the way we get above the valley—the means by which we "set [our] hearts on things above" (COL. 3:1). As we do, the Lord enables us to rise above our circumstances and find courage and calmness for the day. As the apostle Paul wrote, "I have learned to be content whatever the circumstances" (PHIL. 4:11).

We can climb out of our misery and gloom. We can sit for a time on the mountainside and through Christ who gives us strength (V. 13) we can gain a different perspective. 🌿 *DAVID ROPER*

> **Although I** can't always see You or what You're doing, Lord,
> I rest in Your love for me.

Faith can lift you above your fears.

¹ God is our refuge and strength,
    an ever-present help in trouble.
² Therefore we will not fear, though the earth give way
    and the mountains fall into the heart of the sea,
³ though its waters roar and foam
    and the mountains quake with their surging.
⁴ There is a river whose streams make glad the city of God,
    the holy place where the Most High dwells.
⁵ God is within her, she will not fall;
    God will help her at break of day.
⁶ Nations are in uproar, kingdoms fall;
    he lifts his voice, the earth melts.
⁷ The LORD Almighty is with us;
    the God of Jacob is our fortress.
⁸ Come and see what the LORD has done,
    the desolations he has brought on the earth.
⁹ He makes wars cease
    to the ends of the earth.
He breaks the bow and shatters the spear;
    he burns the shields with fire.
¹⁰ He says, "Be still, and know that I am God;
    I will be exalted among the nations,
    I will be exalted in the earth."
¹¹ The LORD Almighty is with us;
    the God of Jacob is our fortress.

Be Still

Years ago I responded to letters within a couple of weeks and kept my correspondents happy. Then came the fax machine, and they seemed content with receiving a response within a couple of days. Today, with email, instant messaging, and mobile phones, a response is expected the same day!

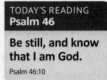

TODAY'S READING
Psalm 46

Be still, and know that I am God.

Psalm 46:10

"Be still, and know that I am God." In this familiar verse from Psalm 46 I read two commands of equal importance. First, we must be still, something that modern life conspires against. In this hectic, buzzing world, even a few moments of quiet do not come naturally to us. And stillness prepares us for the second command: "Know that I am God; I will be exalted among the nations, I will be exalted in the earth." In the midst of a world that colludes to suppress, not exalt, God, how do I carve out time and allow Him to nourish my inner life?

"Prayer," writes Patricia Hampl, "is a habit of attention brought to bear on all that is." Ah, prayer . . . a habit of attention. *Be still and know.* The first step in prayer is to acknowledge or to "know" that God is God. And in that attention, that focus, all else comes into focus. Prayer allows us to admit our failures, weaknesses, and limitations to the One who responds to human vulnerability with infinite mercy. ❂　　　*PHILIP YANCEY*

Dear Lord, help me to be still.
Nourish my soul as I spend time with You in prayer.

In prayer, God can quiet our minds.

¹ Jesus entered Jericho and was passing through. ² A man was there by the name of Zacchaeus; he was a chief tax collector and was wealthy. ³ He wanted to see who Jesus was, but because he was short he could not see over the crowd. ⁴ So he ran ahead and climbed a sycamore-fig tree to see him, since Jesus was coming that way.

⁵ When Jesus reached the spot, he looked up and said to him, "Zacchaeus, come down immediately. I must stay at your house today." ⁶ So he came down at once and welcomed him gladly.

⁷ All the people saw this and began to mutter, "He has gone to be the guest of a sinner."

⁸ But Zacchaeus stood up and said to the Lord, "Look, Lord! Here and now I give half of my possessions to the poor, and if I have cheated anybody out of anything, I will pay back four times the amount."

⁹ Jesus said to him, "Today salvation has come to this house, because this man, too, is a son of Abraham. ¹⁰ For the Son of Man came to seek and to save the lost."

A Better View

As a child, I loved to climb trees. The higher I climbed, the more I could see. Occasionally, in search of a better view, I might inch out along a branch until I felt it bend under my weight. Not surprisingly, my tree-climbing days are over. I suppose it isn't very safe—or dignified.

Zacchaeus, a wealthy man, set aside his dignity (and perhaps ignored his safety) when he climbed a tree one day in Jericho. Jesus was traveling through the city, and Zacchaeus wanted to get a look at Him. However, "because he was short he could not see over the crowd" (LUKE 19:3). Fortunately, those things did not stop him from seeing and even talking with Christ. Zacchaeus's plan worked! And when he met Jesus, his life was changed forever. "Salvation has come to this house," Jesus said (V. 9).

TODAY'S READING
Luke 19:1–10

Because he was short he could not see over the crowd.
Luke 19:3

We too can be prevented from seeing Jesus. Pride can blind us from seeing Him as the Wonderful Counselor. Anxiety keeps us from knowing Him as the Prince of Peace (ISA. 9:6). Hunger for status and stuff can prevent us from seeing Him as the true source of satisfaction—the Bread of Life (JOHN 6:48).

What are you willing to do to get a better view of Jesus? Any sincere effort to get closer to Him will have a good result. God rewards people who earnestly seek Him (HEB. 11:6). 🕊

JENNIFER BENSON SCHULDT

Thank You Jesus for all that You are.
Show me more of Yourself as I read the Bible and pray.
Help me to pursue You with all of my heart and mind.

To strengthen your faith in God, seek the face of God.

²¹ On the eighth day, when it was time to circumcise the child, he was named Jesus, the name the angel had given him before he was conceived.

²² When the time came for the purification rites required by the Law of Moses, Joseph and Mary took him to Jerusalem to present him to the Lord ²³ (as it is written in the Law of the Lord, "Every firstborn male is to be consecrated to the Lord", ²⁴ and to offer a sacrifice in keeping with what is said in the Law of the Lord: "a pair of doves or two young pigeons."

²⁵ Now there was a man in Jerusalem called Simeon, who was righteous and devout. He was waiting for the consolation of Israel, and the Holy Spirit was on him. ²⁶ It had been revealed to him by the Holy Spirit that he would not die before he had seen the Lord's Messiah. ²⁷ Moved by the Spirit, he went into the temple courts. When the parents brought in the child Jesus to do for him what the custom of the Law required,

²⁸ Simeon took him in his arms and praised God, saying:

²⁹ "Sovereign Lord, as you have promised,
    you may now dismiss your servant in peace.
³⁰ For my eyes have seen your salvation,
³¹ which you have prepared in the sight of all nations:
³² a light for revelation to the Gentiles,
    and the glory of your people Israel."

³³ The child's father and mother marveled at what was said about him. ³⁴ Then Simeon blessed them and said to Mary, his mother: "This child is destined to cause the falling and rising of many in Israel, and to be a sign that will be spoken against, ³⁵ so that the thoughts of many hearts will be revealed. And a sword will pierce your own soul too."

The Forward Look

When the great Dutch painter Rembrandt died unexpectedly at age 63, an unfinished painting was found on his easel. It focuses on Simeon's emotion in holding the baby Jesus when He was brought to the temple in Jerusalem, 40 days after His birth. Yet the background and normal detail remain unfinished. Some art experts believe that Rembrandt knew the end of his life was near and—like Simeon—was ready to "be dismissed" (LUKE 2:29).

TODAY'S READING
Luke 2:21–35

Simeon . . . was righteous and devout . . . and the Holy Spirit was on him. Luke 2:25

The Holy Spirit was upon Simeon (V. 25), so it was no coincidence that he was in the temple when Mary and Joseph presented their firstborn son to God. Simeon, who had been looking for the promised Messiah, took the baby in his arms and praised God, saying: "Sovereign Lord, as you have promised, you may now dismiss your servant in peace. For my eyes have seen your salvation, which you have prepared in the sight of all nations: a light for revelation to the Gentiles, and the glory of your people Israel" (VV. 29–32).

Simeon was not longing for the glory days of Israel's history, but was looking ahead for the promised Messiah, who would come to redeem all nations.

Like Simeon, we can have an expectant, forward look in life because we know that one day we will see the Lord. 🌱

DAVID MCCASLAND

Father, may we, like Simeon, be always looking ahead
for the appearing of Jesus our Lord.

Even so, come, Lord Jesus! REVELATION 22:20

³⁹ When Moses reported this to all the Israelites, they mourned bitterly. ⁴⁰ Early the next morning they set out for the highest point in the hill country, saying, "Now we are ready to go up to the land the LORD promised. Surely we have sinned!"

⁴¹ But Moses said, "Why are you disobeying the LORD's command? This will not succeed! ⁴² Do not go up, because the LORD is not with you. You will be defeated by your enemies, ⁴³ for the Amalekites and the Canaanites will face you there. Because you have turned away from the LORD, he will not be with you and you will fall by the sword."

⁴⁴ Nevertheless, in their presumption they went up toward the highest point in the hill country, though neither Moses nor the ark of the LORD's covenant moved from the camp.

⁴⁵ Then the Amalekites and the Canaanites who lived in that hill country came down and attacked them and beat them down all the way to Hormah.

Go Fever

On January 28, 1986, after five weather-related delays, the space shuttle *Challenger* lumbered heavenward amid a thunderous overture of noise and flame. A mere 73 seconds later, system failure tore the shuttle apart, and all seven crewmembers perished.

TODAY'S READING
Numbers 14:39–45

Be still before the LORD and wait patiently for him.

Psalm 37:7

The disaster was attributed to an O-ring seal known to have vulnerabilities. Insiders referred to the fatal mistake as "go fever"—the tendency to ignore vital precautions in the rush to a grand goal.

Our ambitious human nature relentlessly tempts us to make ill-advised choices. Yet we are also prone to a fear that can make us overly cautious. The ancient Israelites demonstrated both traits. When the 12 scouts returned from spying out the Promised Land, 10 of the 12 saw only the obstacles (NUM. 13:26–33). "We can't attack those people; they are stronger than we are," they said (V. 31). After a fearful rebellion against the Lord that led to the death of the 10 spies, the people suddenly developed a case of "go fever." They said, "Now we are ready to go up to the land the LORD promised" (14:40). Without God, the ill-timed invasion failed miserably (VV. 41–45).

When we take our eyes off the Lord, we'll slide into one of two extremes. We'll impatiently rush ahead without Him, or we'll cower and complain in fear. Focusing on Him brings courage tempered with His wisdom. ❧ *TIM GUSTAFSON*

Before making a quick decision, consider why you want to make it quickly. Consider if it will honor God and what it might cost others. If you are afraid to make a decision, think about why that might be. Most of all, pray!

A moment of patience can prevent a great disaster.

⁴ Even to your old age and gray hairs
    I am he, I am he who will sustain you.
  I have made you and I will carry you;
    I will sustain you and I will rescue you.

⁵ "With whom will you compare me or count me equal?
    To whom will you liken me that we may be compared?
⁶ Some pour out gold from their bags
    and weigh out silver on the scales;
  they hire a goldsmith to make it into a god,
    and they bow down and worship it.
⁷ They lift it to their shoulders and carry it;
    they set it up in its place, and there it stands.
    From that spot it cannot move.
  Even though someone cries out to it, it cannot answer;
    it cannot save them from their troubles.

⁸ "Remember this, keep it in mind,
    take it to heart, you rebels.
⁹ Remember the former things, those of long ago;
    I am God, and there is no other;
    I am God, and there is none like me.
¹⁰ I make known the end from the beginning,
    from ancient times, what is still to come.
  I say, 'My purpose will stand,
    and I will do all that I please.'
¹¹ From the east I summon a bird of prey;
    from a far-off land, a man to fulfill my purpose.
  What I have said, that I will bring about;
    what I have planned, that I will do.
¹² Listen to me, you stubborn-hearted,
    you who are now far from my righteousness.
¹³ I am bringing my righteousness near,
    it is not far away;
    and my salvation will not be delayed.
  I will grant salvation to Zion,
    my splendor to Israel.

How to Grow Old

"**H**ow are you today,** Mama?" I asked casually. My 84-year-old friend, pointing to aches and pains in her joints, whispered, "Old age is tough!" Then she added earnestly, "But God has been good to me."

"Growing old has been the greatest surprise of my life," says Billy Graham in his book *Nearing Home*. "I am an old man now, and believe me, it's not easy." However, Graham notes, "While the Bible doesn't gloss over the problems we face as we grow older, neither does it paint old age as a time to be despised or a burden to be

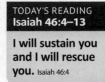

TODAY'S READING
Isaiah 46:4–13

I will sustain you and I will rescue you. Isaiah 46:4

endured with gritted teeth." He then mentions some of the questions he has been forced to deal with as he has aged, such as, "How can we not only learn to cope with the fears and struggles and growing limitations we face but also actually grow stronger inwardly in the midst of these difficulties?"

In Isaiah 46 we have God's assurance: "Even to your old age and gray hairs . . . I am he who will sustain you. I have made you and I will carry you; I will sustain you and I will rescue you" (v. 4).

We don't know how many years we will live on this earth or what we might face as we age. But one thing is certain: God will care for us throughout our life. 🌱

LAWRENCE DARMANI

Lord, please teach us to number our days so that we may gain a heart of wisdom.

(SEE PSALM 90:12)

Don't be afraid to grow old; God goes with you!

¹ The LORD said to Job:

² "Will the one who contends with the Almighty
correct him?
  Let him who accuses God answer him!"

³ Then Job answered the LORD:

⁴ "I am unworthy—how can I reply to you?
  I put my hand over my mouth.

⁵ I spoke once, but I have no answer—
  twice, but I will say no more."

⁶ Then the LORD spoke to Job out of the storm:

⁷ "Brace yourself like a man;
  I will question you,
  and you shall answer me.

⁸ "Would you discredit my justice?
  Would you condemn me to justify yourself?

⁹ Do you have an arm like God's,
  and can your voice thunder like his?

¹⁰ Then adorn yourself with glory and splendor,
  and clothe yourself in honor and majesty.

¹¹ Unleash the fury of your wrath,
  look at all who are proud and bring them low,

¹² look at all who are proud and humble them,
  crush the wicked where they stand.

¹³ Bury them all in the dust together;
  shroud their faces in the grave.

¹⁴ Then I myself will admit to you
  that your own right hand can save you.

_____

_____

_____

_____

_____

Taking Notice

When I clean my house for a special event, I become discouraged because I think that guests won't notice what I clean, only what I don't clean. This brings to mind a larger philosophical and spiritual question: Why do humans more quickly see what's wrong than what's right? We are more likely to remember rudeness than kindness. Crimes seem to receive more attention than acts of generosity. And disasters grab our attention more quickly than the profound beauty all around us.

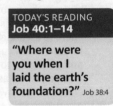

TODAY'S READING
Job 40:1–14

"Where were you when I laid the earth's foundation?" Job 38:4

But then I realize I am the same way with God. I tend to focus on what He hasn't done rather than on what He has, on what I don't have rather than on what I have, on the situations that He has not yet resolved rather than on the many He has.

When I read the book of Job, I am reminded that the Lord doesn't like this any more than I do. After years of experiencing prosperity, Job suffered a series of disasters. Suddenly those became the focus of his life and conversations. Finally, God intervened and asked Job some hard questions, reminding him of His sovereignty and of everything Job didn't know and hadn't seen (JOB 38–40).

Whenever I start focusing on the negative, I hope I remember to stop, consider the life of Job, and take notice of all the wonders God has done and continues to do. ❂   *JULIE ACKERMAN LINK*

Consider keeping a "thanks" journal.
Write down each day one thing God has done for you.

When you think of all that's good, give thanks to God.

¹ As a prisoner for the Lord, then, I urge you to live a life worthy of the calling you have received. ² Be completely humble and gentle; be patient, bearing with one another in love. ³ Make every effort to keep the unity of the Spirit through the bond of peace. ⁴ There is one body and one Spirit, just as you were called to one hope when you were called; ⁵ one Lord, one faith, one baptism; ⁶ one God and Father of all, who is over all and through all and in all.

⁷ But to each one of us grace has been given as Christ apportioned it. ⁸ This is why it says:

"When he ascended on high,
　he took many captives
　and gave gifts to his people."

⁹ (What does "he ascended" mean except that he also descended to the lower, earthly regions? ¹⁰ He who descended is the very one who ascended higher than all the heavens, in order to fill the whole universe.) ¹¹ So Christ himself gave the apostles, the prophets, the evangelists, the pastors and teachers, ¹² to equip his people for works of service, so that the body of Christ may be built up ¹³ until we all reach unity in the faith and in the knowledge of the Son of God and become mature, attaining to the whole measure of the fullness of Christ.

¹⁴ Then we will no longer be infants, tossed back and forth by the waves, and blown here and there by every wind of teaching and by the cunning and craftiness of people in their deceitful scheming. ¹⁵ Instead, speaking the truth in love, we will grow to become in every respect the mature body of him who is the head, that is, Christ. ¹⁶ From him the whole body, joined and held together by every supporting ligament, grows and builds itself up in love, as each part does its work.

Growing Up

Watching my young grandson and his friends play T-Ball is entertaining. In this version of baseball, young players often run to the wrong base or don't know what to do with the ball if they happen to catch it. If we were watching a professional baseball game, these mistakes would not be so funny.

It's all a matter of maturity.

It's okay for young athletes to struggle—not knowing what to do or not getting everything exactly right. They are trying and learning. So we coach them and patiently guide them toward maturity. Then we celebrate their success as later they play with skill as a team.

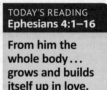

TODAY'S READING
Ephesians 4:1–16

From him the whole body... grows and builds itself up in love.

Ephesians 4:16

Something similar happens in the life of those who follow Jesus. Paul pointed out that the church needs people who will "be patient, bearing with one another in love" (EPH. 4:2). And we need a variety of "coaches" (pastors, teachers, spiritual mentors) to help us all move toward "unity in the faith" as we strive to "become mature" (V. 13).

The goal as we listen to preaching and teaching and enjoy life together in the church is to grow up to maturity in Christ (V. 15). Each of us is on this journey, and we can encourage each other on the road to maturity in Jesus. 🌱   *DAVE BRANON*

Lord, help me to strive for maturity. Thank You for equipping the church
with men and women who can help me grow in my faith.
Show me who I can encourage today.

There's joy in the journey as we walk alongside each other.

⁴ As you come to him, the living Stone—rejected by humans but chosen by God and precious to him— ⁵ you also, like living stones, are being built into a spiritual house to be a holy priesthood, offering spiritual sacrifices acceptable to God through Jesus Christ. ⁶ For in Scripture it says:

"See, I lay a stone in Zion,
    a chosen and precious cornerstone,
and the one who trusts in him
    will never be put to shame."

⁷ Now to you who believe, this stone is precious. But to those who do not believe,

"The stone the builders rejected
    has become the cornerstone,"

⁸ and, "A stone that causes people to stumble
    and a rock that makes them fall."

They stumble because they disobey the message—which is also what they were destined for.

⁹ But you are a chosen people, a royal priesthood, a holy nation, God's special possession, that you may declare the praises of him who called you out of darkness into his wonderful light. ¹⁰ Once you were not a people, but now you are the people of God; once you had not received mercy, but now you have received mercy.

Leaning into the Light

O ne day I received a bouquet of pink tulips. Their heads bobbed on thick stems as I settled them into a vase, which I placed at the center of our kitchen table. The next day, I noticed that the flowers were facing a different direction. The blossoms that once faced upward were now leaning to the side, opening and reaching toward sunlight that streamed in through a nearby window.

TODAY'S READING
1 Peter 2:4–10

In one sense, we all were made to be like those flowers. God has called us to turn to the light of His love. Peter writes of the wonder of being called "out of darkness into [God's] wonderful light"

> **[He] called you out of darkness into his wonderful light.**
> 1 Peter 2:9

(1 PETER 2:9). Before we come to know God, we live in the shadows of sin and death, which keep us separated from Him (EPH. 2:1–7). However, because of God's mercy and love, He made a way for us to escape spiritual darkness through the death and resurrection of His Son (COL. 1:13–14).

Jesus is the Light of the world, and everyone who trusts Him for the forgiveness of sin will receive eternal life. Only as we turn to Him will we increasingly reflect His goodness and truth (EPH. 5:8–9).

May we never forget to lean into the Light. 🌸

JENNIFER BENSON SCHULDT

Joyful, joyful we adore You, God of glory, Lord of love;
hearts unfold like flowers before You, opening to the sun above.
HENRY VAN DYKE

Salvation from sin means moving from spiritual darkness to God's light.

¹ That night all the members of the community raised their voices and wept aloud. ² All the Israelites grumbled against Moses and Aaron, and the whole assembly said to them, "If only we had died in Egypt! Or in this wilderness! ³ Why is the LORD bringing us to this land only to let us fall by the sword? Our wives and children will be taken as plunder. Wouldn't it be better for us to go back to Egypt?" ⁴ And they said to each other, "We should choose a leader and go back to Egypt."

⁵ Then Moses and Aaron fell facedown in front of the whole Israelite assembly gathered there. ⁶ Joshua son of Nun and Caleb son of Jephunneh, who were among those who had explored the land, tore their clothes ⁷ and said to the entire Israelite assembly, "The land we passed through and explored is exceedingly good. ⁸ If the LORD is pleased with us, he will lead us into that land, a land flowing with milk and honey, and will give it to us. ⁹ Only do not rebel against the LORD. And do not be afraid of the people of the land, because we will devour them. Their protection is gone, but the LORD is with us. Do not be afraid of them."

Lurking Lions

When I was young, my dad would "scare" us by hiding in the bush and growling like a lion. Even though we lived in rural Ghana in the 1960s, it was almost impossible that a lion lurked nearby. My brother and I would laugh and seek out the source of the noise, thrilled that playtime with Dad had arrived.

One day a young friend came for a visit. As we played, we heard the familiar growl. Our friend screamed and ran. My brother and I knew the sound of my father's voice—any "danger" was merely a phantom lion—but a funny thing happened. We ran with her. My dad felt terrible that our friend had been frightened, and my brother and I learned not to be influenced by the panicked reaction of others.

TODAY'S READING
Numbers 14:1–9

The LORD is with us. Do not be afraid of them.

Numbers 14:9

Caleb and Joshua stand out as men unfazed by the panic of others. As Israel was poised to enter the Promised Land, Moses commissioned 12 scouts to spy out the region. They all saw a beautiful territory, but 10 focused on the obstacles and discouraged the entire nation (NUM. 13:27–33). In the process, they started a panic (14:1–4). Only Caleb and Joshua accurately assessed the situation (VV. 6–9). They knew the history of their Father and trusted Him to bring them success.

Some "lions" pose a genuine threat. Others are phantoms. Regardless, as followers of Jesus our confidence is in the One whose voice and deeds we know and trust. 🌿   *TIM GUSTAFSON*

Lord, we face many fears today. Help us distinguish between
real danger and empty threats, and help us trust You with all of it.
May we live not in fear, but in faith.

*The wicked flee though no one pursues,
but the righteous are as bold as a lion.* PROVERBS 28:1

¹ These are the commands, decrees and laws the LORD your God directed me to teach you to observe in the land that you are crossing the Jordan to possess, ² so that you, your children and their children after them may fear the LORD your God as long as you live by keeping all his decrees and commands that I give you, and so that you may enjoy long life. ³ Hear, Israel, and be careful to obey so that it may go well with you and that you may increase greatly in a land flowing with milk and honey, just as the LORD, the God of your ancestors, promised you.

⁴ Hear, O Israel: The LORD our God, the LORD is one. ⁵ Love the LORD your God with all your heart and with all your soul and with all your strength. ⁶ These commandments that I give you today are to be on your hearts. ⁷ Impress them on your children. Talk about them when you sit at home and when you walk along the road, when you lie down and when you get up. ⁸ Tie them as symbols on your hands and bind them on your foreheads. ⁹ Write them on the doorframes of your houses and on your gates.

¹⁰ When the LORD your God brings you into the land he swore to your fathers, to Abraham, Isaac and Jacob, to give you—a land with large, flourishing cities you did not build, ¹¹ houses filled with all kinds of good things you did not provide, wells you did not dig, and vineyards and olive groves you did not plant—then when you eat and are satisfied, ¹² be careful that you do not forget the LORD, who brought you out of Egypt, out of the land of slavery.

Written on Our Hearts

n my neighborhood, religious inscriptions abound—on plaques, walls, doorposts, commercial vehicles, and even as registered names of businesses. *By the Grace of God* reads an inscription on a mini-bus; *God's Divine Favor Bookshop* adorns a business signboard. The other day I couldn't help smiling at this one on a Mercedes Benz: *Keep Off—Angels on Guard!*

But religious inscriptions, whether on wall plaques, jewelry, or T-shirts, are not a reliable indicator of a person's love for God. It's not the words on the outside that count but the truth we carry on the inside that reveals our desire to be changed by God.

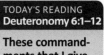

TODAY'S READING
Deuteronomy 6:1–12

These commandments that I give you today are to be on your hearts.

Deuteronomy 6:6

I recall a program sponsored by a local ministry that distributed cards with Bible verses written on both sides that helped people memorize God's Word. Such a practice is in keeping with the instructions Moses gave the Israelites when he told them to write the commandments of God "on the doorframes of your houses and on your gates" (DEUT. 6:9). We are to treasure God's Word in our hearts (V. 6), to impress it on our children, and to talk about it "when [we] walk along the road, when [we] lie down and when [we] get up" (V. 7).

May our faith be real and our commitment true, so we can love the Lord our God with all our heart, soul, and strength (V. 5). 🕮

LAWRENCE DARMANI

Father, may Your words be more than nice sayings to us.
May they be written on our hearts so that we will love You and others.

When God's Word is hidden in our heart, His ways will become our ways.

² Consider it pure joy, my brothers and sisters, whenever you face trials of many kinds, ³ because you know that the testing of your faith produces perseverance. ⁴ Let perseverance finish its work so that you may be mature and complete, not lacking anything.

For His Time

When South African pastor Andrew Murray was visiting England in 1895, he began to suffer pain from a previous back injury. While he was recuperating, his hostess told him of a woman who was in great trouble and wanted to know if he had any counsel for her. Murray said, "Give her this paper which I have been writing for my own [encouragement]. It may be that she will find it helpful." This is what Murray wrote:

TODAY'S READING
James 1:2–4

My times are in your hands.
Psalm 31:15

"In time of trouble say:

First—God brought me here. It is by His will I am in this strait place. In that I will rest.

Next—He will keep me in His love and give me grace in this trial to behave as His child.

Then—He will make the trial a blessing, teaching me lessons He intends me to learn, and working in me the grace He means to bestow.

Last—In His good time He can bring me out again—how and when He knows.

I am here—by God's appointment, in His keeping, under His training, for His time."

We want the instant solution, the quick fix, but some things cannot be disposed of so readily; they can only be accepted. God will keep us by His love. By His grace, we can rest in Him. ✿

DAVID ROPER

Dear Lord, it's hard to endure times of illness and suffering. Comfort me and help me to trust You.

When God permits suffering, He also provides comfort.

⁹ Now Sennacherib received a report that Tirhakah, the king of Cush, was marching out to fight against him. So he again sent messengers to Hezekiah with this word: ¹⁰ "Say to Hezekiah king of Judah: Do not let the god you depend on deceive you when he says, 'Jerusalem will not be given into the hands of the king of Assyria.' ¹¹ Surely you have heard what the kings of Assyria have done to all the countries, destroying them completely. And will you be delivered? ¹² Did the gods of the nations that were destroyed by my predecessors deliver them—the gods of Gozan, Harran, Rezeph and the people of Eden who were in Tel Assar? ¹³ Where is the king of Hamath or the king of Arpad? Where are the kings of Lair, Sepharvaim, Hena and Ivvah?"

¹⁴ Hezekiah received the letter from the messengers and read it. Then he went up to the temple of the LORD and spread it out before the LORD. ¹⁵ And Hezekiah prayed to the LORD: "LORD, the God of Israel, enthroned between the cherubim, you alone are God over all the kingdoms of the earth. You have made heaven and earth. ¹⁶ Give ear, LORD, and hear; open your eyes, LORD, and see; listen to the words Sennacherib has sent to ridicule the living God.

¹⁷ "It is true, LORD, that the Assyrian kings have laid waste these nations and their lands. ¹⁸ They have thrown their gods into the fire and destroyed them, for they were not gods but only wood and stone, fashioned by human hands. ¹⁹ Now, LORD our God, deliver us from his hand, so that all the kingdoms of the earth may know that you alone, LORD, are God."

²⁰ Then Isaiah son of Amoz sent a message to Hezekiah: "This is what the LORD, the God of Israel, says: I have heard your prayer concerning Sennacherib king of Assyria.

Forward to God

I n the days before telephones, email, and mobile phones, the telegram was usually the fastest means of communication. But only important news was sent by telegram, and such news was usually bad. Hence the saying, "The telegram boy always brings bad news."

It was wartime in ancient Israel when Hezekiah was king of Judah. Sennacherib, king of Assyria, had invaded and captured the cities of Judah. He then sent a letter to Hezekiah, a bad-news "telegram" urging his surrender. Hezekiah described the moment as "a day of distress and rebuke and disgrace" (2 KINGS 19:3).

TODAY'S READING
2 Kings 19:9–20

Give ear, LORD, and hear; open your eyes, LORD, and see. 2 Kings 19:16

With taunts and scoffs, Sennacherib boasted of his past military campaigns, belittling the God of Israel and threatening mayhem (VV. 11–13). In that dreadful moment, King Hezekiah did an unusual thing with the bad-news letter: "He went up to the temple of the LORD and spread it out before the LORD" (V. 14). Then he prayed earnestly, acknowledging the power of God over their gloomy situation (VV. 15–19). God intervened in a powerful way (VV. 35–36).

Bad news can reach us at any time. In those moments, Hezekiah's action is a good example to follow. Spread out the news before the Lord in prayer and hear His reassurance: "I have heard your prayer" (V. 20). 🌼

LAWRENCE DARMANI

Heavenly Father, when people attack us, we tend to react defensively. Teach us to turn to You instead of taking matters into our own hands. We trust You and love You. Defend us today.

Prayer is the child's helpless cry to the Father's attentive ear.

¹² Therefore, as God's chosen people, holy and dearly loved, clothe yourselves with compassion, kindness, humility, gentleness and patience. ¹³ Bear with each other and forgive one another if any of you has a grievance against someone. Forgive as the Lord forgave you. ¹⁴ And over all these virtues put on love, which binds them all together in perfect unity.

¹⁵ Let the peace of Christ rule in your hearts, since as members of one body you were called to peace. And be thankful. ¹⁶ Let the message of Christ dwell among you richly as you teach and admonish one another with all wisdom through psalms, hymns, and songs from the Spirit, singing to God with gratitude in your hearts. ¹⁷ And whatever you do, whether in word or deed, do it all in the name of the Lord Jesus, giving thanks to God the Father through him.

The Power of God's Music

The *Sound of Music*, one of the most successful musical films ever produced, was released as a motion picture in 1965. It won many accolades, including five Academy Awards, as it captured the hearts and voices of people around the world. More than half a century later, people still attend special showings of the film where viewers come dressed as their favorite character and sing along during the performance.

TODAY'S READING
Colossians 3:12–17

Let the message of Christ dwell among you richly . . . with all wisdom through psalms, hymns, and songs from the Spirit. Colossians 3:16

Music is deeply rooted in our souls. And for followers of Jesus, it is a powerful means of encouraging each other along the journey of faith. Paul urged the believers in Colosse, "Let Christ's teaching live in your hearts, making you rich in the true wisdom. Teach and help one another along the right road with your psalms and hymns and Christian songs, singing God's praises with joyful hearts" (COL. 3:16 PHILLIPS).

Singing together to the Lord embeds the message of His love in our minds and souls. It is a powerful ministry of teaching and encouragement that we share together. Whether our hearts cry out, "Create in me a pure heart, O God" (PS. 51:10), or joyfully shout, "And he will reign forever and ever" (REV. 11:15), the power of music that exalts God lifts our spirits and grants us peace.

Let us sing to the Lord today. 🕮   *DAVID MCCASLAND*

Thank You, Lord, for Your gift of music.
We sing Your praise together and learn more of Your love and power.
What is your favorite hymn or worship song?

Music washes from the soul the dust of everyday life.

⁶ This is a copy of the letter that Tattenai, governor of Trans-Euphrates, and Shethar-Bozenai and their associates, the officials of Trans-Euphrates, sent to King Darius. ⁷ The report they sent him read as follows:

To King Darius:

Cordial greetings.

⁸ The king should know that we went to the district of Judah, to the temple of the great God. The people are building it with large stones and placing the timbers in the walls. The work is being carried on with diligence and is making rapid progress under their direction.

⁹ We questioned the elders and asked them, "Who authorized you to rebuild this temple and to finish it?" ¹⁰ We also asked them their names, so that we could write down the names of their leaders for your information.

¹¹ This is the answer they gave us:

"We are the servants of the God of heaven and earth, and we are rebuilding the temple that was built many years ago, one that a great king of Israel built and finished. ¹² But because our ancestors angered the God of heaven, he gave them into the hands of Nebuchadnezzar the Chaldean, king of Babylon, who destroyed this temple and deported the people to Babylon.

¹³ "However, in the first year of Cyrus king of Babylon, King Cyrus issued a decree to rebuild this house of God.

¹⁴ He even removed from the temple of Babylon the gold and silver articles of the house of God, which Nebuchadnezzar had taken from the temple in Jerusalem and brought to the temple in Babylon. Then King Cyrus gave them to a man named Sheshbazzar, whom he had appointed governor, ¹⁵ and he told him, 'Take these articles and go and deposit them in the temple in Jerusalem. And rebuild the house of God on its site.'

¹⁶ "So this Sheshbazzar came and laid the foundations of the house of God in Jerusalem. From that day to the present it has been under construction but is not yet finished."

¹⁷ Now if it pleases the king, let a search be made in the royal archives of Babylon to see if King Cyrus did in fact issue a decree to rebuild this house of God in Jerusalem. Then let the king send us his decision in this matter.

With Respect

The citizens of Israel were having some trouble with the government. It was the late 500s BC, and the Jewish people were eager to complete their temple that had been destroyed in 586 BC by Babylon. However, the governor of their region was not sure they should be doing that, so he sent a note to King Darius (EZRA 5:6-17).

In the letter, the governor says he found the Jews working on the temple and asks the king if they had permission to do so. The letter also records the Jews' respectful response that they had indeed been given permission by an earlier king (Cyrus) to rebuild. When the king checked out their story, he found it to be true: King Cyrus had said they could build the temple. So Darius not only gave them permission to rebuild, but he

TODAY'S READING
Ezra 5:6-17

If it pleases the king, let a search be made in the royal archives of Babylon to see if King Cyrus . . . issue[d] a decree.
Ezra 5:17

also paid for it! (SEE 6:1-12). After the Jews finished building the temple, they "celebrated with joy" because they knew God had "[changed] the attitude of the king" (6:22).

When we see a situation that needs to be addressed, we honor God when we plead our case in a respectful way, trust that He is in control of every situation, and express gratitude for the outcome.   *DAVE BRANON*

Lord, help us to respond respectfully to situations around us.
We need Your wisdom for this.
May we always honor, trust, and praise You.

Respect for authority brings glory to God.

⁵ Your love, LORD, reaches to the heavens,
   your faithfulness to the skies.
⁶ Your righteousness is like the highest mountains,
   your justice like the great deep.
 You, LORD, preserve both people and animals.
⁷ How priceless is your unfailing love, O God!
 People take refuge in the shadow of your wings.
⁸ They feast on the abundance of your house;
   you give them drink from your river of delights.
⁹ For with you is the fountain of life;
   in your light we see light.
¹⁰ Continue your love to those who know you,
   your righteousness to the upright in heart.
¹¹ May the foot of the proud not come against me,
   nor the hand of the wicked drive me away.
¹² See how the evildoers lie fallen—
   thrown down, not able to rise!

Abundant Supply

We have a hummingbird feeder in the garden, and we love to see the little birds come and drink from its sugary water. Recently, however, we went on a short trip and forgot to replenish its contents. When we came back, it was completely dry. *Poor birds!* I thought. *Because of my forgetfulness, they haven't had any nourishment.* Then I was reminded that I am not the one who feeds them: God is.

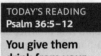

TODAY'S READING
Psalm 36:5–12

You give them drink from your river of delights.
Psalm 36:8

Sometimes we may feel that all of the demands of life have depleted our strength and there is no one to replenish it. But others don't feed our souls: God does.

In Psalm 36 we read about God's lovingkindness. It describes those who put their trust in Him and are abundantly satisfied. God gives them water from His "river of delights" (V. 8). He is the fountain of life!

We can go to God every day for the supply of our needs. As Charles Spurgeon wrote, "The springs of my faith and all my graces; the springs of my life and all my pleasures; the springs of my activity and all its right doings; the springs of my hope, and all its heavenly anticipations, all lie in thee, my Lord."

Let us be filled with His abundant supply. His fountain will never run dry. ❀   *KEILA OCHOA*

Lord, I come to You with the confidence that You will fill me
with what I need.

God's love is abundant.

19 Therefore, brothers and sisters, since we have confidence to enter the Most Holy Place by the blood of Jesus, 20 by a new and living way opened for us through the curtain, that is, his body, 21 and since we have a great priest over the house of God, 22 let us draw near to God with a sincere heart and with the full assurance that faith brings, having our hearts sprinkled to cleanse us from a guilty conscience and having our bodies washed with pure water.

23 Let us hold unswervingly to the hope we profess, for he who promised is faithful. 24 And let us consider how we may spur one another on toward love and good deeds, 25 not giving up meeting together, as some are in the habit of doing, but encouraging one another—and all the more as you see the Day approaching.

Please Come In

Jenny's house is situated on a little country lane, which is often used in rush hour by drivers who want to avoid the nearby main road and traffic lights. A few weeks ago workmen arrived to repair the badly damaged road surface, bringing with them large barriers and "No Entry" signs. "I was really worried at first," said Jenny, "thinking that I would be unable to get my car out until the road work was finished. But then I went to look at the signs more closely and realized that they said 'No Entry: Access for Residents Only.' No detours or barriers for me. I had the right to go in and out whenever I liked because I lived there. I felt very special!"

> TODAY'S READING
> Hebrews 10:19–25
>
> **Let us draw near to God . . . with the full assurance that faith brings.**
> Hebrews 10:22

In the Old Testament, access to God in the tabernacle and the temple was strictly limited. Only the high priest could go in through the curtain and offer sacrifices in the Most Holy Place, and then only once a year (LEV. 16:2–20; HEB. 9:25–26). But at the very moment Jesus died, the curtain of the temple was torn in two from top to bottom, showing that the barrier between man and God was destroyed forever (MARK 15:38).

Because of Christ's sacrifice for our sins, all those who love and follow Him can come into His presence at any time. He has given us the right of access. ✒️ *MARION STROUD*

Lord, thank You for paying such a price to enable me to have unrestricted entry into Your presence!

Access to God's throne is always open.

⁸ By faith Abraham, when called to go to a place he would later receive as his inheritance, obeyed and went, even though he did not know where he was going.

⁹ By faith he made his home in the promised land like a stranger in a foreign country; he lived in tents, as did Isaac and Jacob, who were heirs with him of the same promise. ¹⁰ For he was looking forward to the city with foundations, whose architect and builder is God. ¹¹ And by faith even Sarah, who was past childbearing age, was enabled to bear children because she considered him faithful who had made the promise. ¹² And so from this one man, and he as good as dead, came descendants as numerous as the stars in the sky and as countless as the sand on the seashore.

¹³ All these people were still living by faith when they died. They did not receive the things promised; they only saw them and welcomed them from a distance, admitting that they were foreigners and strangers on earth. ¹⁴ People who say such things show that they are looking for a country of their own. ¹⁵ If they had been thinking of the country they had left, they would have had opportunity to return. ¹⁶ Instead, they were longing for a better country—a heavenly one. Therefore God is not ashamed to be called their God, for he has prepared a city for them.

Strangers and Foreigners

parked my bicycle, fingering my map of Cambridge for reassurance. Directions not being my strength, I knew I could easily get lost in this maze of roads bursting with historic buildings.

Life should have felt idyllic, for I had just married my Englishman and moved to the UK. But I felt adrift. When I kept my mouth closed I blended in, but when I spoke I immediately felt branded as an American tourist. I didn't yet know what my role was, and I quickly realized that blending two stubborn people into one shared life was harder than I had anticipated.

TODAY'S READING
Hebrews 11:8–16

He was looking forward to the city with foundations, whose architect and builder is God.

Hebrews 11:10

I related to Abraham, who left all that he knew as he obeyed the Lord's call to live as a foreigner and stranger in a new land (GEN. 12:1). He pressed through the cultural challenges while keeping faith in God, and 2,000 years later the writer to the Hebrews named him a hero (11:9). Like the other men and women listed in this chapter, Abraham lived by faith, longing for things promised, hoping and waiting for his heavenly home.

Perhaps you've always lived in the same town, but as Christ-followers we're all foreigners and strangers on this earth. By faith we press forward, knowing that God will lead and guide us, and by faith we believe He will never leave nor abandon us. By faith we long for home. ●   *AMY BOUCHER PYE*

Father God, I want to live by faith, believing Your promises and knowing that You welcome me into Your kingdom. Enlarge my faith, I pray.

God calls us to live by faith, believing that He will fulfill His promises.

¹ Therefore, since we are surrounded by such a great cloud of witnesses, let us throw off everything that hinders and the sin that so easily entangles. And let us run with perseverance the race marked out for us, ² fixing our eyes on Jesus, the pioneer and perfecter of faith. For the joy set before him he endured the cross, scorning its shame, and sat down at the right hand of the throne of God. ³ Consider him who endured such opposition from sinners, so that you will not grow weary and lose heart.

⁴ In your struggle against sin, you have not yet resisted to the point of shedding your blood. ⁵ And have you completely forgotten this word of encouragement that addresses you as a father addresses his son? It says,

"My son, do not make light of the Lord's discipline,
    and do not lose heart when he rebukes you,
⁶ because the Lord disciplines the one he loves,
    and he chastens everyone he accepts as his son."

⁷ Endure hardship as discipline; God is treating you as his children. For what children are not disciplined by their father? ⁸ If you are not disciplined—and everyone undergoes discipline—then you are not legitimate, not true sons and daughters at all. ⁹ Moreover, we have all had human fathers who disciplined us and we respected them for it. How much more should we submit to the Father of spirits and live!

¹⁰ They disciplined us for a little while as they thought best; but God disciplines us for our good, in order that we may share in his holiness. ¹¹ No discipline seems pleasant at the time, but painful. Later on, however, it produces a harvest of righteousness and peace for those who have been trained by it.

Don't Quit!

In 1952 Florence Chadwick attempted to swim 26 miles from the coast of California to Catalina Island. After 15 hours, a heavy fog began to block her view, she became disoriented, and she gave up. To her chagrin, Chadwick learned that she had quit just 1 mile short of her destination.

Two months later Chadwick tried a second time to swim to Catalina Island from the coast. Again a thick fog settled in, but this time she reached her destination, becoming the first woman to swim the Catalina Channel. Chadwick said she kept an image of the shoreline in her mind even when she couldn't see it.

TODAY'S READING
Hebrews 12:1–11

Let us run with
perseverance the
race marked out
for us, fixing our
eyes on Jesus,
the pioneer and
perfecter of faith.

Hebrews 12:1–2

When the problems of life cloud our vision, we have an opportunity to learn to see our goal with the eyes of faith. The New Testament letter to the Hebrews urges us to "run with perseverance the race marked out for us, fixing our eyes on Jesus, the pioneer and perfecter of faith" (12:1–2). When we feel like quitting, this is our signal to remember not only what Jesus suffered for us but what He now helps us to endure—until the day we see Him face to face. 🌿

DENNIS FISHER

Dear Father, sometimes the challenges of life seem insurmountable.
Help me to fix my eyes on You and trust You.
I'm thankful You are bringing about Your good purposes in me.

We can finish strong when we focus on Christ.

¹⁴ One of the servants told Abigail, Nabal's wife, "David sent messengers from the wilderness to give our master his greetings, but he hurled insults at them. ¹⁵ Yet these men were very good to us. They did not mistreat us, and the whole time we were out in the fields near them nothing was missing. ¹⁶ Night and day they were a wall around us the whole time we were herding our sheep near them. ¹⁷ Now think it over and see what you can do, because disaster is hanging over our master and his whole household. He is such a wicked man that no one can talk to him." ¹⁸ Abigail acted quickly. She took two hundred loaves of bread, two skins of wine, five dressed sheep, five seahs of roasted grain, a hundred cakes of raisins and two hundred cakes of pressed figs, and loaded them on donkeys. ¹⁹ Then she told her servants, "Go on ahead; I'll follow you." But she did not tell her husband Nabal. ²⁰ As she came riding her donkey into a mountain ravine, there were David and his men descending toward her, and she met them. ²¹ David had just said, "It's been useless—all my watching over this fellow's property in the wilderness so that nothing of his was missing. He has paid me back evil for good. ²² May God deal with David, be it ever so severely, if by morning I leave alive one male of all who belong to him!" ²³ When Abigail saw David, she quickly got off her donkey and bowed down before David with her face to the ground. ²⁴ She fell at his feet and said: "Pardon your servant, my lord, and let me speak to you; hear what your servant has to say. ²⁵ Please pay no attention, my lord, to that wicked man Nabal. He is just like his name—his name means Fool, and folly goes with him. And as for me, your servant, I did not see the men my lord sent. ²⁶ And now, my lord, as surely as the Lᴏʀᴅ your God lives and as you live, since the Lᴏʀᴅ has kept you from bloodshed and from avenging yourself with your own hands, may your enemies and all who are intent on harming my lord be like Nabal. ²⁷ And let this gift, which your servant has brought to my lord, be given to the men who follow you. ²⁸ "Please forgive your servant's presumption. The Lᴏʀᴅ your God will certainly make a lasting dynasty for my lord, because you fight the Lᴏʀᴅ's battles, and no wrongdoing will be found in you as long as you live. ²⁹ Even though someone is pursuing you to take your life, the life of my lord will be bound securely in the bundle of the living by the Lᴏʀᴅ your God, but the lives of your enemies he will hurl away as from the pocket of a sling. ³⁰ When the Lᴏʀᴅ has fulfilled for my lord every good thing he promised concerning him and has appointed him ruler over Israel, ³¹ my lord will not have on his conscience the staggering burden of needless bloodshed or of having avenged himself. And when the Lord your God has brought my lord success, remember your servant." ³² David said to Abigail, "Praise be to the Lord, the God of Israel, who has sent you today to meet me. ³³ May you be blessed for your good judgment and for keeping me from bloodshed this day and from avenging myself with my own hands.

Abigail's Reminder

David and 400 of his warriors thundered through the countryside in search of Nabal, a prosperous brute who had harshly refused to lend them help. David would have murdered him if he hadn't first encountered Abigail, Nabal's wife. She had packed up enough food to feed an army and traveled out to meet the troops, hoping to head off disaster.

She respectfully reminded David that guilt would haunt him if he followed through with his vengeful plan (1 SAM. 25:31). David realized she was right and blessed her for her good judgment.

David's anger was legitimate—he had protected Nabal's shepherds in the wilderness (VV. 14–17) and had been repaid evil for good. However, his anger was leading him into sin. David's first instinct was to sink his sword into Nabal, even though he knew God did not approve of murder and revenge (EX. 20:13; LEV. 19:18).

> TODAY'S READING
> **1 Samuel 25:14–33**
>
> **When the LORD takes pleasure in anyone's way, he causes their enemies to make peace with them.**
> Proverbs 16:7

When we've been offended, it's good to compare our instincts with God's intent for human behavior. We may be inclined to strike at people verbally, isolate ourselves, or escape through any number of ways. However, choosing a gracious response will help us avoid regret, and most important it will please God. When our desire is to honor God in our relationships, He is able to make even our enemies to be at peace with us (SEE PROV. 16:7). 🌱

JENNIFER BENSON SCHULDT

Lord, thank You for holding back Your anger and having mercy on me. Help me to walk in step with Your Spirit so that my actions please You in every situation.

We can endure life's wrongs because we know that God will make things right.

¹⁴ When his father-in-law saw all that Moses was doing for the people, he said, "What is this you are doing for the people? Why do you alone sit as judge, while all these people stand around you from morning till evening?"

¹⁵ Moses answered him, "Because the people come to me to seek God's will. ¹⁶ Whenever they have a dispute, it is brought to me, and I decide between the parties and inform them of God's decrees and instructions."

¹⁷ Moses' father-in-law replied, "What you are doing is not good. ¹⁸ You and these people who come to you will only wear yourselves out. The work is too heavy for you; you cannot handle it alone. ¹⁹ Listen now to me and I will give you some advice, and may God be with you. You must be the people's representative before God and bring their disputes to him. ²⁰ Teach them his decrees and instructions, and show them the way they are to live and how they are to behave. ²¹ But select capable men from all the people—men who fear God, trustworthy men who hate dishonest gain—and appoint them as officials over thousands, hundreds, fifties and tens. ²² Have them serve as judges for the people at all times, but have them bring every difficult case to you; the simple cases they can decide themselves. That will make your load lighter, because they will share it with you. ²³ If you do this and God so commands, you will be able to stand the strain, and all these people will go home satisfied."

²⁴ Moses listened to his father-in-law and did everything he said.

Self-Care

After my husband underwent heart surgery, I spent an anxious night by his hospital bed. Mid-morning, I remembered a scheduled haircut. "I'll have to cancel," I said, raking my fingers distractedly through my straggly hair.

"Mom, just wash your face and go to your appointment," my daughter said.

"No, no," I insisted. "It doesn't matter. I need to be *here*."

"I'll stay," Rosie said. "Self-care, Mom. . . . *Self-care.* You're of more use to Dad if you take care of yourself."

TODAY'S READING
Exodus 18:14–24

Come with me by yourselves to a quiet place and get some rest. Mark 6:31

Moses was wearing himself out serving alone as judge over the Israelites. Jethro cautioned his son-in-law Moses: "You will only wear [yourself] out. The work is too heavy . . . you cannot handle it alone" (EX. 18:18). He then explained ways that Moses could delegate his work and share his heavy load with others.

Though it may seem paradoxical for the Christian, self-care is essential for a healthy life (MATT. 22:37–39; EPH. 5:29–30). Yes, we must love God first and love others as well, but we also need to get adequate rest to renew our body and spirit. Sometimes self-care means stepping away and graciously allowing others to help us with our burdens.

Jesus often slipped away to rest and pray (MARK 6:30–32). When we follow His example, we will be more effective in our relationships and better able to give care to others. 🌱

CINDY HESS KASPER

Dear Lord, refresh my spirit today. Help me to bring balance to my life as I juggle my responsibilities. Thank You for Your love and care.

Don't try to do everything—take time to refresh your body and spirit.

⁴⁰ Now when Jesus returned, a crowd welcomed him, for they were all expecting him. ⁴¹ Then a man named Jairus, a synagogue leader, came and fell at Jesus' feet, pleading with him to come to his house ⁴² because his only daughter, a girl of about twelve, was dying.

As Jesus was on his way, the crowds almost crushed him. ⁴³ And a woman was there who had been subject to bleeding for twelve years, but no one could heal her. ⁴⁴ She came up behind him and touched the edge of his cloak, and immediately her bleeding stopped.

⁴⁵ "Who touched me?" Jesus asked.

When they all denied it, Peter said, "Master, the people are crowding and pressing against you."

⁴⁶ But Jesus said, "Someone touched me; I know that power has gone out from me."

⁴⁷ Then the woman, seeing that she could not go unnoticed, came trembling and fell at his feet. In the presence of all the people, she told why she had touched him and how she had been instantly healed. ⁴⁸ Then he said to her, "Daughter, your faith has healed you. Go in peace."

THE BIBLE in ONE YEAR
DEUT. 23–25 and MARK 14:1–26

My Personal Space

An industrial design graduate from a Singapore university was challenged in a workshop to come up with a novel solution to a common problem using only ordinary objects. She created a vest to protect one's personal space from being invaded while traveling in the crush of crowded public trains and buses. The vest was covered with long, flexible plastic spikes normally used to keep birds and cats away from plants.

TODAY'S READING
Luke 8:40–48

We do not have a high priest who is unable to empathize with our weaknesses.

Hebrews 4:15

Jesus knew what it was like to lose His personal space in the commotion of crowds desperate to see and touch Him. A woman who had suffered from constant bleeding for 12 years and could find no cure touched the fringe of His robe. Immediately, her bleeding stopped (LUKE 8:43–44).

Jesus's question, "Who touched me?" (V. 45) isn't as strange as it sounds. He felt power come out of Him (V. 46). That touch was different from those who merely happened to accidentally touch Him.

While we must admit that we do sometimes wish to keep our personal space and privacy, the only way we help a world of hurting people is to let them get close enough to be touched by the encouragement, comfort, and grace of Christ in us. *C. P. HIA*

Lord Jesus, I want to be near You and know You so that when I'm in contact with others they can see You through me.

A Christian's life is the window through which others can see Jesus.

¹ Praise the LORD.
 Praise the LORD, my soul.
² I will praise the LORD all my life;
 I will sing praise to my God as long as I live.
³ Do not put your trust in princes,
 in human beings, who cannot save.
⁴ When their spirit departs, they return to the ground;
 on that very day their plans come to nothing.
⁵ Blessed are those whose help is the God of Jacob,
 whose hope is in the LORD their God.
⁶ He is the Maker of heaven and earth,
 the sea, and everything in them—
 he remains faithful forever.
⁷ He upholds the cause of the oppressed
 and gives food to the hungry.
The LORD sets prisoners free,
⁸ the LORD gives sight to the blind,
the LORD lifts up those who are bowed down,
 the LORD loves the righteous.
⁹ The LORD watches over the foreigner
 and sustains the fatherless and the widow,
 but he frustrates the ways of the wicked.
¹⁰ The LORD reigns forever,
 your God, O Zion, for all generations.
Praise the LORD.

Looking Up

An article in the *Surgical Technology International* journal says that looking down at a smart phone with your head bent forward is the equivalent of having a 60-pound weight on your neck. When we consider that millions of people around the world spend an average of 2-4 hours daily reading and texting, the resulting damage to neck and spine becomes a growing health concern.

TODAY'S READING
Psalm 146:1–10

The LORD lifts up those who are bowed down.
Psalm 146:8

It is also easy to become spiritually bowed down by the burdens of life. How often we find ourselves discouraged by the problems we face and the needs of those we love. The psalmist understood this weight of concern yet saw hope as he wrote about "the Maker of heaven and earth, the sea, and everything in them—[who] remains faithful forever. He upholds the cause of the oppressed and gives food to the hungry. The LORD sets prisoners free, the LORD gives sight to the blind, the LORD lifts up those who are bowed down, the LORD loves the righteous" (PS. 146:6–8).

When we consider God's care, His great power, and His loving heart, we can begin to look up and praise Him. We can walk through each day knowing that "the LORD reigns forever . . . for all generations" (V. 10).

He lifts us up when we are bowed down. Praise the Lord! 🏵

DAVID MCCASLAND

O Lord, lift our eyes to see Your power and love today
so we can raise our heads and our hearts in grateful praise to You.

Faith in God's goodness puts a song in your heart.

²⁵ "Therefore I tell you, do not worry about your life, what you will eat or drink; or about your body, what you will wear. Is not life more than food, and the body more than clothes? ²⁶ Look at the birds of the air; they do not sow or reap or store away in barns, and yet your heavenly Father feeds them. Are you not much more valuable than they? ²⁷ Can any one of you by worrying add a single hour to your life?

²⁸ "And why do you worry about clothes? See how the flowers of the field grow. They do not labor or spin. ²⁹ Yet I tell you that not even Solomon in all his splendor was dressed like one of these. ³⁰ If that is how God clothes the grass of the field, which is here today and tomorrow is thrown into the fire, will he not much more clothe you—you of little faith? ³¹ So do not worry, saying, 'What shall we eat?' or 'What shall we drink?' or 'What shall we wear?' ³² For the pagans run after all these things, and your heavenly Father knows that you need them.

³³ But seek first his kingdom and his righteousness, and all these things will be given to you as well. ³⁴ Therefore do not worry about tomorrow, for tomorrow will worry about itself. Each day has enough trouble of its own.

Deeply Loved

Years ago I had an office in Boston that looked out on the Granary Burying Ground where many prominent American heroes are buried. There one can find the gravestones for John Hancock and Samuel Adams, two signers of the Declaration of Independence, and just a few feet beyond that is Paul Revere's marker.

But no one really knows *where* in this burial ground each body is buried because the stones have been moved many times—sometimes to make the grounds more picturesque and other times so lawn mowers could fit between them. And while the Granary features approximately 2,300 markers, closer to 5,000 people are buried there! Even in death, it seems, some people are not fully known.

TODAY'S READING
Matthew 6:25–34

Your heavenly Father feeds [the birds of the air]. Are you not much more valuable than they? Matthew 6:26

There may be times when we feel as if we are like those unmarked residents of the Granary, unknown and unseen. Loneliness can make us feel unseen by others—and maybe even by God. But we must remind ourselves that even though we may feel forgotten by our Creator God, we are not. God not only made us in His image (GEN. 1:26–27), but He also values each of us individually and sent His Son to save us (JOHN 3:16).

Even in our darkest hours, we can rest in the knowledge we are never alone, for our loving God is with us. RANDY KILGORE

Thank You, Lord, that You never leave me alone and
that You know all about me. Make me aware of Your presence so I may
share that comfort with others who are feeling alone too.

We are important because God loves us.

¹¹ Now what I am commanding you today is not too difficult for you or beyond your reach. ¹² It is not up in heaven, so that you have to ask, "Who will ascend into heaven to get it and proclaim it to us so we may obey it?" ¹³ Nor is it beyond the sea, so that you have to ask, "Who will cross the sea to get it and proclaim it to us so we may obey it?" ¹⁴ No, the word is very near you; it is in your mouth and in your heart so you may obey it.

¹⁵ See, I set before you today life and prosperity, death and destruction. ¹⁶ For I command you today to love the LORD your God, to walk in obedience to him, and to keep his commands, decrees and laws; then you will live and increase, and the LORD your God will bless you in the land you are entering to possess.

¹⁷ But if your heart turns away and you are not obedient, and if you are drawn away to bow down to other gods and worship them, ¹⁸ I declare to you this day that you will certainly be destroyed. You will not live long in the land you are crossing the Jordan to enter and possess.

¹⁹ This day I call the heavens and the earth as witnesses against you that I have set before you life and death, blessings and curses. Now choose life, so that you and your children may live ²⁰ and that you may love the LORD your God, listen to his voice, and hold fast to him. For the LORD is your life, and he will give you many years in the land he swore to give to your fathers, Abraham, Isaac and Jacob.

Positive Repetition

journalist had a quirky habit of not using blue pens. So when his colleague asked him if he needed anything from the store, he asked for some pens. "But not blue pens," he said. "I don't want blue pens. I don't like blue. Blue is too heavy. So please purchase 12 ballpoint pens for me— anything but blue!" The next day his colleague passed him the pens—and they were all blue. When asked to explain, he said, "You kept saying 'blue, blue.' That's the word that left the deepest impression!" The journalist's use of repetition had an effect, but not the one he desired.

Moses, the lawgiver of Israel, also used repetition in his requests to his people. More than 30 times he urged his

TODAY'S READING
Deuteronomy 30:11–20

I command you today to love the LORD your God, to walk in obedience to him.

Deuteronomy 30:16

people to remain true to the law of their God. Yet the result was the opposite of what he asked for. He told them that obedience would lead them to life and prosperity, but disobedience would lead to destruction (DEUT. 30:15–18).

When we love God, we want to walk in His ways not because we fear the consequences but because it is our joy to please the One we love. That's a good word to remember. 🌼 POH FANG CHIA

Dear Lord, as we read Your inspired story,
may Your Spirit be our teacher. Help us to walk the path of obedience
as we hear the voice of Your heart.

Love for God will cause you to live for God.

¹ Now Joseph had been taken down to Egypt. Potiphar, an Egyptian who was one of Pharaoh's officials, the captain of the guard, bought him from the Ishmaelites who had taken him there.

² The LORD was with Joseph so that he prospered, and he lived in the house of his Egyptian master. ³ When his master saw that the LORD was with him and that the LORD gave him success in everything he did, ⁴ Joseph found favor in his eyes and became his attendant. Potiphar put him in charge of his household, and he entrusted to his care everything he owned.

⁵ From the time he put him in charge of his household and of all that he owned, the LORD blessed the household of the Egyptian because of Joseph. The blessing of the LORD was on everything Potiphar had, both in the house and in the field. ⁶ So Potiphar left everything he had in Joseph's care; with Joseph in charge, he did not concern himself with anything except the food he ate.

Now Joseph was well-built and handsome, ⁷ and after a while his master's wife took notice of Joseph and said, "Come to bed with me!"

⁸ But he refused. "With me in charge," he told her, "my master does not concern himself with anything in the house; everything he owns he has entrusted to my care. ⁹ No one is greater in this house than I am. My master has withheld nothing from me except you, because you are his wife. How then could I do such a wicked thing and sin against God?"

¹⁰ And though she spoke to Joseph day after day, he refused to go to bed with her or even be with her.

¹¹ One day he went into the house to attend to his duties, and none of the household servants was inside. ¹² She caught him by his cloak and said, "Come to bed with me!" But he left his cloak in her hand and ran out of the house.

When to Walk Away

When my father became a Christian in his old age, he fascinated me with his plan for overcoming temptation. Sometimes he just walked away! For example, whenever a disagreement between him and a neighbor began to degenerate into a quarrel, my father just walked away for a time rather than be tempted to advance the quarrel.

TODAY'S READING
Genesis 39:1–12

God is faithful; he will not let you be tempted beyond what you can bear.

1 Corinthians 10:13

One day he met with some friends who ordered *pito* (a locally brewed alcoholic beer). My father had formerly struggled with alcohol and had decided he was better off without it. So he simply stood up, said his goodbyes, and left the gathering of old friends for another day.

In Genesis, we read how Potiphar's wife tempted Joseph. He immediately recognized that giving in would cause him to "sin against God," so he fled (GEN. 39:9–12).

Temptation knocks often at our door. Sometimes it comes from our own desires, other times through the situations and people we encounter. As Paul told the Corinthians, "No temptation has overtaken you except what is common to mankind." But he also wrote, "God is faithful; he will not let you be tempted beyond what you can bear. But when you are tempted, he will also provide a way out so that you can endure it" (1 COR. 10:13).

The "way out" may include removing the objects of temptation or fleeing from them. Our best course of action may be to simply walk away. ✤

LAWRENCE DARMANI

Lord, please give me the wisdom and strength to know when to walk away from situations and people that tempt me to do wrong.

Every temptation is an opportunity to flee to God.

²⁷ Whatever happens, conduct yourselves in a manner worthy of the gospel of Christ. Then, whether I come and see you or only hear about you in my absence, I will know that you stand firm in the one Spirit, striving together as one for the faith of the gospel ²⁸ without being frightened in any way by those who oppose you. This is a sign to them that they will be destroyed, but that you will be saved—and that by God. ²⁹ For it has been granted to you on behalf of Christ not only to believe in him, but also to suffer for him, ³⁰ since you are going through the same struggle you saw I had, and now hear that I still have.

Ignore No More

don't know how these people find me, but I keep getting more and more flyers in the mail from folks asking me to show up at their events so they can teach me about retirement benefits. It started several years ago when I began getting invitations to join an organization that works on behalf of retirees. These reminders all serve to say: "You're getting older. Get ready!"

I have ignored them all along, but soon enough I'm going to have to break down and go to one of their meetings. I really should be taking action on their suggestions.

TODAY'S READING
Philippians 1:27–30

The commands of the LORD are radiant, giving light to the eyes. Psalm 19:8

Sometimes I hear a similar reminder in the wisdom of Scripture. We know that what the passage says is true about us, but we are just not ready to respond. Maybe it's a passage like Romans 14:13 that says, "Let us stop passing judgment on one another." Or the reminder in 2 Corinthians 9:6, which tells us, "Whoever sows generously will also reap generously." Or this reminder in Philippians 1: "Stand firm in the one Spirit, striving together as one for the faith of the gospel without being frightened" (VV. 27–28).

As we read God's Word, we get vital reminders. Let's take these seriously as from the heart of the Father who knows what honors Him and is best for us. ❧

DAVE BRANON

Thank You, Lord, for Your gentle reminders.
We know that the things You tell us to do in Your Word
are for our good and for Your glory. Help us to step up and do the things
that bring honor to Your name.

*Holiness is simply Christ in us fulfilling
the will and commands of the Father.*

¹ Meanwhile, Saul was still breathing out murderous threats against the Lord's disciples. He went to the high priest ² and asked him for letters to the synagogues in Damascus, so that if he found any there who belonged to the Way, whether men or women, he might take them as prisoners to Jerusalem. ³ As he neared Damascus on his journey, suddenly a light from heaven flashed around him.

⁴ He fell to the ground and heard a voice say to him, "Saul, Saul, why do you persecute me?"

⁵ "Who are you, Lord?" Saul asked.

"I am Jesus, whom you are persecuting," he replied. ⁶ "Now get up and go into the city, and you will be told what you must do."

⁷ The men traveling with Saul stood there speechless; they heard the sound but did not see anyone. ⁸ Saul got up from the ground, but when he opened his eyes he could see nothing. So they led him by the hand into Damascus. ⁹ For three days he was blind, and did not eat or drink anything.

¹⁰ In Damascus there was a disciple named Ananias. The Lord called to him in a vision, "Ananias!"

"Yes, Lord," he answered.

¹¹ The Lord told him, "Go to the house of Judas on Straight Street and ask for a man from Tarsus named Saul, for he is praying. ¹² In a vision he has seen a man named Ananias come and place his hands on him to restore his sight."

¹³ "Lord," Ananias answered, "I have heard many reports about this man and all the harm he has done to your holy people in Jerusalem. ¹⁴ And he has come here with authority from the chief priests to arrest all who call on your name."

¹⁵ But the Lord said to Ananias, "Go! This man is my chosen instrument to proclaim my name to the Gentiles and their kings and to the people of Israel. ¹⁶ I will show him how much he must suffer for my name."

Surprised by Grace

A woman from Grand Rapids, Michigan, fell asleep on the couch after her husband had gone to bed. An intruder sneaked in through the sliding door, which the couple had forgotten to lock, and crept through the house. He entered the bedroom where the husband was sleeping and picked up the television set. The sleeping man woke up, saw a figure standing there, and whispered, "Honey, come to bed." The burglar panicked, put down the TV, grabbed a stack of money from the dresser, and ran out.

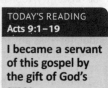

TODAY'S READING
Acts 9:1–19

I became a servant of this gospel by the gift of God's grace. Ephesians 3:7

The thief was in for a big surprise! The money turned out to be a stack of Christian pamphlets with a likeness of a $20 bill on one side and an explanation of the love and forgiveness God offers to people on the other side. Instead of the cash he expected, the intruder got the story of God's love for him.

I wonder what Saul expected when he realized it was Jesus appearing to him on the road to Damascus, since he had been persecuting and even killing Jesus's followers? (ACTS 9:1–9). Saul, later called Paul, must have been surprised by God's grace toward him, which he called "a gift": "I became a servant of this gospel by the gift of God's grace given me through the working of his power" (EPH. 3:7).

Have you been surprised by God's gift of grace in your life as He shows you His love and forgiveness? 🌿   *ANNE CETAS*

Lord, Your grace is amazing to me.
I'm grateful that in spite of my sinfulness,
You offer Your love to me.

Never measure God's unlimited power by your limited expectations.

¹ Follow God's example, therefore, as dearly loved children ² and walk in the way of love, just as Christ loved us and gave himself up for us as a fragrant offering and sacrifice to God.

³ But among you there must not be even a hint of sexual immorality, or of any kind of impurity, or of greed, because these are improper for God's holy people. ⁴ Nor should there be obscenity, foolish talk or coarse joking, which are out of place, but rather thanksgiving. ⁵ For of this you can be sure: No immoral, impure or greedy person—such a person is an idolater—has any inheritance in the kingdom of Christ and of God. ⁶ Let no one deceive you with empty words, for because of such things God's wrath comes on those who are disobedient. ⁷ Therefore do not be partners with them.

⁸ For you were once darkness, but now you are light in the Lord. Live as children of light ⁹ (for the fruit of the light consists in all goodness, righteousness and truth) ¹⁰ and find out what pleases the Lord. ¹¹ Have nothing to do with the fruitless deeds of darkness, but rather expose them. ¹² It is shameful even to mention what the disobedient do in secret. ¹³ But everything exposed by the light becomes visible—and everything that is illuminated becomes a light. ¹⁴ This is why it is said:

"Wake up, sleeper,
    rise from the dead,
        and Christ will shine on you."

¹⁵ Be very careful, then, how you live—not as unwise but as wise, ¹⁶ making the most of every opportunity, because the days are evil.

Full Sun

know better, but I still keep trying. The instructions on the label are clear: "Needs full sun." Our yard has mostly shade. It is not suitable for plants that need full sun. But I like the plant. I like its color, the shape of the leaves, the size, the scent. So I buy it, bring it home, plant it, and take really good care of it. But the plant is not happy at my house. My care and attention are not enough. It needs sunlight, which I cannot provide. I thought I could make up for lack of light by giving the plant some other kind of attention. But it doesn't work that way. Plants need what they need.

TODAY'S READING
Ephesians 5:1–16

Live as children of light. Ephesians 5:8

And so do people. Although we can survive for a while in less-than-ideal conditions, we can't thrive. In addition to our basic physical needs, we also have spiritual needs that can't be met by any substitute.

Scripture says that believers are children of light. This means that we need to live in the full light of God's presence to thrive (PS. 89:15). If we try to live in darkness, we will produce nothing but "fruitless deeds" (SEE EPH. 5:3–4, 11). But if we are living in the light of Jesus, the Light of the world, we will produce the fruit of His light, which is good, faithful, and true. ❧　　　*JULIE ACKERMAN LINK*

Dear Lord, thank You for redeeming me and giving me new life.
Help me to live as a child of the Light.

Children of the Light walk in His light.

¹ Since, then, you have been raised with Christ, set your hearts on things above, where Christ is, seated at the right hand of God. ² Set your minds on things above, not on earthly things. ³ For you died, and your life is now hidden with Christ in God. ⁴ When Christ, who is your life, appears, then you also will appear with him in glory.

⁵ Put to death, therefore, whatever belongs to your earthly nature: sexual immorality, impurity, lust, evil desires and greed, which is idolatry. ⁶ Because of these, the wrath of God is coming. ⁷ You used to walk in these ways, in the life you once lived. ⁸ But now you must also rid yourselves of all such things as these: anger, rage, malice, slander, and filthy language from your lips. ⁹ Do not lie to each other, since you have taken off your old self with its practices ¹⁰ and have put on the new self, which is being renewed in knowledge in the image of its Creator. ¹¹ Here there is no Gentile or Jew, circumcised or uncircumcised, barbarian, Scythian, slave or free, but Christ is all, and is in all.

The Best Is Yet to Come

In our family, March means more than the end of winter. It means that the college basketball extravaganza called "March Madness" has arrived. As avid fans, we watch the tournament and enthusiastically root for our favorite teams. If we tune in early we get a chance to listen to the broadcasters talk about the upcoming game and to enjoy some of the pre-game drills where players shoot practice shots and warm up with teammates.

TODAY'S READING
Colossians 3:1–11

Set your minds on things above, not on earthly things.
Colossians 3:2

Our life on earth is like the pre-game in basketball. Life is interesting and full of promise, but it doesn't compare to what lies ahead. Just think of the pleasure of knowing that even when life is good, the best is yet to come! Or that when we give cheerfully to those in need, it's an investment in heavenly treasure. In times of suffering and sorrow, we can find hope as we reflect on the truth that a pain-free, tearless eternity awaits us. It's no wonder that Paul exhorts: "Set your minds on things above" (COL. 3:2).

The future God has promised us enables us to see all of life in new dimensions. While this may be a great life, the best life is still to come. It is a wonderful privilege to live *here* in the light of *there*. 🌿

JOE STOWELL

Let us then be true and faithful, trusting, serving every day;
just one glimpse of Him in glory will the toils of life repay.
When we all get to heaven, what a day of rejoicing that will be!
ELIZA E. HEWITT

Living for the future puts today in perspective.

¹¹ But when Christ came as high priest of the good things that are now already here, he went through the greater and more perfect tabernacle that is not made with human hands, that is to say, is not a part of this creation. ¹² He did not enter by means of the blood of goats and calves; but he entered the Most Holy Place once for all by his own blood, thus obtaining eternal redemption. ¹³ The blood of goats and bulls and the ashes of a heifer sprinkled on those who are ceremonially unclean sanctify them so that they are outwardly clean. ¹⁴ How much more, then, will the blood of Christ, who through the eternal Spirit offered himself unblemished to God, cleanse our consciences from acts that lead to death, so that we may serve the living God!

¹⁵ For this reason Christ is the mediator of a new covenant, that those who are called may receive the promised eternal inheritance—now that he has died as a ransom to set them free from the sins committed under the first covenant.

Stories in a Cabin

The vintage cabin, expertly constructed from hand-hewn logs, was worthy of a magazine cover. But the structure itself was only half the treasure. Inside, family heirlooms clung to the walls, infusing the home with memories. On the table sat a hand-woven egg basket, an ancient biscuit board, and an oil lamp. A weathered pork pie hat perched over the front door. "There's a story behind everything," the proud owner said.

TODAY'S READING
Hebrews 9:11–15

[Christ] went through the greater and more perfect tabernacle that is not made with human hands. Hebrews 9:11

When God gave Moses instructions for constructing the tabernacle, there was a "story" behind everything (EX. 25-27). The tabernacle had only one entrance, just as we have only one way to God (SEE ACTS 4:12). The thick inner curtain separated the people from the Most Holy Place where God's presence dwelt: Our sin separates us from God. Inside the Most Holy Place was the ark of the covenant, which symbolized God's presence. The high priest was a forerunner of the greater Priest to come—Jesus Himself. The blood of the sacrifices foreshadowed Christ's perfect sacrifice: "He entered the Most Holy Place once for all by his own blood, thus obtaining eternal redemption" (HEB. 9:12).

All these things told the story of Christ and the work He would accomplish on our behalf. He did it so that "those who are called may receive the promised eternal inheritance" (V. 15). Jesus invites us to be a part of His story. ❖   *TIM GUSTAFSON*

What items have special meaning for me and why? What stories do I tell about them? How can they help point people to Jesus?

Jesus took our sin that we might have salvation.

¹ Early in the morning, Jerub-Baal (that is, Gideon) and all his men camped at the spring of Harod. The camp of Midian was north of them in the valley near the hill of Moreh. ² The LORD said to Gideon, "You have too many men. I cannot deliver Midian into their hands, or Israel would boast against me, 'My own strength has saved me.' ³ Now announce to the army, 'Anyone who trembles with fear may turn back and leave Mount Gilead.'" So twenty-two thousand men left, while ten thousand remained.

⁴ But the LORD said to Gideon, "There are still too many men. Take them down to the water, and I will thin them out for you there. If I say, 'This one shall go with you,' he shall go; but if I say, 'This one shall not go with you,' he shall not go."

⁵ So Gideon took the men down to the water. There the LORD told him, "Separate those who lap the water with their tongues as a dog laps from those who kneel down to drink."

⁶ Three hundred of them drank from cupped hands, lapping like dogs. All the rest got down on their knees to drink.

⁷ The LORD said to Gideon, "With the three hundred men that lapped I will save you and give the Midianites into your hands. Let all the others go home." ⁸ So Gideon sent the rest of the Israelites home but kept the three hundred, who took over the provisions and trumpets of the others.

Now the camp of Midian lay below him in the valley.

God of My Strength

No one could have mistaken the ancient Babylonian soldiers for gentlemen. They were ruthless, resilient, and vicious, and they attacked other nations the way an eagle overtakes its prey. Not only were they powerful, they were prideful as well. They practically worshiped their own combat abilities. In fact, the Bible says that their "strength [was] their god" (HAB. 1:11).

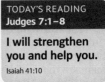

TODAY'S READING
Judges 7:1–8

I will strengthen you and help you.
Isaiah 41:10

God did not want this kind of self-reliance to infect Israel's forces as they prepared to battle the Midianites. So He told Gideon, Israel's army commander, "You have too many men. I cannot deliver Midian into their hands, or Israel would boast against me, 'My own strength has saved me' " (JUDG. 7:2). As a result, Gideon discharged anyone who was fearful. Twenty-two thousand men hightailed it home, while 10,000 fighters stayed. God continued to downsize the army until only 300 men remained (VV. 3–7).

Having fewer troops meant that Israel was dramatically outnumbered—their enemies, who populated a nearby valley, were as "thick as locusts" (V. 12). Despite this, God gave Gideon's forces victory.

At times, God may allow our resources to dwindle so that we rely on His strength to keep going. Our needs showcase His power, but He is the One who says, "I will strengthen you and help you; I will uphold you with my righteous right hand" (ISA. 41:10). 🌱

JENNIFER BENSON SCHULDT

Dear God, I am thankful for Your strength. You carry me when I am weak. Help me to give You the credit for every victory in life.

God wants us to depend on His strength, not our own.

¹ In the beginning was the Word, and the Word was with God, and the Word was God. ² He was with God in the beginning. ³ Through him all things were made; without him nothing was made that has been made.

⁴ In him was life, and that life was the light of all mankind. ⁵ The light shines in the darkness, and the darkness has not overcome it.

⁶ There was a man sent from God whose name was John. ⁷ He came as a witness to testify concerning that light, so that through him all might believe. ⁸ He himself was not the light; he came only as a witness to the light.

⁹ The true light that gives light to everyone was coming into the world. ¹⁰ He was in the world, and though the world was made through him, the world did not recognize him. ¹¹ He came to that which was his own, but his own did not receive him. ¹² Yet to all who did receive him, to those who believed in his name, he gave the right to become children of God— ¹³ children born not of natural descent, nor of human decision or a husband's will, but born of God.

¹⁴ The Word became flesh and made his dwelling among us. We have seen his glory, the glory of the one and only Son, who came from the Father, full of grace and truth.

When the Water Blushed

Why did Jesus come to Earth before the invention of photography and video? Couldn't He have reached more people if everyone could see Him? After all, a picture is worth a thousand words.

"No," says Ravi Zacharias, who asserts that a word can be worth "a thousand pictures." As evidence, he quotes poet Richard Crashaw's magnificent line, "The conscious water saw its Master and blushed." In one simple line, Crashaw captures the essence of Jesus's first miracle (JOHN 2:1–11). Creation itself recognizes Jesus as the Creator. No mere carpenter could turn water to wine.

TODAY'S READING
John 1:1–14

In the beginning was the Word.... Through him all things were made.

John 1:1, 3

Another time, when Christ calmed a storm with the words, "Quiet! Be still," His stunned disciples asked, "Who is this? Even the wind and the waves obey him!" (MARK 4:39, 41). Later, Jesus told the Pharisees that if the crowd did not praise Him, "the stones will cry out" (LUKE 19:40). Even the rocks know who He is.

John tells us, "The Word became flesh and made his dwelling among us. We have seen His glory" (JOHN 1:14). Out of that eyewitness experience John also wrote, "We proclaim to you the one who existed from the beginning, whom we have heard and seen. . . . He is the Word of life" (1 JOHN 1:1 NLT). Like John, we can use our words to introduce others to Jesus whom wind and water obey. ❂

TIM GUSTAFSON

Jesus, we acknowledge You as the Creator who knows and loves His creation. Yet You wait for us to invite You into every aspect of our lives. Forgive us for those times we keep You at a safe distance. Today we choose to risk knowing You more completely.

The written Word reveals the Living Word.

¹³ Once again Jesus went out beside the lake. A large crowd came to him, and he began to teach them. ¹⁴ As he walked along, he saw Levi son of Alphaeus sitting at the tax collector's booth. "Follow me," Jesus told him, and Levi got up and followed him.

¹⁵ While Jesus was having dinner at Levi's house, many tax collectors and sinners were eating with him and his disciples, for there were many who followed him. ¹⁶ When the teachers of the law who were Pharisees saw him eating with the sinners and tax collectors, they asked his disciples: "Why does he eat with tax collectors and sinners?"

¹⁷ On hearing this, Jesus said to them, "It is not the healthy who need a doctor, but the sick. I have not come to call the righteous, but sinners."

Follow Me

Health clubs offer many different programs for those who want to lose weight and stay healthy. One fitness center caters only to those who want to lose at least 50 pounds and develop a healthy lifestyle. One member says that she quit her previous fitness club because she felt the slim and fit people were staring at her and judging her out-of-shape body. She now works out 5 days a week and is achieving healthy weight loss in a positive and welcoming environment.

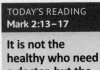

TODAY'S READING
Mark 2:13–17

It is not the healthy who need a doctor, but the sick. Mark 2:17

Two thousand years ago, Jesus came to call the spiritually unfit to follow Him. Levi was one such person. Jesus saw him sitting in his tax collector's booth and said, "Follow me" (MARK 2:14). His words captured Levi's heart, and he followed Jesus. Tax collectors were often greedy and dishonest in their dealings and were considered religiously unclean. When the religious leaders saw Jesus having dinner at Levi's house with other tax collectors, they asked, "Why does he eat with tax collectors and sinners?" (2:16). Jesus replied, "I have not come to call the righteous, but sinners" (2:17).

Jesus came to save sinners, which includes all of us. He loves us, welcomes us into His presence, and calls us to follow Him. As we walk with Him, we grow more and more spiritually fit. ✿

MARVIN WILLIAMS

Read Acts 9:10-19 and see how one man obeyed God and welcomed someone who was considered spiritually unfit. What were the results? How can you reach out to those who need the Savior? How can you help your church become a more welcoming place for the spiritually unfit?

Jesus's arms of welcome are always open.

¹ Shout for joy to the LORD, all the earth.
²   Worship the LORD with gladness;
      come before him with joyful songs.
³ Know that the LORD is God.
  It is he who made us, and we are his;
  we are his people, the sheep of his pasture.
⁴ Enter his gates with thanksgiving
  and his courts with praise;
  give thanks to him and praise his name.
⁵ For the LORD is good and his love endures forever;
  his faithfulness continues through all generations.

The Gallery of God

Psalm 100 is like a work of art that helps us celebrate our unseen God. While the focus of our worship is beyond view, His people make Him known.

Imagine the artist with brush and palette working the colorful words of this psalm onto a canvas. What emerges before our eyes is a world—"all the earth"—shouting for joy to the Lord (V. 1). Joy. Because it is the delight of our God to redeem us from death. "For the joy that was set before Him," Jesus endured the cross (HEB. 12:2 NKJV).

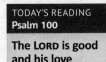

TODAY'S READING
Psalm 100

The LORD is good and his love endures forever.

Psalm 100:5

As our eyes move across the canvas we see an all-world choir of countless members singing "with gladness" and "joyful songs" (PS. 100:2). Our heavenly Father's heart is pleased when His people worship Him for who He is and what He has done.

Then we see images of ourselves, fashioned from dust in the hands of our Creator, and led like sheep into green pasture (V. 3). We, His people, have a loving Shepherd.

Finally, we see God's great and glorious dwelling place—and the gates through which His rescued people enter His unseen presence, while giving Him thanks and praise (V. 4).

What a picture, inspired by our God. Our good, loving, and faithful God. No wonder it will take forever to enjoy His greatness! 🌿

DAVE BRANON

Great God of heaven, thank You for life, for joy, for protection, and for promising us a future with You forever. Help us to live with thoughts of Your greatness always on our hearts and minds.

Nothing is more awesome than to know God.

¹ My son, do not forget my teaching,
  but keep my commands in your heart,
² for they will prolong your life many years
  and bring you peace and prosperity.
³ Let love and faithfulness never leave you;
  bind them around your neck,
  write them on the tablet of your heart.
⁴ Then you will win favor and a good name
  in the sight of God and man.
⁵ Trust in the LORD with all your heart
  and lean not on your own understanding;
⁶ in all your ways submit to him,
  and he will make your paths straight.
⁷ Do not be wise in your own eyes;
  fear the LORD and shun evil.
⁸ This will bring health to your body
  and nourishment to your bones.
⁹ Honor the LORD with your wealth,
  with the firstfruits of all your crops;
¹⁰ then your barns will be filled to overflowing,
  and your vats will brim over with new wine.
¹¹ My son, do not despise the LORD's discipline,
  and do not resent his rebuke,
¹² because the LORD disciplines those he loves,
  as a father the son he delights in.
¹³ Blessed are those who find wisdom,
  those who gain understanding,
¹⁴ for she is more profitable than silver
  and yields better returns than gold.
¹⁵ She is more precious than rubies;
  nothing you desire can compare with her.
¹⁶ Long life is in her right hand;
  in her left hand are riches and honor.
¹⁷ Her ways are pleasant ways,
  and all her paths are peace.
¹⁸ She is a tree of life to those who take hold of her;
  those who hold her fast will be blessed.

Too Close

grew up in Oklahoma where severe weather is common from early spring through the end of summer. I recall one evening when the sky boiled with dark clouds, the TV weather forecaster warned of an approaching tornado, and the electricity went out. Very quickly, my parents, my sister, and I climbed down the wooden ladder into the storm cellar behind our house where we stayed until the storm passed by.

TODAY'S READING
Proverbs 3:1–18

In all your ways submit to him, and he will make your paths straight.

Proverbs 3:6

Today "storm chasing" has become a hobby for many people and a profitable business for others. The goal is to get as close as possible to a tornado without being harmed. Many storm chasers are skilled forecasters with accurate information, but I won't sign up for a tornado tour anytime soon.

In moral and spiritual areas of my life, however, I can foolishly pursue dangerous things God tells me to avoid because of His love for me, all the time believing I won't be harmed. A wiser approach is to read the book of Proverbs, which contains many positive ways to elude these snares of life.

"Trust in the LORD with all your heart and lean not on your own understanding," Solomon wrote. "In all your ways submit to him, and he will make your paths straight" (PROV. 3:5–6).

Our Lord is the master of the adventure of living, and following His wisdom leads us to fullness of life. DAVID MCCASLAND

Father, Your wisdom leads us along the path of life.
Help us to follow Your guidance today.

Every temptation is an occasion to trust God.

³² They went to a place called Gethsemane, and Jesus said to his disciples, "Sit here while I pray." ³³ He took Peter, James and John along with him, and he began to be deeply distressed and troubled. ³⁴ "My soul is overwhelmed with sorrow to the point of death," he said to them. "Stay here and keep watch."

³⁵ Going a little farther, he fell to the ground and prayed that if possible the hour might pass from him. ³⁶ "Abba, Father," he said, "everything is possible for you. Take this cup from me. Yet not what I will, but what you will."

³⁷ Then he returned to his disciples and found them sleeping. "Simon," he said to Peter, "are you asleep? Couldn't you keep watch for one hour? ³⁸ Watch and pray so that you will not fall into temptation. The spirit is willing, but the flesh is weak."

³⁹ Once more he went away and prayed the same thing.

The Olive Press

If you visit the village of Capernaum beside the Sea of Galilee, you will find an exhibit of ancient olive presses. Formed from basalt rock, the olive press consists of two parts: a base and a grinding wheel. The base is large, round, and has a trough carved out of it. The olives were placed in this trough, and then the wheel, also made from heavy stone, was rolled over the olives to extract the oil.

TODAY'S READING
Mark 14:32–39

They went to a place called Gethsemane.
Mark 14:32

On the night before His death, Jesus went to the Mount of Olives overlooking the city of Jerusalem. There, in the garden called Gethsemane, He prayed to the Father, knowing what lay ahead of Him.

The word *Gethsemane* means "place of the olive press"— and that perfectly describes those first crushing hours of Christ's suffering on our behalf. There, "in anguish, he prayed . . . and his sweat was like drops of blood falling to the ground" (LUKE 22:44).

Jesus the Son suffered and died to take away "the sin of the world" (JOHN 1:29) and restore our broken relationship with God the Father. "Surely he took up our pain and bore our suffering . . . . He was pierced for our transgressions, he was crushed for our iniquities, the punishment that brought us peace was on him, and by his wounds we are healed" (ISA. 53:4–5).

Our hearts cry out in worship and gratitude. ❖ *BILL CROWDER*

Father, help me understand what Your Son endured for me.
Help me appreciate the depths of love that would allow my Lord and
Christ to be crushed for my wrongs and my rescue.

*Gone my transgressions, and now I am free—all because Jesus was
wounded for me.* W. G. OVENS

28 And we know that in all things God works for the good of those who love him, who have been called according to his purpose. 29 For those God foreknew he also predestined to be conformed to the image of his Son, that he might be the firstborn among many brothers and sisters. 30 And those he predestined, he also called; those he called, he also justified; those he justified, he also glorified.

31 What, then, shall we say in response to these things? If God is for us, who can be against us? 32 He who did not spare his own Son, but gave him up for us all—how will he not also, along with him, graciously give us all things? 33 Who will bring any charge against those whom God has chosen? It is God who justifies. 34 Who then is the one who condemns? No one. Christ Jesus who died—more than that, who was raised to life—is at the right hand of God and is also interceding for us. 35 Who shall separate us from the love of Christ? Shall trouble or hardship or persecution or famine or nakedness or danger or sword? 36 As it is written:

"For your sake we face death all day long;
    we are considered as sheep to be slaughtered."

37 No, in all these things we are more than conquerors through him who loved us. 38 For I am convinced that neither death nor life, neither angels nor demons, neither the present nor the future, nor any powers, 39 neither height nor depth, nor anything else in all creation, will be able to separate us from the love of God that is in Christ Jesus our Lord.

Three-Word Obituary

Before **Stig Kernell** died, he told the local funeral home that he didn't want a traditional obituary. Instead, the Swedish man instructed them to publish only three words noting his passing: "I am dead." When Mr. Kernell died at age 92, that's exactly what appeared. The audacity and simplicity of his unusual death notice captured the attention of newspapers around the world. In a strange twist, the international curiosity about the man with the three-word obituary caused more attention to his death than he intended.

> **TODAY'S READING**
> Romans 8:28–39
>
> **Christ Jesus who died—more than that, who was raised to life—is at the right hand of God.** Romans 8:34

When Jesus was crucified, the Lord's obituary could have read, "He is dead." But after 3 days, it would have been changed to front-page news saying, "He is risen!" Much of the New Testament is devoted to proclaiming and explaining the results of Christ's resurrection. "Christ Jesus who died—more than that, who was raised to life—is at the right hand of God and is also interceding for us. Who shall separate us from the love of Christ? . . . We are more than conquerors through him who loved us" (ROM. 8:34–37).

The three-word obituary of Jesus, "He is dead," has been transformed into an eternal anthem of praise to our Savior. He is risen! He is risen indeed! 🌿   *DAVID MCCASLAND*

Lord, we rejoice in Your great victory over sin and death through Your resurrection. May we live in light of it every day.

Jesus sacrificed His life for ours.

¹ My God, my God, why have you forsaken me?
   Why are you so far from saving me,
      so far from my cries of anguish?
² My God, I cry out by day, but you do not answer,
   by night, but I find no rest.

³ Yet you are enthroned as the Holy One;
   you are the one Israel praises.
⁴ In you our ancestors put their trust;
   they trusted and you delivered them.
⁵ To you they cried out and were saved;
   in you they trusted and were not put to shame.

⁶ But I am a worm and not a man,
   scorned by everyone, despised by the people.
⁷ All who see me mock me;
   they hurl insults, shaking their heads.
⁸ "He trusts in the LORD," they say,
   "let the LORD rescue him.
Let him deliver him,
   since he delights in him."

⁹ Yet you brought me out of the womb;
   you made me trust in you, even at my mother's breast.
¹⁰ From birth I was cast on you;
   from my mother's womb you have been my God.

Never Forsaken

Russian writer **Fyodor Dostoyevsky** said, "The degree of civilization in a society can be judged by entering its prisons." With that in mind, I read an online article describing "The Top 8 Deadliest Prisons in the World." In one of these prisons *every* prisoner is held in solitary confinement.

We are intended to live and relate in relationships and community, not in isolation. This is what makes solitary confinement such a harsh punishment.

Isolation is the agony Christ suffered when His eternal relationship with the Father was broken on the cross. We hear this in His cry captured in Matthew 27:46: "About three in the afternoon Jesus cried out in a loud voice, '*Eli, Eli, lema sabachthani?*' (which means, 'My God, my God, why have you forsaken me?')." As He suffered and died under the burden of our sins, Christ was suddenly alone, forsaken, isolated, cut off from His relationship with the Father. Yet His suffering in isolation secured for us the promise of the Father: "Never will I leave you; never will I forsake you" (HEB. 13:5).

> **TODAY'S READING**
> Psalm 22:1–10
>
> **Jesus cried out in a loud voice, . . . "My God, my God, why have you forsaken me?"**
> Matthew 27:46

Christ endured the agony and abandonment of the cross for us so that we would never be alone or abandoned by our God. Ever. 🌐

BILL CROWDER

Father, thank You for making it possible for me to be Your child. I will be eternally grateful for the price Jesus paid to make that relationship possible. Thank You for the promise that You will never abandon me.

Those who know Jesus are never alone.

²⁴ Now Thomas (also known as Didymus), one of the Twelve, was not with the disciples when Jesus came.

²⁵ So the other disciples told him, "We have seen the Lord!" But he said to them, "Unless I see the nail marks in his hands and put my finger where the nails were, and put my hand into his side, I will not believe."

²⁶ A week later his disciples were in the house again, and Thomas was with them. Though the doors were locked, Jesus came and stood among them and said, "Peace be with you!"

²⁷ Then he said to Thomas, "Put your finger here; see my hands. Reach out your hand and put it into my side. Stop doubting and believe."

²⁸ Thomas said to him, "My Lord and my God!"

²⁹ Then Jesus told him, "Because you have seen me, you have believed; blessed are those who have not seen and yet have believed."

³⁰ Jesus performed many other signs in the presence of his disciples, which are not recorded in this book. ³¹ But these are written that you may believe that Jesus is the Messiah, the Son of God, and that by believing you may have life in his name.

Easter Start

One detail in the Easter story has always intrigued me. Why did Jesus keep the scars from His crucifixion? Presumably He could have had any resurrected body He wanted, and yet He chose one identifiable mainly by scars that could be seen and touched. Why?

I believe the story of Easter would be incomplete without those scars on the hands, the feet, and the side of Jesus (JOHN 20:27). Human beings dream of pearly straight teeth and wrinkle-free skin and ideal body shapes. We dream of an unnatural state: the perfect body. But for Jesus, being confined in a skeleton and human skin *was* the unnatural state. The scars are a permanent reminder of His days of confinement and suffering on our planet.

TODAY'S READING
John 20:24–31

Reach out your hand and put it into my side. Stop doubting and believe. John 20:27

From the perspective of heaven, those scars represent the most horrible event that has ever happened in the history of the universe. Even that event, though, turned into a memory. Because of Easter, we can hope that the tears we shed, the struggles we endure, the emotional pain, the heartache over lost friends and loved ones—all these will become memories, like Jesus's scars. Scars never completely go away, but neither do they hurt any longer. Someday we will have re-created bodies and a re-created heaven and earth (REV. 21:4). We will have a new start, an Easter start. 🌿

PHILIP YANCEY

Thank You, Lord, for the hope that the resurrection of Jesus brings—
for now and for eternity. I put my trust in You today.

Christ's resurrection is the guarantee of our own.

13 Now that same day two of them were going to a village called Emmaus, about seven miles from Jerusalem. 14 They were talking with each other about everything that had happened. 15 As they talked and discussed these things with each other, Jesus himself came up and walked along with them; 16 but they were kept from recognizing him. 17 He asked them, "What are you discussing together as you walk along?" They stood still, their faces downcast. 18 One of them, named Cleopas, asked him, "Are you the only one visiting Jerusalem who does not know the things that have happened there in these days?" 19 "What things?" he asked. "About Jesus of Nazareth," they replied. "He was a prophet, powerful in word and deed before God and all the people. 20 The chief priests and our rulers handed him over to be sentenced to death, and they crucified him; 21 but we had hoped that he was the one who was going to redeem Israel. And what is more, it is the third day since all this took place. 22 In addition, some of our women amazed us. They went to the tomb early this morning 23 but didn't find his body. They came and told us that they had seen a vision of angels, who said he was alive. 24 Then some of our companions went to the tomb and found it just as the women had said, but they did not see Jesus." 25 He said to them, "How foolish you are, and how slow to believe all that the prophets have spoken! 26 Did not the Messiah have to suffer these things and then enter his glory?" 27 And beginning with Moses and all the Prophets, he explained to them what was said in all the Scriptures concerning himself. 28 As they approached the village to which they were going, Jesus continued on as if he were going farther. 29 But they urged him strongly, "Stay with us, for it is nearly evening; the day is almost over." So he went in to stay with them. 30 When he was at the table with them, he took bread, gave thanks, broke it and began to give it to them. 31 Then their eyes were opened and they recognized him, and he disappeared from their sight. 32 They asked each other, "Were not our hearts burning within us while he talked with us on the road and opened the Scriptures to us?" 33 They got up and returned at once to Jerusalem. There they found the Eleven and those with them, assembled together 34 and saying, "It is true! The Lord has risen and has appeared to Simon." 35 Then the two told what had happened on the way, and how Jesus was recognized by them when he broke the bread.

Surprised!

Michelangelo Merisi da Caravaggio (1571–1610), an Italian artist, was known for his fiery temperament and unconventional technique. He used ordinary working people as models for his saints and was able to make viewers of his paintings feel they were a part of the scene. The *Supper at Emmaus* shows an innkeeper standing while Jesus and two of His followers are seated at a table when they recognize Him as the risen Lord (LUKE 24:31). One disciple is pushing himself to a standing position while the other's arms are outstretched and his hands open in astonishment.

TODAY'S READING
Luke 24:13–35

Then their eyes were opened and they recognized him. Luke 24:31

Luke, who records these events in his gospel, tells us that the two men immediately returned to Jerusalem where they found the eleven disciples and others assembled together and saying, " 'It is true! The Lord has risen and has appeared to Simon.' Then the two told what had happened on the way, and how Jesus was recognized by them when he broke the bread" (VV. 33–35).

Oswald Chambers said, "Jesus rarely comes where we expect Him; He appears where we least expect Him, and always in the most illogical connections. The only way a worker can keep true to God is by being ready for the Lord's surprise visits."

Whatever road we are on today, may we be ready for Jesus to make Himself known to us in new and surprising ways. 🌿

DAVID MCCASLAND

Lord Jesus, open our eyes to see You, the risen Christ, alongside us and at work in the circumstances of our lives today.

To find the Lord Jesus Christ we must be willing to seek Him.

¹ Then the LORD said to Moses, ² "See, I have chosen Bezalel son of Uri, the son of Hur, of the tribe of Judah, ³ and I have filled him with the Spirit of God, with wisdom, with understanding, with knowledge and with all kinds of skills— ⁴ to make artistic designs for work in gold, silver and bronze, ⁵ to cut and set stones, to work in wood, and to engage in all kinds of crafts. ⁶ Moreover, I have appointed Oholiab son of Ahisamak, of the tribe of Dan, to help him. Also I have given ability to all the skilled workers to make everything I have commanded you: ⁷ the tent of meeting, the ark of the covenant law with the atonement cover on it, and all the other furnishings of the tent— ⁸ the table and its articles, the pure gold lampstand and all its accessories, the altar of incense, ⁹ the altar of burnt offering and all its utensils, the basin with its stand— ¹⁰ and also the woven garments, both the sacred garments for Aaron the priest and the garments for his sons when they serve as priests, ¹¹ and the anointing oil and fragrant incense for the Holy Place. They are to make them just as I commanded you."

The Blacksmith and the King

I n 1878, when Scotsman Alexander Mackay arrived in what is now Uganda to serve as a missionary, he first set up a blacksmith forge among a tribe ruled by King Mutesa. Villagers gathered around this stranger who worked with his hands, puzzled because everyone "knew" that work was for women. At that time, men in Uganda never worked with their hands. They raided other villages to capture slaves, selling them to outsiders. Yet here was this foreign man at work forging farming tools.

Mackay's work ethic and life resulted in relationships with the villagers and gained him an audience with the king. Mackay challenged King Mutesa to end the slave trade, and he did.

TODAY'S READING
Exodus 31:1–11

Whatever you do, work at it with all your heart, as working for the Lord, not for human masters.

Colossians 3:23

In Scripture, we read of Bezalel and Oholiab, who were chosen and gifted by God to work with their hands designing the tent of meeting and all its furnishings for worship (EX. 31:1–11). Like Mackay, they honored and served God with their talent and labor.

We tend to categorize our work as either church work or secular. In truth, there is no distinction. God designs each of us in ways that make our contributions to the kingdom unique and meaningful. Even when we have little choice in where or how we work, God calls us to know Him more fully—and He will show us how to serve Him—right now. ❂   *RANDY KILGORE*

Father, grant me an awareness of my place in Your work.
Help me to see You at work in the people and places where I
spend my time.

God will show us how to serve Him—wherever we are.

¹ James, a servant of God and of the Lord Jesus Christ,
To the twelve tribes scattered among the nations:
Greetings.

² Consider it pure joy, my brothers and sisters,
whenever you face trials of many kinds, ³ because you know
that the testing of your faith produces perseverance. ⁴ Let
perseverance finish its work so that you may be mature and
complete, not lacking anything. ⁵ If any of you lacks wisdom,
you should ask God, who gives generously to all without
finding fault, and it will be given to you. ⁶ But when you ask,
you must believe and not doubt, because the one who doubts
is like a wave of the sea, blown and tossed by the wind. ⁷ That
person should not expect to receive anything from the Lord.

⁸ Such a person is double-minded and unstable in all they
do.

Wisdom and Grace

On April 4, 1968, American civil rights leader Dr. Martin Luther King Jr., was assassinated, leaving millions angry and disillusioned. In Indianapolis, a largely African-American crowd had gathered to hear Robert F. Kennedy speak. Many had not yet heard of Dr. King's death, so Kennedy had to share the tragic news. He appealed for calm by acknowledging not only their pain but his own abiding grief over the murder of his brother, President John F. Kennedy.

Kennedy then quoted a variation of an ancient poem by Aeschylus (526–456 BC):

Even in our sleep, pain which cannot forget falls drop by drop upon the heart until, in our own despair, against our will, comes wisdom through the awful grace of God.

"Wisdom through the awful grace of God" is a remarkable statement. It means that God's grace fills us with awe and gives us the opportunity to grow in wisdom during life's most difficult moments.

> **TODAY'S READING**
> James 1:1–8
>
> **If any of you lacks wisdom, you should ask of God, who gives generously to all without finding fault.** James 1:5

James wrote, "If any of you lacks wisdom, you should ask of God, who gives generously to all without finding fault, and it will be given to you" (JAMES 1:5). James says that this wisdom is grown in the soil of hardship (VV. 2–4), for there we not only learn from the wisdom of God, we rest in the grace of God. 🍂   *BILL CROWDER*

Father, in the face of life's sometimes awful circumstances, may we find Your grace to be a source of awe and wonder. Instruct us in our trials, and carry us in Your arms when we are overwhelmed.

The darkness of trials only makes God's grace shine brighter.

⁴ The word of the LORD came to me, saying,

⁵ "Before I formed you in the womb I knew you,
    before you were born I set you apart;
    I appointed you as a prophet to the nations."

⁶ "Alas, Sovereign LORD," I said, "I do not know how to speak; I am too young."

⁷ But the LORD said to me, "Do not say, 'I am too young.' You must go to everyone I send you to and say whatever I command you. ⁸ Do not be afraid of them, for I am with you and will rescue you," declares the LORD.

⁹ Then the LORD reached out his hand and touched my mouth and said to me, "I have put my words in your mouth.

Don't Walk Away

In 1986, John Piper nearly quit as minister of a large church. At that time he admitted in his journal: "I am so discouraged. I am so blank. I feel like there are opponents on every hand." But Piper didn't walk away, and God used him to lead a thriving ministry that would eventually reach far beyond his church.

Although *success* is a word easily misunderstood, we might call John Piper successful. But what if his ministry had never flourished?

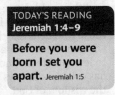

TODAY'S READING
Jeremiah 1:4–9

Before you were born I set you apart. Jeremiah 1:5

God gave the prophet Jeremiah a direct call. "Before I formed you in the womb I knew you," God said. "Before you were born I set you apart" (JER. 1:5). God encouraged him not to fear his enemies, "for I am with you and will rescue you" (V. 8).

Jeremiah later lamented his commission with ironic language for a man with a prenatal calling. "Alas, my mother, that you gave me birth, a man with whom the whole land strives and contends!" (15:10).

God did protect Jeremiah, but his ministry never thrived. His people never repented. He saw them slaughtered, enslaved, and scattered. Yet despite a lifetime of discouragement and rejection, he never walked away. He knew that God didn't call him to success but to faithfulness. He trusted the God who called him. Jeremiah's resilient compassion shows us the heart of the Father, who yearns for everyone to turn to Him. 🕮 *TIM GUSTAFSON*

Do you sense a call from God? Where in your calling have you encountered discouragement? How do you define success, and how do you react to it when you experience it?

Beware of giving up too soon. Our emotions are not reliable guides. JOHN PIPER

¹⁸ For the message of the cross is foolishness to those who are perishing, but to us who are being saved it is the power of God. ¹⁹ For it is written:

"I will destroy the wisdom of the wise;
the intelligence of the intelligent I will frustrate."

²⁰ Where is the wise person? Where is the teacher of the law? Where is the philosopher of this age? Has not God made foolish the wisdom of the world? ²¹ For since in the wisdom of God the world through its wisdom did not know him, God was pleased through the foolishness of what was preached to save those who believe. ²² Jews demand signs and Greeks look for wisdom, ²³ but we preach Christ crucified: a stumbling block to Jews and foolishness to Gentiles, ²⁴ but to those whom God has called, both Jews and Greeks, Christ the power of God and the wisdom of God. ²⁵ For the foolishness of God is wiser than human wisdom, and the weakness of God is stronger than human strength.

²⁶ Brothers and sisters, think of what you were when you were called. Not many of you were wise by human standards; not many were influential; not many were of noble birth.

²⁷ But God chose the foolish things of the world to shame the wise; God chose the weak things of the world to shame the strong. ²⁸ God chose the lowly things of this world and the despised things—and the things that are not—to nullify the things that are, ²⁹ so that no one may boast before him. ³⁰ It is because of him that you are in Christ Jesus, who has become for us wisdom from God—that is, our righteousness, holiness and redemption. ³¹ Therefore, as it is written: "Let the one who boasts boast in the Lord.

The Hollywood Hills Cross

One of the most recognizable images in the US is the "HOLLYWOOD" sign in Southern California. People from all over the globe come to "Tinseltown" to gaze at cement footprints of stars and perhaps catch a glimpse of celebrities who might pass by. It's hard for these visitors to miss the sign anchored in the foothills nearby.

Less well known in the Hollywood hills is another easily recognized symbol—one with eternal significance. Known as the Hollywood Pilgrimage Memorial Monument, this 32-foot cross looks out over the city. The cross was placed there in memory of Christine Wetherill Stevenson, a wealthy heiress who in the 1920s established the Pilgrimage Theatre (now the John Anson Ford Theatre). The site served as the venue for *The Pilgrimage Play*, a drama about Christ.

TODAY'S READING
1 Corinthians 1:18–31

May I never boast except in the cross of our Lord Jesus Christ. Galatians 6:14

The two icons showcase an interesting contrast. Movies good and bad will come and go. Their entertainment value, artistic contributions, and relevance are temporary at best.

The cross, however, reminds us of a drama eternal in scope. The work of Christ is a story of the loving God who pursues us and invites us to accept His offer of complete forgiveness. The high drama of Jesus's death is rooted in history. His resurrection conquered death and has an eternal impact for all of us. The cross will never lose its meaning and power. 🌿 *DENNIS FISHER*

Thank You, Father, for the eternal significance of the cross.
Help us to understand and appreciate the love that caused Your Son
to embrace His cross for our sakes.

To know the meaning of the cross, you must know the One who died there.

¹ After David was settled in his palace, he said to Nathan the prophet, "Here I am, living in a house of cedar, while the ark of the covenant of the LORD is under a tent." ² Nathan replied to David, "Whatever you have in mind, do it, for God is with you."

³ But that night the word of God came to Nathan, saying: ⁴ "Go and tell my servant David, 'This is what the LORD says: You are not the one to build me a house to dwell in. ⁵ I have not dwelt in a house from the day I brought Israel up out of Egypt to this day. I have moved from one tent site to another, from one dwelling place to another. ⁶ Wherever I have moved with all the Israelites, did I ever say to any of their leaders whom I commanded to shepherd my people, "Why have you not built me a house of cedar?"' ⁷ "Now then, tell my servant David, 'This is what the LORD Almighty says: I took you from the pasture, from tending the flock, and appointed you ruler over my people Israel. ⁸ I have been with you wherever you have gone, and I have cut off all your enemies from before you. Now I will make your name like the names of the greatest men on earth. ⁹ And I will provide a place for my people Israel and will plant them so that they can have a home of their own and no longer be disturbed. Wicked people will not oppress them anymore, as they did at the beginning ¹⁰ and have done ever since the time I appointed leaders over my people Israel. I will also subdue all your enemies. "'I declare to you that the LORD will build a house for you: ¹¹ When your days are over and you go to be with your ancestors, I will raise up your offspring to succeed you, one of your own sons, and I will establish his kingdom. ¹² He is the one who will build a house for me, and I will establish his throne forever. ¹³ I will be his father, and he will be my son. I will never take my love away from him, as I took it away from your predecessor. ¹⁴ I will set him over my house and my kingdom forever; his throne will be established forever.'" ¹⁵ Nathan reported to David all the words of this entire revelation.

¹⁶ Then King David went in and sat before the LORD, and he said: "Who am I, LORD God, and what is my family, that you have brought me this far? ¹⁷ And as if this were not enough in your sight, my God, you have spoken about the future of the house of your servant. You, LORD God, have looked on me as though I were the most exalted of men. ¹⁸ "What more can David say to you for honoring your servant? For you know your servant, ¹⁹ LORD. For the sake of your servant and according to your will, you have done this great thing and made known all these great promises. ²⁰ "There is no one like you, LORD, and there is no God but you, as we have heard with our own ears.

His Plans or Ours?

When my husband was 18 years old, he started a car-cleaning business. He rented a garage, hired helpers, and created advertising brochures. The business prospered. His intention was to sell it and use the proceeds to pay for college, so he was thrilled when a buyer expressed interest. After some negotia-tions, it seemed that the transaction would happen. But at the last minute, the deal collapsed. It wouldn't be until several months later that his plan to sell the business would succeed.

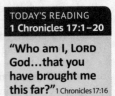

TODAY'S READING
1 Chronicles 17:1–20

"Who am I, LORD God…that you have brought me this far." 1 Chronicles 17:16

It's normal to be disappointed when God's timing and design for our lives do not match our expectations. When David wanted to build the Lord's temple, he had the right motives, the leadership ability, and the resources. Yet God said he could not undertake the proj-ect because he had killed too many people in battle (1 CHRON. 22:8).

David could have shaken his fist at the sky in anger. He could have pouted or plowed ahead with his own plans. But he humbly said, "Who am I, LORD God . . . that you have brought me this far?" (17:16). David went on to praise God and affirm his devotion to Him. He valued his relationship with God more than his ambition.

What is more important—achieving our hopes and dreams, or our love for God? 🌢

JENNIFER BENSON SCHULDT

Dear heavenly Father, I commit all of my plans to You.
Thank You for bringing me this far. You mean more to me than
anything in the world.

True satisfaction is found in yielding ourselves to the will of God.

¹⁷ On his arrival, Jesus found that Lazarus had already been in the tomb for four days. ¹⁸ Now Bethany was less than two miles from Jerusalem, ¹⁹ and many Jews had come to Martha and Mary to comfort them in the loss of their brother. ²⁰ When Martha heard that Jesus was coming, she went out to meet him, but Mary stayed at home.

²¹ "Lord," Martha said to Jesus, "if you had been here, my brother would not have died. ²² But I know that even now God will give you whatever you ask."

²³ Jesus said to her, "Your brother will rise again."

²⁴ Martha answered, "I know he will rise again in the resurrection at the last day."

²⁵ Jesus said to her, "I am the resurrection and the life. The one who believes in me will live, even though they die; ²⁶ and whoever lives by believing in me will never die. Do you believe this?"

²⁷ "Yes, Lord," she replied, "I believe that you are the Messiah, the Son of God, who is to come into the world."

In Transition

People post obituary notices on billboards and concrete block walls in Ghana regularly. Headlines such as *Gone Too Soon, Celebration of Life,* and *What a Shock!* announce the passing away of loved ones and the approaching funerals. One I read—*In Transition*—points to life beyond the grave.

When a close relative or friend dies, we sorrow as Mary and Martha did for their brother Lazarus (JOHN 11:17–27). We miss the departed so much that our hearts break and we weep, as Jesus wept at the passing of His friend (V. 35).

TODAY'S READING
John 11:17–27

We will be with the Lord forever.
1 Thessalonians 4:17

Yet, it was at this sorrowful moment Jesus made a delightful statement on life after death: "I am the resurrection and the life. The one who believes in me will live, even though they die; and whoever lives by believing in me will never die" (V. 25).

On the basis of this we give departed believers only a temporary farewell. For they "will be with the Lord forever," Paul emphasizes (1 THESS. 4:17). Of course, farewells are painful, but we can rest assured that they are in the Lord's safe hands.

In Transition suggests that we are only changing from one situation to another. Though life on earth ends for us, we will continue to live forever and better in the next life where Jesus is. "Therefore encourage one another with these words" (V. 18). ❤

LAWRENCE DARMANI

It is because of You, Jesus, that we have hope and are sure of a forever life. We're grateful.

Because of Jesus, we can live forever.

⁸ We are hard pressed on every side, but not crushed; perplexed, but not in despair; ⁹ persecuted, but not abandoned; struck down, but not destroyed. ¹⁰ We always carry around in our body the death of Jesus, so that the life of Jesus may also be revealed in our body. ¹¹ For we who are alive are always being given over to death for Jesus' sake, so that his life may also be revealed in our mortal body. ¹² So then, death is at work in us, but life is at work in you.

¹³ It is written: "I believed; therefore I have spoken." Since we have that same spirit of faith, we also believe and therefore speak, ¹⁴ because we know that the one who raised the Lord Jesus from the dead will also raise us with Jesus and present us with you to himself. ¹⁵ All this is for your benefit, so that the grace that is reaching more and more people may cause thanksgiving to overflow to the glory of God.

¹⁶ Therefore we do not lose heart. Though outwardly we are wasting away, yet inwardly we are being renewed day by day. ¹⁷ For our light and momentary troubles are achieving for us an eternal glory that far outweighs them all. ¹⁸ So we fix our eyes not on what is seen, but on what is unseen, since what is seen is temporary, but what is unseen is eternal.

Take Heart!

like to watch birds at play, so years ago I built a small sanctuary in our backyard to attract them. For several months I enjoyed the sight of my feathered friends feeding and flitting about—until a Cooper's Hawk made my bird refuge his private hunting reserve.

Such is life: Just about the time we settle down to take our ease, something or someone comes along to unsettle our nests. Why, we ask, must so much of life be a vale of tears?

I've heard many answers to that old question, but lately I'm satisfied with just one: "All the discipline of the world is to make [us] children, that God may be revealed to [us]" (George MacDonald, *Life Essential*). When we become like children, we begin trusting, resting solely in the love of our Father in heaven, seeking to know Him and to be like Him.

> TODAY'S READING
> **2 Corinthians 4:8–18**
>
> **In this world you will have trouble. But take heart! I have overcome the world.** John 16:33

Cares and sorrow may follow us all the days of our lives, but "we do not lose heart. . . . For our light and momentary troubles are achieving for us an eternal glory that far outweighs them all. So we fix our eyes not on what is seen, but on what is unseen, since what is seen is temporary, but what is unseen is eternal" (2 COR. 4:16–18).

Can we not rejoice, then, with such an end in view? ⊘

DAVID ROPER

Lord, we do rejoice even in our struggles because we are rejoicing in who You are and Your good purposes for us. You are powerful, loving, in control, and eternal. We trust You and love You.

Heaven's delights will far outweigh earth's difficulties.

⁷ The LORD said, "I have indeed seen the misery of my people in Egypt. I have heard them crying out because of their slave drivers, and I am concerned about their suffering. ⁸ So I have come down to rescue them from the hand of the Egyptians and to bring them up out of that land into a good and spacious land, a land flowing with milk and honey—the home of the Canaanites, Hittites, Amorites, Perizzites, Hivites and Jebusites. ⁹ And now the cry of the Israelites has reached me, and I have seen the way the Egyptians are oppressing them. ¹⁰ So now, go. I am sending you to Pharaoh to bring my people the Israelites out of Egypt."

¹¹ But Moses said to God, "Who am I that I should go to Pharaoh and bring the Israelites out of Egypt?"

¹² And God said, "I will be with you. And this will be the sign to you that it is I who have sent you: When you have brought the people out of Egypt, you will worship God on this mountain."

¹³ Moses said to God, "Suppose I go to the Israelites and say to them, 'The God of your fathers has sent me to you,' and they ask me, 'What is his name?' Then what shall I tell them?"

¹⁴ God said to Moses, "I AM WHO I AM. This is what you are to say to the Israelites: 'I am has sent me to you.'"

¹⁵ God also said to Moses, "Say to the Israelites, 'The LORD, the God of your fathers—the God of Abraham, the God of Isaac and the God of Jacob—has sent me to you.'

"This is my name forever,
　　the name you shall call me
　　from generation to generation.

¹⁶ "Go, assemble the elders of Israel and say to them, 'The LORD, the God of your fathers—the God of Abraham, Isaac and Jacob—appeared to me and said: I have watched over you and have seen what has been done to you in Egypt. ¹⁷ And I have promised to bring you up out of your misery in Egypt into the land of the Canaanites, Hittites, Amorites, Perizzites, Hivites and Jebusites—a land flowing with milk and honey.'

Sweet Reminders

When the tomb of Egyptian King Tutankhamen was discovered in 1922, it was filled with things ancient Egyptians thought were needed in the afterlife. Among items such as golden shrines, jewelry, clothing, furniture, and weapons was a pot filled with honey—still edible after 3,200 years!

Today we think of honey primarily as a sweetener, but in the ancient world it had many other uses. Honey is one of the only foods known to have all the nutrients needed to sustain life, so it was eaten for nutrition. In addition, honey has medicinal value. It is one of the oldest known wound dressings because it has properties that prevent infection.

TODAY'S READING
Exodus 3:7–17

Gracious words are a honeycomb, sweet to the soul and healing to the bones. Proverbs 16:24

When God rescued the children of Israel from Egyptian captivity, He promised to lead them to a "land flowing with milk and honey" (EX. 3:8, 17), a metaphor for abundance. When their journey was prolonged due to sin, God fed them bread (manna) that tasted like honey (16:31). The Israelites grumbled about having to eat the same food for so long, but it's likely that God was kindly reminding them of what they would enjoy in the Promised Land.

God still uses honey to remind us that His ways and words are sweeter than the honeycomb (PS. 19:10). So then the words we speak should also be like the honey we eat—both sweet and healing. 🌿

JULIE ACKERMAN LINK

Read these verses about the use of words: Proverbs 12:18; Proverbs 13:3; Ephesians 4:29; Colossians 3:8. Which truths might God want you to put into practice in your life today?

Spend time counting your blessings, not airing your complaints.

⁴ And I saw that all toil and all achievement spring from one person's envy of another. This too is meaningless, a chasing after the wind.

⁵ Fools fold their hands and ruin themselves.

⁶ Better one handful with tranquillity
than two handfuls with toil
and chasing after the wind.

⁷ Again I saw something meaningless under the sun:

⁸ There was a man all alone;
he had neither son nor brother.
There was no end to his toil,
yet his eyes were not content with his wealth.
"For whom am I toiling," he asked,
"and why am I depriving myself of enjoyment?"
This too is meaningless— a miserable business!

⁹ Two are better than one,
because they have a good return for their labor:

¹⁰ If either of them falls down, one can help the other up.
But pity anyone who falls
and has no one to help them up.

¹¹ Also, if two lie down together, they will keep warm.
But how can one keep warm alone?

¹² Though one may be overpowered,
two can defend themselves.
A cord of three strands is not quickly broken.

¹³ Better a poor but wise youth than an old but foolish king who no longer knows how to heed a warning. ¹⁴ The youth may have come from prison to the kingship, or he may have been born in poverty within his kingdom. ¹⁵ I saw that all who lived and walked under the sun followed the youth, the king's successor. ¹⁶ There was no end to all the people who were before them. But those who came later were not pleased with the successor. This too is meaningless, a chasing after the wind.

Who Am I Working For?

Henry worked 70 hours a week. He loved his job and brought home a sizeable paycheck to provide good things for his family. He always had plans to slow down but he never did. One evening he came home with great news—he had been promoted to the highest position in his company. But no one was home. Over the years, his children had grown up and moved out, his wife had found a career of her own, and now the house was empty. There was no one to share the good news with.

Solomon talked about the need to keep a balance in life with our work. He wrote, "Fools fold their hands and ruin themselves" (ECCL. 4:5). We don't want to go to the extreme of being lazy, but neither do we want to fall into the trap of being a workaholic. "Better one handful with tranquillity than two handfuls with toil and chasing after the wind" (V. 6). In other words, it is better to have less and enjoy it more. Sacrificing relationships at the altar of success is unwise. Achievement is fleeting, while relationships are what make our life meaningful, rewarding, and enjoyable (VV. 7–12).

> TODAY'S READING
> **Ecclesiastes 4:4–16**
>
> **"For whom am I toiling," he asked, "and why am I depriving myself of enjoyment?"**
>
> Ecclesiastes 4:8

We can learn to work to live and not live to work by choosing to apportion our time wisely. The Lord can give us this wisdom as we seek Him and trust Him to be our Provider. 🖋

POH FANG CHIA

Lord, show me if my priorities are skewed and where I need to make changes. Thank You for the gift of family and friends.

To spend time wisely, invest it in eternity.

¹ Adam made love to his wife Eve, and she became pregnant and gave birth to Cain. She said, "With the help of the LORD I have brought forth a man." ² Later she gave birth to his brother Abel.

Now Abel kept flocks, and Cain worked the soil. ³ In the course of time Cain brought some of the fruits of the soil as an offering to the LORD. ⁴ And Abel also brought an offering—fat portions from some of the firstborn of his flock. The LORD looked with favor on Abel and his offering, ⁵ but on Cain and his offering he did not look with favor. So Cain was very angry, and his face was downcast.

⁶ Then the LORD said to Cain, "Why are you angry? Why is your face downcast? ⁷ If you do what is right, will you not be accepted? But if you do not do what is right, sin is crouching at your door; it desires to have you, but you must rule over it."

⁸ Now Cain said to his brother Abel, "Let's go out to the field." While they were in the field, Cain attacked his brother Abel and killed him.

Resisting the Trap

A **Venus flytrap** can digest an insect in about 10 days. The process begins when an unsuspecting bug smells nectar on the leaves that form the trap. When the insect investigates, it crawls into the jaws of the plant. The leaves clamp shut within half a second and digestive juices dissolve the bug.

This meat-eating plant reminds me of the way sin can devour us if we are lured into it. Sin is hungry for us. Genesis 4:7 says, "If you do not do what is right, sin is crouching at your door; it desires to have you." God spoke these words to Cain just before he killed his brother Abel.

> TODAY'S READING
> Genesis 4:1–8
>
> **Sin is crouching at your door; it desires to have you, but you must rule over it.** Genesis 4:7

Sin may try to entice us by tempting us with a new experience, convincing us that living right doesn't matter, or appealing to our physical senses. However, there is a way for us to rule over sin instead of letting it consume our lives. The Bible says, "Walk by the Spirit, and you will not gratify the desires of the flesh" (GAL. 5:16). When we face temptation, we don't face it alone. We have supernatural assistance. Relying on God's Spirit supplies the power to live for Him and others. 🌱

JENNIFER BENSON SCHULDT

Dear God, at times I let down my guard and indulge in sin.
Please help me to listen to Your warnings and obey Your Word.
Protect me from my own impulses and conform me to Your image.
Thank You for Your work in me.

We fall into temptation when we don't flee from it.

²² Then Jesus said to his disciples: "Therefore I tell you, do not worry about your life, what you will eat; or about your body, what you will wear. ²³ For life is more than food, and the body more than clothes. ²⁴ Consider the ravens: They do not sow or reap, they have no storeroom or barn; yet God feeds them. And how much more valuable you are than birds! ²⁵ Who of you by worrying can add a single hour to your life? ²⁶ Since you cannot do this very little thing, why do you worry about the rest?

²⁷ "Consider how the wild flowers grow. They do not labor or spin. Yet I tell you, not even Solomon in all his splendor was dressed like one of these. ²⁸ If that is how God clothes the grass of the field, which is here today, and tomorrow is thrown into the fire, how much more will he clothe you—you of little faith! ²⁹ And do not set your heart on what you will eat or drink; do not worry about it. ³⁰ For the pagan world runs after all such things, and your Father knows that you need them. ³¹ But seek his kingdom, and these things will be given to you as well.

³² "Do not be afraid, little flock, for your Father has been pleased to give you the kingdom. ³³ Sell your possessions and give to the poor. Provide purses for yourselves that will not wear out, a treasure in heaven that will never fail, where no thief comes near and no moth destroys. ³⁴ For where your treasure is, there your heart will be also.

Heart Check

When commuting into Chicago on the train, I always followed the "unwritten codes of conduct"—such as, no conversations with people sitting next to you if you don't know them. That was tough on a guy like me who has never met a stranger. I love talking to new people! Although I kept the code of silence, I realized that you can still learn something about people based on the section of the newspaper they read. So I'd watch to see what they turned to first: The business section? Sports? Politics? Current events? Their choices revealed their interests.

TODAY'S READING
Luke 12:22–34

Where your treasure is, there your heart will be also. Luke 12:34

Our choices are always revealing. Of course, God doesn't need to wait to see our choices in order for Him to know what's in our hearts. But the things that occupy our time and attention are telling. As Jesus said, "Where your treasure is, there your heart will be also" (LUKE 12:34). Regardless of what we want Him to think of us, the true condition of our heart becomes clear based on how we use our time, our money, and our talents. When we invest these resources in the things He cares about, then it reveals that our hearts are in tune with His.

God's heart is with the needs of people and the advancement of His kingdom. What do your choices tell Him and others about where your heart is? 🌱

JOE STOWELL

Lord, I want my heart to be in tune with Yours.
Forgive me for giving it to things of far less value, and teach me the joy of investing my time in opportunities to serve You. Thank You.

Where is your treasure?

19 Open for me the gates of the righteous;
    I will enter and give thanks to the LORD.
20 This is the gate of the LORD
    through which the righteous may enter.
21 I will give you thanks, for you answered me;
    you have become my salvation.
22 The stone the builders rejected
    has become the cornerstone;
23 the LORD has done this,
    and it is marvelous in our eyes.
24 The LORD has done it this very day;
    let us rejoice today and be glad.
25 LORD, save us!
    LORD, grant us success!
26 Blessed is he who comes in the name of the LORD.
    From the house of the LORD we bless you.
27 The LORD is God,
    and he has made his light shine on us.
With boughs in hand, join in the festal procession
    up to the horns of the altar.
28 You are my God, and I will praise you;
    you are my God, and I will exalt you.
29 Give thanks to the LORD, for he is good;
    his love endures forever.

This Is the Day

I n 1940, **Dr. Virginia Connally**, age 27, braved opposition and criticism to become the first female physician in Abilene, Texas. A few months before her 100th birthday in 2012, the Texas Medical Association presented her with its Distinguished Service Award, Texas's highest physician honor. Between those two landmark events, Dr. Connally has enthusiastically embraced a passion for spreading the gospel around the world through her many medical mission trips while living a life of service to God and to others—one day at a time.

> **TODAY'S READING**
> **Psalm 118:19–29**
>
> **This is the day the LORD has made; we will rejoice and be glad in it.** Psalm 118:24 NKJV

Dr. Connally's pastor, Phil Christopher, said, "Every day for her is a gift." He recalled a letter in which she wrote, "Every tour, trip, effort, I wonder if this will be my last and ultimate? Only God knows. And this is enough."

The psalmist wrote, "This is the day the LORD has made; we will rejoice and be glad in it" (PS. 118:24 NKJV). So often we focus on the disappointments of yesterday or the uncertainties of tomorrow and miss God's matchless gift to us: Today!

Dr. Connally said of her journey with Christ, "As you live a life of faith, you're not looking for the results. I was just doing the things that God planted in my life and heart."

God made today. Let's celebrate it and make the most of every opportunity to serve others in His name. ❧ *DAVID MCCASLAND*

Lord, thank You for today. May I embrace it as Your gift, celebrate Your faithfulness, and live this day fully for You.

Welcome each day as a gift from God.

⁵ Therefore, when Christ came into the world, he said:
"Sacrifice and offering you did not desire,
    but a body you prepared for me;
⁶ with burnt offerings and sin offerings
    you were not pleased.
⁷ Then I said, 'Here I am—it is written about me in the scroll—
    I have come to do your will, my God.'"

⁸ First he said, "Sacrifices and offerings, burnt offerings and sin offerings you did not desire, nor were you pleased with them"—though they were offered in accordance with the law. ⁹ Then he said, "Here I am, I have come to do your will." He sets aside the first to establish the second. ¹⁰ And by that will, we have been made holy through the sacrifice of the body of Jesus Christ once for all.

¹¹ Day after day every priest stands and performs his religious duties; again and again he offers the same sacrifices, which can never take away sins. ¹² But when this priest had offered for all time one sacrifice for sins, he sat down at the right hand of God, ¹³ and since that time he waits for his enemies to be made his footstool. ¹⁴ For by one sacrifice he has made perfect forever those who are being made holy.

¹⁵ The Holy Spirit also testifies to us about this. First he says:
¹⁶ "This is the covenant I will make with them
    after that time, says the Lord.
I will put my laws in their hearts,
    and I will write them on their minds."
¹⁷ Then he adds:
"Their sins and lawless acts
    I will remember no more."
¹⁸ And where these have been forgiven, sacrifice for sin is no longer necessary.

Great Sacrifice

W.T. Stead, an innovative English journalist at the turn of the 20th century, was known for writing about controversial social issues. Two of the articles he published addressed the danger of ships operating with an insufficient ratio of lifeboats to passengers. Ironically, Stead was aboard the *Titanic* when it struck an iceberg in the North Atlantic on April 15, 1912. According to one report, after helping women and children into lifeboats, Stead sacrificed his own life by giving up his life vest and a place in the lifeboats so others could be rescued.

TODAY'S READING
Hebrews 10:5–18

The Lord Jesus Christ...gave himself for our sins to rescue us.
Galatians 1:3–4

There is something very stirring about self-sacrifice. No greater example of that can be found than in Christ Himself. The writer of Hebrews says, "This Man, after He had offered one sacrifice for sins forever, sat down at the right hand of God .... For by one offering He has perfected forever those who are being sanctified" (HEB. 10:12, 14 NKJV). In his letter to the Galatians, Paul opened with words describing this great sacrifice: "The Lord Jesus Christ ... gave himself for our sins to rescue us from the present evil age" (GAL. 1:3–4).

Jesus's offering of Himself on our behalf is the measure of His love for us. That willing sacrifice continues to rescue men and women and offer assurance of eternity with Him. 🌀

BILL CROWDER

God of love and grace, words can never capture the wonder of the sacrifice that Christ offered on our behalf. May our love respond to You with faith and worship—for Your Son who was slain is worthy of our praise.

Jesus laid down His life to show His love for us.

¹ After this, the Moabites and Ammonites with some of the Meunites came to wage war against Jehoshaphat.
² Some people came and told Jehoshaphat, "A vast army is coming against you from Edom, from the other side of the Dead Sea. It is already in Hazezon Tamar" (that is, En Gedi). ³ Alarmed, Jehoshaphat resolved to inquire of the LORD, and he proclaimed a fast for all Judah. ⁴ The people of Judah came together to seek help from the LORD; indeed, they came from every town in Judah to seek him.

⁵ Then Jehoshaphat stood up in the assembly of Judah and Jerusalem at the temple of the LORD in the front of the new courtyard ⁶ and said:

"LORD, the God of our ancestors, are you not the God who is in heaven? You rule over all the kingdoms of the nations. Power and might are in your hand, and no one can withstand you. ⁷ Our God, did you not drive out the inhabitants of this land before your people Israel and give it forever to the descendants of Abraham your friend? ⁸ They have lived in it and have built in it a sanctuary for your Name, saying, ⁹ 'If calamity comes upon us, whether the sword of judgment, or plague or famine, we will stand in your presence before this temple that bears your Name and will cry out to you in our distress, and you will hear us and save us.'

¹⁰ "But now here are men from Ammon, Moab and Mount Seir, whose territory you would not allow Israel to invade when they came from Egypt; so they turned away from them and did not destroy them. ¹¹ See how they are repaying us by coming to drive us out of the possession you gave us as an inheritance. ¹² Our God, will you not judge them? For we have no power to face this vast army that is attacking us. We do not know what to do, but our eyes are on you."

¹³ All the men of Judah, with their wives and children and little ones, stood there before the LORD.

Unconventional Tactics

In 1980, a woman hopped on a subway during the Boston Marathon. No big deal, except for one small detail. She was supposed to be *running* the marathon! Later, witnesses saw her jump into the race less than a mile from the finish line. She finished well ahead of all the other female runners, and oddly, she wasn't winded or even sweating much. For a brief time she looked like the winner.

TODAY'S READING
2 Chronicles 20:1–13

We do not know what to do, but our eyes are on you. 2 Chronicles 20:12

In a conflict long ago, a people who were losing a battle found a more honorable way to win. When messengers told King Jehoshaphat, "A vast army is coming against you from Edom," he was terrified (2 CHRON. 20:2–3). But instead of turning to typical military tactics, Jehoshaphat turned to God. He acknowledged God's supremacy and admitted his own fear and confusion. "We do not know what to do, but our eyes are on you" (V. 12). Then the king chose singers to lead the army into battle. Instead of a war cry, they sang of God's love (V. 21). The result was startling. Their enemies turned on each other (VV. 22–24). In the end, "The kingdom of Jehoshaphat was at peace, for his God had given him rest on every side" (V. 30).

Life can ambush us with overwhelming challenges. Yet our fear and uncertainties give us the opportunity to turn to our all-powerful God. He specializes in the unconventional. 🌿

TIM GUSTAFSON

Lord, You are not the source of confusion or fear,
but of strength and peace. We exchange our panicky plans for Your
amazing answers. Encourage us as we wait for You.

Our God is never predictable, but He is unfailingly reliable.

⁴² They devoted themselves to the apostles' teaching and to fellowship, to the breaking of bread and to prayer. ⁴³ Everyone was filled with awe at the many wonders and signs performed by the apostles. ⁴⁴ All the believers were together and had everything in common. ⁴⁵ They sold property and possessions to give to anyone who had need. ⁴⁶ Every day they continued to meet together in the temple courts. They broke bread in their homes and ate together with glad and sincere hearts, ⁴⁷ praising God and enjoying the favor of all the people. And the Lord added to their number daily those who were being saved.

Chameleon Crawl

When we think of the chameleon, we probably think of its ability to change color according to its surroundings. But this lizard has another interesting characteristic. On several occasions I've watched a chameleon walk along a pathway and wondered how it ever reached its destination. Reluctantly, the chameleon stretches out one leg, seems to change its mind, attempts again, and then carefully plants a hesitant foot, as if afraid the ground will collapse under it. That was why I couldn't help laughing when I heard someone say, "Do not be a chameleon church member who says, 'Let me go to church today; no, let me go next week; no, let me wait for a while!'"

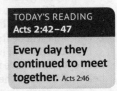

TODAY'S READING
Acts 2:42–47

Every day they continued to meet together. Acts 2:46

"The house of the LORD" at Jerusalem was King David's place of worship, and he was far from being a "chameleon" worshiper. Rather, he rejoiced with those who said, "Let us go to the house of the LORD" (PS. 122:1). The same was true for believers in the early church. "They devoted themselves to the apostles' teaching and to fellowship, to the breaking of bread and to prayer.... Every day they continued to meet together in the temple courts" (ACTS 2:42, 46).

What a joy it is to join with others in worship and fellowship! Praying and worshiping together, studying the Scriptures together, and caring for one another are essential for our spiritual growth and unity as believers. 🌼 *LAWRENCE DARMANI*

Before our Father's throne we pour our ardent prayers; our fears,
our hopes, our aims are one, our comforts and our cares.
JOHN FAWCETT

Worshiping together brings strength and joy.

¹ Then I looked up, and there before me was a man with a measuring line in his hand. ² I asked, "Where are you going?"

He answered me, "To measure Jerusalem, to find out how wide and how long it is."

³ While the angel who was speaking to me was leaving, another angel came to meet him ⁴ and said to him: "Run, tell that young man, 'Jerusalem will be a city without walls because of the great number of people and animals in it.

⁵ And I myself will be a wall of fire around it,' declares the LORD, 'and I will be its glory within.'

⁶ "Come! Come! Flee from the land of the north," declares the LORD, "for I have scattered you to the four winds of heaven," declares the LORD.

⁷ "Come, Zion! Escape, you who live in Daughter Babylon!" ⁸ For this is what the LORD Almighty says: "After the Glorious One has sent me against the nations that have plundered you—for whoever touches you touches the apple of his eye—

⁹ I will surely raise my hand against them so that their slaves will plunder them. Then you will know that the LORD Almighty has sent me.

¹⁰ "Shout and be glad, Daughter Zion. For I am coming, and I will live among you," declares the LORD. ¹¹ "Many nations will be joined with the LORD in that day and will become my people. I will live among you and you will know that the LORD Almighty has sent me to you. ¹² The LORD will inherit Judah as his portion in the holy land and will again choose Jerusalem. ¹³ Be still before the LORD, all mankind, because he has roused himself from his holy dwelling.

The Apple of His Eye

A **friend's baby** was suffering seizures, so they sped to the hospital in an ambulance, the mother's heart racing as she prayed for her daughter. Her fierce love for this child hit her afresh as she held her tiny fingers, recalling too how much more the Lord loves us and how we are "the apple of His eye."

TODAY'S READING
Zechariah 2

Whoever touches you touches the apple of his eye.
Zechariah 2:8

The prophet Zechariah employs this phrase in his word to God's people who had returned to Jerusalem after their captivity in Babylon. He calls them to repent, to rebuild the temple, and to renew their hearts of love for the true God. For the Lord loves His people greatly; they are the apple of His eye.

Hebrew scholars suggest this phrase from Zechariah 2 denotes one's reflection in the pupil of another's eye, with the word "apple" emerging because it's a common spherical object. So with eyes being precious and fragile, they need protecting, and that's how the Lord wants to love and protect His people—by holding them close to His heart.

The Lord who dwells in our midst pours out His love on us—even, amazingly, far more than a loving mother who does all she can for her ailing child. We are the apple of His eye, His beloved. ✒

AMY BOUCHER PYE

Father God, You love us so much that You gave us Your only Son to die that we might live. May we receive Your love this day and live in it.

A parent's love for a child reflects our Father's love for us.

¹ As the deer pants for streams of water,
    so my soul pants for you, my God.
² My soul thirsts for God, for the living God.
    When can I go and meet with God?
³ My tears have been my food
    day and night,
while people say to me all day long,
    "Where is your God?"
⁴ These things I remember
    as I pour out my soul:
how I used to go to the house of God
    under the protection of the Mighty One
with shouts of joy and praise
    among the festive throng.
⁵ Why, my soul, are you downcast?
    Why so disturbed within me?
Put your hope in God,
    for I will yet praise him,
    my Savior and my God.
⁶ My soul is downcast within me;
    therefore I will remember you
from the land of the Jordan,
    the heights of Hermon—from Mount Mizar.
⁷ Deep calls to deep
    in the roar of your waterfalls;
all your waves and breakers
    have swept over me.
⁸ By day the LORD directs his love,
    at night his song is with me—
    a prayer to the God of my life.
⁹ I say to God my Rock,
    "Why have you forgotten me?
Why must I go about mourning,
    oppressed by the enemy?"

The God Who Paints

Nezahualcoyotl (1402–1472) may have had a difficult name to pronounce, but his name is full of significance. It means "Hungry Coyote," and this man's writings show a spiritual hunger. As a poet and ruler in Mexico before the arrival of the Europeans, he wrote, "Truly the gods, which I worship, are idols of stone that do not speak nor feel. . . . Some very powerful, hidden and unknown god is the creator of the entire universe. He is the only one that can console me in my affliction and help me in such anguish as my heart feels; I want him to be my helper and protection."

TODAY'S READING
Psalm 42

My soul thirsts for God, for the living God. Psalm 42:2

We cannot know if Nezahualcoyotl found the Giver of life. But during his reign he built a pyramid to the "God who paints things with beauty," and he banned human sacrifices in his city.

The writers of Psalm 42 cried out, "My soul thirsts for God, for the living God" (V. 2). Every human being desires the true God, just as "the deer pants for streams of water" (V. 1).

Today there are many Hungry Coyotes who know that the idols of fame, money, and relationships can't fill the void in their souls. The Living God has revealed Himself through Jesus, the only One who gives us meaning and fulfillment. This is good news for those who are hungry for the God who paints things with beauty.

KEILA OCHOA

Lord, You are the One my soul needs. Only You can bring meaning
and fulfillment to my life. You are the One my heart cries out for.
I put my hope in You.

Beneath all of our longings is a deep desire for God.

¹ When Moses finished setting up the tabernacle, he anointed and consecrated it and all its furnishings. He also anointed and consecrated the altar and all its utensils. ² Then the leaders of Israel, the heads of families who were the tribal leaders in charge of those who were counted, made offerings. ³ They brought as their gifts before the LORD six covered carts and twelve oxen—an ox from each leader and a cart from every two. These they presented before the tabernacle.

⁴ The LORD said to Moses, ⁵ "Accept these from them, that they may be used in the work at the tent of meeting. Give them to the Levites as each man's work requires."

⁶ So Moses took the carts and oxen and gave them to the Levites. ⁷ He gave two carts and four oxen to the Gershonites, as their work required, ⁸ and he gave four carts and eight oxen to the Merarites, as their work required. They were all under the direction of Ithamar son of Aaron, the priest. ⁹ But Moses did not give any to the Kohathites, because they were to carry on their shoulders the holy things, for which they were responsible.

God's Way

We really needed to hear from God. Having been asked to foster two young children as an emergency measure just for 3 months, a decision had to be made about their future. With three older children of our own, becoming foster parents to preschoolers didn't seem to fit with our life plan and having our family almost double in size had been hard work. Our book of daily readings by the veteran missionary Amy Carmichael directed us to some unfamiliar verses in Numbers 7.

TODAY'S READING
Numbers 7:1–9

They were to carry on their shoulders the holy things, for which they were responsible.

Numbers 7:9

"I wonder how the Kohathites felt?" Amy wrote. "All the other priests had ox-carts to carry their parts of the tabernacle through the desert. But the sons of Kohath had to trudge along the rocky tracks and through the burning sand, with the 'holy things for which they were responsible' on their shoulders. Did they ever grumble inwardly, feeling that the other priests had an easier task? Perhaps! But God knows that some things are too precious to be carried on ox-carts and then He asks us to carry them on our shoulders."

My husband and I knew this was our answer. We had often thought of sponsoring a child from an undeveloped country, but we hadn't done so. That would have been easier, much like the ox-cart. Now we had two needy children in our own home to carry "on our shoulders" because they were so precious to Him.

God has different plans for each of us. We might feel that others have an easier assignment, or a more glamorous role to play. But if our loving Father has handpicked us for our task, who are we to whisper, "I can't do this"? 🌿   *MARION STROUD*

God uses ordinary people to carry out His extraordinary plans.

¹ Now a man named Lazarus was sick. He was from Bethany, the village of Mary and her sister Martha. ² (This Mary, whose brother Lazarus now lay sick, was the same one who poured perfume on the Lord and wiped his feet with her hair.) ³ So the sisters sent word to Jesus, "Lord, the one you love is sick."

⁴ When he heard this, Jesus said, "This sickness will not end in death. No, it is for God's glory so that God's Son may be glorified through it."

³⁸ Jesus, once more deeply moved, came to the tomb. It was a cave with a stone laid across the entrance. ³⁹ "Take away the stone," he said.

"But, Lord," said Martha, the sister of the dead man, "by this time there is a bad odor, for he has been there four days."

⁴⁰ Then Jesus said, "Did I not tell you that if you believe, you will see the glory of God?"

⁴¹ So they took away the stone. Then Jesus looked up and said, "Father, I thank you that you have heard me. ⁴² I knew that you always hear me, but I said this for the benefit of the people standing here, that they may believe that you sent me."

⁴³ When he had said this, Jesus called in a loud voice, "Lazarus, come out!" ⁴⁴ The dead man came out, his hands and feet wrapped with strips of linen, and a cloth around his face.

Jesus said to them, "Take off the grave clothes and let him go."

Jesus Wept

I was engrossed in a book when a friend bent over to see what I was reading. Almost immediately, she recoiled and looked at me aghast. "What a gloomy title!" she said. I was reading "The Glass Coffin" in *Grimm's Fairy Tales,* and the word *coffin* disturbed her. Most of us don't like to be reminded of our mortality. But the reality is that out of 1,000 people, 1,000 people will die.

Death always elicits a deep emotional response. It was at the funeral of one of His dear friends that Jesus displayed strong emotions. When He saw Mary, whose brother had recently died, "he was deeply moved in spirit and troubled" (JOHN 11:33). Another translation says, "a deep anger welled up within him" (NLT).

Jesus was troubled—even angry—but at what? Possibly, He was indignant at sin and its consequences. God didn't make a world filled with sickness, suffering, and death. But sin entered the world and marred God's beautiful plan.

> **TODAY'S READING**
> John 11:1–4, 38–44
>
> **The sting of death is sin....But thanks be to God! He gives us the victory through our Lord Jesus Christ.**
>
> 1 Corinthians 15:56–57

The Lord comes alongside us in our grief, weeping with us in our sorrow (V. 35). But more than that, Christ defeated sin and death by dying in our place and rising from the dead (1 COR. 15:56–57).

Jesus promises, "The one who believes in me will live, even though they die" (JOHN 11:25). As believers we enjoy fellowship with our Savior now, and we look forward to an eternity with Him where there will be no more tears, pain, sickness, or death. 🌿

POH FANG CHIA

Christ's empty tomb guarantees our victory over death.

¹⁹ For the creation waits in eager expectation for the children of God to be revealed. ²⁰ For the creation was subjected to frustration, not by its own choice, but by the will of the one who subjected it, in hope ²¹ that the creation itself will be liberated from its bondage to decay and brought into the freedom and glory of the children of God.

²² We know that the whole creation has been groaning as in the pains of childbirth right up to the present time. ²³ Not only so, but we ourselves, who have the firstfruits of the Spirit, groan inwardly as we wait eagerly for our adoption to sonship, the redemption of our bodies. ²⁴ For in this hope we were saved. But hope that is seen is no hope at all. Who hopes for what they already have? ²⁵ But if we hope for what we do not yet have, we wait for it patiently.

²⁶ In the same way, the Spirit helps us in our weakness. We do not know what we ought to pray for, but the Spirit himself intercedes for us through wordless groans. ²⁷ And he who searches our hearts knows the mind of the Spirit, because the Spirit intercedes for God's people in accordance with the will of God.

The Spirit Delivers

Until recently, many towns in rural Ireland didn't use house numbers or postal codes. So if there were three Patrick Murphys in town, the newest resident with that name would not get his mail until it was first delivered to the other two Patrick Murphys who had lived there longer. "My neighbors would get it first," said Patrick Murphy (the newest resident). "They'd have a good read, and they'd go, 'No, it's probably not us.'" To end all this mail-delivery confusion, the Irish government recently instituted its first postal-code system which will ensure the proper delivery of the mail.

TODAY'S READING
Romans 8:19–27

Sometimes when we pray we feel like we need help delivering to God what is on our heart. We may not know the right words to say or how to express our deep longings. The apostle Paul says in Romans 8 that the Holy Spirit helps us and intercedes for us by taking our unspeakable

> The Spirit helps us in our weakness. We do not know what we ought to pray for, but the Spirit himself intercedes for us through wordless groans. Romans 8:26

"groanings" and presenting them to the Father. "We do not know what we ought to pray for, but the Spirit himself intercedes for us through wordless groans" (V. 26). The Spirit always prays according to God's will, and the Father knows the mind of the Spirit.

Be encouraged that God hears us when we pray and He knows our deepest needs.

MARVIN WILLIAMS

Thank You, Father, for giving me Your Spirit to help me when I pray.
Thank You for hearing my prayers and for loving me.

When you can't put your prayers into words, God hears your heart.

⁸⁹ Your word, LORD, is eternal;
    it stands firm in the heavens.
⁹⁰ Your faithfulness continues through all generations;
    you established the earth, and it endures.
⁹¹ Your laws endure to this day,
    for all things serve you.
⁹² If your law had not been my delight,
    I would have perished in my affliction.
⁹³ I will never forget your precepts,
    for by them you have preserved my life.
⁹⁴ Save me, for I am yours;
    I have sought out your precepts.
⁹⁵ The wicked are waiting to destroy me,
    but I will ponder your statutes.
⁹⁶ To all perfection I see a limit,
    but your commands are boundless.

God's Enduring Word

At the beginning of World War II, aerial bombings flattened much of Warsaw, Poland. Cement blocks, ruptured plumbing, and shards of glass lay strewn across the great city. In the downtown area, however, most of one damaged building still stubbornly stood. It was the Polish headquarters for the British and Foreign Bible Society. Still legible on a surviving wall were these words: "Heaven and earth will pass away, but my words will never pass away" (MATT. 24:35).

TODAY'S READING
Psalm 119:89–96

> Heaven and earth
> will pass away,
> but my words will
> never pass away.
>
> Matthew 24:35

Jesus made that statement to encourage His disciples when they asked Him about the "end of the age" (V. 3). But His words also give us courage in the midst of our embattled situation today. Standing in the rubble of our shattered dreams, we can still find confidence in God's indestructible character, sovereignty, and promises.

The psalmist wrote: "Your word, LORD, is eternal; it stands firm in the heavens" (PS. 119:89). But it is more than the word of the Lord; it is His very character. That is why the psalmist could also say, "Your faithfulness continues through all generations" (V. 90).

As we face devastating experiences, we can define them either in terms of despair or of hope. Because God will not abandon us to our circumstances, we can confidently choose hope. His enduring Word assures us of His unfailing love. 🌱 *DENNIS FISHER*

Thank You, Lord, for the gift of Your Word. Thank You for its truth,
its timelessness, and the guidance You give us by that Word.
Help us believe and trust everything You say.

We can trust God's unchanging Word.

³ We ought always to thank God for you, brothers and sisters, and rightly so, because your faith is growing more and more, and the love all of you have for one another is increasing. ⁴ Therefore, among God's churches we boast about your perseverance and faith in all the persecutions and trials you are enduring.

⁵ All this is evidence that God's judgment is right, and as a result you will be counted worthy of the kingdom of God, for which you are suffering. ⁶ God is just: He will pay back trouble to those who trouble you ⁷ and give relief to you who are troubled, and to us as well. This will happen when the Lord Jesus is revealed from heaven in blazing fire with his powerful angels. ⁸ He will punish those who do not know God and do not obey the gospel of our Lord Jesus. ⁹ They will be punished with everlasting destruction and shut out from the presence of the Lord and from the glory of his might ¹⁰ on the day he comes to be glorified in his holy people and to be marveled at among all those who have believed. This includes you, because you believed our testimony to you.

¹¹ With this in mind, we constantly pray for you, that our God may make you worthy of his calling, and that by his power he may bring to fruition your every desire for goodness and your every deed prompted by faith. ¹² We pray this so that the name of our Lord Jesus may be glorified in you, and you in him, according to the grace of our God and the Lord Jesus Christ.

Relief for the Troubled

One of my favorite scenes in literature occurs when a feisty aunt confronts an evil stepfather over the abuse of her nephew, David Copperfield. This scene takes place in Charles Dickens's novel named after the main character.

When David Copperfield shows up at his aunt's house, his stepfather is not far behind. Aunt Betsy Trotwood is not pleased to see the malicious Mr. Murdstone. She recounts a list of offenses and does not let him slither out of his responsibility for each act of cruelty. Her

TODAY'S READING
2 Thessalonians 1:3–12

[God will] give relief to you who are troubled.

2 Thessalonians 1:7

charges are so forceful and truthful that Mr. Murdstone—a normally aggressive person—finally leaves without a word. Through the strength and goodness of Aunt Betsy's character, David finally receives justice.

There is Someone else who is strong and good, and who will one day right the wrongs in our world. When Jesus returns, He will come down from heaven with a group of powerful angels. He will "give relief to you who are troubled," and He will not ignore those who have created problems for His children (2 THESS. 1:6–7). Until that day, Jesus wants us to stand firm and have courage. No matter what we endure on earth, we are safe for eternity. 🌱   *JENNIFER BENSON SCHULDT*

Dear God, please protect us and give us wisdom through Your Holy Spirit. Help us to be just and fair in everything we do so that we are good representatives for You.

One day God will right every wrong.

26 "To the faithful you show yourself faithful,
  to the blameless you show yourself blameless,
27 to the pure you show yourself pure,
  but to the devious you show yourself shrewd.
28 You save the humble,
  but your eyes are on the haughty to bring them low.
29 You, LORD, are my lamp;
  the LORD turns my darkness into light.
30 With your help I can advance against a troop;
  with my God I can scale a wall.
31 "As for God, his way is perfect:
  The LORD's word is flawless;
  he shields all who take refuge in him.
32 For who is God besides the LORD?
  And who is the Rock except our God?
33 It is God who arms me with strength
  and keeps my way secure.
34 He makes my feet like the feet of a deer;
  he causes me to stand on the heights.
35 He trains my hands for battle;
  my arms can bend a bow of bronze.
36 You make your saving help my shield;
  your help has made me great.
37 You provide a broad path for my feet,
  so that my ankles do not give way.

Greater than the Mess

A major theme of the Old Testament book of 2 Samuel could easily be "Life is a mess!" It has all the elements of a blockbuster TV miniseries. As David sought to establish his rule as king of Israel, he faced military challenges, political intrigue, and betrayal by friends and family members. And David himself was certainly not without guilt as his relationship with Bathsheba clearly showed (CHS. 11–12).

Yet near the end of 2 Samuel we find David's song of praise to God for His mercy, love, and deliverance. "You, LORD, are my lamp; the LORD turns my darkness into light" (22:29).

TODAY'S READING
2 Samuel 22:26–37

You, LORD, are my lamp; the LORD turns my darkness into light. 2 Samuel 22:29

In many of his difficulties, David turned to the Lord. "With your help I can advance against a troop [run through a barricade]; with my God I can scale a wall" (V. 30).

Perhaps we identify with David's struggles because he, like us, was far from perfect. Yet he knew that God was greater than the most chaotic parts of his life.

With David we can say, "As for God, his way is perfect: the Lord's word is flawless; he shields all who take refuge in him" (V. 31). And that includes us!

Life is messy, but God is greater than the mess. 🌿

DAVID MCCASLAND

Lord, we cannot read about the failures and difficulties of others without being reminded of our own. We bring them all to You, seeking forgiveness and Your power for a fresh start.

It's not too late to make a fresh start with God.

¹ We who are strong ought to bear with the failings of the weak and not to please ourselves. ² Each of us should please our neighbors for their good, to build them up. ³ For even Christ did not please himself but, as it is written: "The insults of those who insult you have fallen on me." ⁴ For everything that was written in the past was written to teach us, so that through the endurance taught in the Scriptures and the encouragement they provide we might have hope.

⁵ May the God who gives endurance and encouragement give you the same attitude of mind toward each other that Christ Jesus had, ⁶ so that with one mind and one voice you may glorify the God and Father of our Lord Jesus Christ.

Meant to Be Understood

enjoy visiting museums such as the National Gallery in London and the State Tretyakov Gallery in Moscow. While most of the art is breathtaking, some of it confuses me. I look at seemingly random splashes of color on canvas and realize I have no idea what I am seeing—even though the artist is a master at his craft.

TODAY'S READING
Romans 15:1–6

Everything that was written in the past was written to teach us. Romans 15:4

Sometimes we can feel the same way about the Scriptures. We wonder, *Is it even possible to understand them? Where do I start?* Perhaps Paul's words can give us some help: "Everything that was written in the past was written to teach us, so that through the endurance taught in the Scriptures and the encouragement they provide we might have hope" (ROM. 15:4).

God has given us the Scriptures for our instruction and encouragement. He has also given us His Spirit to help us to know His mind. Jesus said that He was sending the Spirit to "guide [us] into all the truth" (JOHN 16:13). Paul affirms this in 1 Corinthians 2:12, saying, "What we have received is not the spirit of the world, but the Spirit who is from God, so that we may understand what God has freely given us."

With the help of the Spirit, we can approach the Bible with confidence, knowing that through its pages God wants us to know Him and His ways.

BILL CROWDER

Father, thank You for giving us Your Son to bring us into relationship with You. Thank You for giving us the Scriptures so that we can know You better. And thank You for giving us Your Spirit to guide us into the truth of what we need to know about You and Your great love.

Read the Bible to get to know its Author.

²³ Then he got into the boat and his disciples followed him. ²⁴ Suddenly a furious storm came up on the lake, so that the waves swept over the boat. But Jesus was sleeping. ²⁵ The disciples went and woke him, saying, "Lord, save us! We're going to drown!"

²⁶ He replied, "You of little faith, why are you so afraid?" Then he got up and rebuked the winds and the waves, and it was completely calm.

²⁷ The men were amazed and asked, "What kind of man is this? Even the winds and the waves obey him!"

²⁸ When he arrived at the other side in the region of the Gadarenes, two demon-possessed men coming from the tombs met him. They were so violent that no one could pass that way.

Storms on the Horizon

Our son, Josh, is a commercial salmon fisherman in Kodiak, Alaska. Some time ago he sent me a photograph he took of a tiny vessel a few hundred yards ahead of his boat moving through a narrow pass. Ominous storm clouds loom on the horizon. But a rainbow, the sign of God's providence and loving care, stretches from one side of the pass to the other, encircling the little boat.

The photograph reflects our earthly voyage: We sail into an uncertain future, but we are surrounded by the faithfulness of God!

Jesus's disciples were surrounded by a storm, and He used the experience to teach them about the power and faithfulness of God (MATT. 8:23–27). We seek answers for the uncertainties of life. We watch the future growing closer and wonder what will happen to us there. Puritan poet John Keble captured this in one of his poems in which he watched the future as it drew near. But as he watched he was "waiting to see what God will do."

Whether young or old we all face uncertain futures. Heaven answers: God's love and goodness encircle us no matter what awaits us. We wait and see what God will do! ❖

DAVID ROPER

> TODAY'S READING
> Matthew 8:23–28
>
> **What kind of man is this? Even the winds and the waves obey him!**
>
> Matthew 8:27

What do you need to trust God with today?

We sail into the uncertain future surrounded by the faithfulness of God!

▶ ¹:¹ A prophecy: The word of the LORD to Israel through Malachi. ² "I have loved you," says the LORD.

"But you ask, 'How have you loved us?'

"Was not Esau Jacob's brother?" declares the LORD.

"Yet I have loved Jacob, ³ but Esau I have hated, and I have turned his hill country into a wasteland and left his inheritance to the desert jackals."

⁴ Edom may say, "Though we have been crushed, we will rebuild the ruins." But this is what the LORD Almighty says: "They may build, but I will demolish. They will be called the Wicked Land, a people always under the wrath of the LORD.

⁵ You will see it with your own eyes and say, 'Great is the LORD—even beyond the borders of Israel!' ⁶ "A son honors his father, and a slave his master. If I am a father, where is the honor due me? If I am a master, where is the respect due me?" says the LORD Almighty. "It is you priests who show contempt for my name. "But you ask, 'How have we shown contempt for your name?' ⁷ "By offering defiled food on my altar.

"But you ask, 'How have we defiled you?'

"By saying that the LORD's table is contemptible. ⁸ When you offer blind animals for sacrifice, is that not wrong? When you sacrifice lame or diseased animals, is that not wrong? Try offering them to your governor! Would he be pleased with you? Would he accept you?" says the LORD Almighty.

⁹ "Now plead with God to be gracious to us. With such offerings from your hands, will he accept you?"—says the LORD Almighty. ¹⁰ "Oh, that one of you would shut the temple doors, so that you would not light useless fires on my altar! I am not pleased with you," says the LORD Almighty, "and I will accept no offering from your hands.

⁴:⁵ "See, I will send the prophet Elijah to you before that great and dreadful day of the LORD comes. ⁶ He will turn the hearts of the parents to their children, and the hearts of the children to their parents; or else I will come and strike the land with total destruction."

An Amazing Love

The final major historic acts of the Old Testament are described in Ezra and Nehemiah as God allowed the people of Israel to return from exile and resettle in Jerusalem. The City of David was repopulated with Hebrew families, a new temple was built, and the wall was repaired.

And that brings us to Malachi. This prophet, who was most likely a contemporary of Nehemiah, brings the written portion of the Old Testament to a close. Notice the first thing he said to the people of Israel: " 'I have loved you,' says the LORD." And look at their response: "How have you loved us?" (1:2).

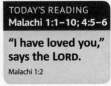

TODAY'S READING
Malachi 1:1–10; 4:5–6

**"I have loved you,"
says the LORD.**

Malachi 1:2

Amazing, isn't it? Their history had proven God's faithfulness, yet after hundreds of years in which God continually provided for His chosen people in both miraculous and mundane ways, they wondered how He had shown His love. As the book continues, Malachi reminds the people of their unfaithfulness (SEE VV. 6–8). They had a long historical pattern of God's provision for them, followed by their disobedience, followed by God's discipline.

It was time, soon, for a new way. The prophet hints at it in Malachi 4:5-6. The Messiah would be coming. There was hope ahead for a Savior who would show us His love and pay the penalty once and for all for our sin.

That Messiah indeed has come! Malachi's hope is now a reality in Jesus. 🌱   *DAVE BRANON*

Thank You, Father, for the story You told in Your Word of the people of Israel. It reminds us to be grateful for what You have done for us. Thank You for loving us so much You sent us Jesus.

Those who put their trust in Jesus will have eternal life.

¹⁴ But thanks be to God, who always leads us as captives in Christ's triumphal procession and uses us to spread the aroma of the knowledge of him everywhere. ¹⁵ For we are to God the pleasing aroma of Christ among those who are being saved and those who are perishing. ¹⁶ To the one we are an aroma that brings death; to the other, an aroma that brings life. And who is equal to such a task? ¹⁷ Unlike so many, we do not peddle the word of God for profit. On the contrary, in Christ we speak before God with sincerity, as those sent from God.

The Fragrance of Christ

Which of the five senses brings back your memories most sharply? For me it is definitely the sense of smell. A certain kind of sun oil takes me instantly to a French beach. The smell of chicken mash brings back childhood visits to my grandmother. A hint of pine says "Christmas," and a certain kind of aftershave reminds me of my son's teenage years.

TODAY'S READING
2 Corinthians 2:14–17

We are to God the pleasing aroma of Christ. 2 Corinthians 2:15

Paul reminded the Corinthians that they were the aroma of Christ: "For we are to God the pleasing aroma of Christ" (2 COR. 2:15). He may have been referring to Roman victory parades. The Romans made sure everyone knew they had been victorious by burning incense on altars throughout the city. For the victors, the aroma was pleasing; for the prisoners it meant certain slavery or death. So as believers, we are victorious soldiers. And when the gospel of Christ is preached, it is a pleasing fragrance to God.

As the aroma of Christ, what perfumes do Christians bring with them as they walk into a room? It's not something that can be bought in a bottle or a jar. When we spend a lot of time with someone, we begin to think and act like that person. Spending time with Jesus will help us spread a pleasing fragrance to those around us. 🌿

MARION STROUD

Lord, please shape my thoughts and actions so people may sense
that I have been with You.

When we walk with God, people will notice.

¹ In the seventh year of Jehu, Joash became king, and he reigned in Jerusalem forty years. His mother's name was Zibiah; she was from Beersheba. ² Joash did what was right in the eyes of the LORD all the years Jehoiada the priest instructed him.

³ The high places, however, were not removed; the people continued to offer sacrifices and burn incense there. ⁴ Joash said to the priests, "Collect all the money that is brought as sacred offerings to the temple of the LORD—the money collected in the census, the money received from personal vows and the money brought voluntarily to the temple. ⁵ Let every priest receive the money from one of the treasurers, then use it to repair whatever damage is found in the temple." ⁶ But by the twenty-third year of King Joash the priests still had not repaired the temple. ⁷ Therefore King Joash summoned Jehoiada the priest and the other priests and asked them, "Why aren't you repairing the damage done to the temple? Take no more money from your treasurers, but hand it over for repairing the temple." ⁸ The priests agreed that they would not collect any more money from the people and that they would not repair the temple themselves.

⁹ Jehoiada the priest took a chest and bored a hole in its lid. He placed it beside the altar, on the right side as one enters the temple of the LORD. The priests who guarded the entrance put into the chest all the money that was brought to the temple of the LORD. ¹⁰ Whenever they saw that there was a large amount of money in the chest, the royal secretary and the high priest came, counted the money that had been brought into the temple of the LORD and put it into bags. ¹¹ When the amount had been determined, they gave the money to the men appointed to supervise the work on the temple. With it they paid those who worked on the temple of the LORD—the carpenters and builders, ¹² the masons and stonecutters. They purchased timber and blocks of dressed stone for the repair of the temple of the LORD, and met all the other expenses of restoring the temple. ¹³ The money brought into the temple was not spent for making silver basins, wick trimmers, sprinkling bowls, trumpets or any other articles of gold or silver for the temple of the LORD; ¹⁴ it was paid to the workers, who used it to repair the temple. ¹⁵ They did not require an accounting from those to whom they gave the money to pay the workers, because they acted with complete honesty.

Doing Right in God's Sight

"**C**owboy builders" is a term many British homeowners use for tradespeople who do shoddy construction work. The term is bandied about with fear or regret, often because of bad experiences.

No doubt there were rogue carpenters, masons, and stonecutters in biblical times, but tucked away in the story of King Joash repairing the temple is a line about the complete honesty of those who oversaw and did the work (2 KINGS 12:15).

> **TODAY'S READING**
> **2 Kings 12:1-15**
>
> **Joash did what was right ... all the years Jehoiada the priest instructed him.** 2 Kings 12:2

However, King Joash "did what was right in the eyes of the LORD" (V. 2) only when Jehoiada the priest instructed him. As we see in 2 Chronicles 24:17-27, after Jehoiada died Joash turned from the Lord and was persuaded to worship other gods.

The mixed legacy of a king who enjoyed a season of fruitfulness only while under the spiritual counsel of a godly priest makes me stop and think. What will our legacies be? Will we continue to grow and develop in our faith throughout our lives, producing good fruit? Or will we become distracted by the things of this world and turn to modern-day idols—such as comfort, materialism, and self-promotion? AMY BOUCHER PYE

Go deeper: How does this passage compare with Jesus's letter to the church at Ephesus in Revelation 2? How do these passages apply to your life?

Living well and doing right require perseverance and spiritual direction.

¹ Further, my brothers and sisters, rejoice in the Lord! It is no trouble for me to write the same things to you again, and it is a safeguard for you. ² Watch out for those dogs, those evildoers, those mutilators of the flesh. ³ For it is we who are the circumcision, we who serve God by his Spirit, who boast in Christ Jesus, and who put no confidence in the flesh— ⁴ though I myself have reasons for such confidence.

If someone else thinks they have reasons to put confidence in the flesh, I have more: ⁵ circumcised on the eighth day, of the people of Israel, of the tribe of Benjamin, a Hebrew of Hebrews; in regard to the law, a Pharisee; ⁶ as for zeal, persecuting the church; as for righteousness based on the law, faultless.

⁷ But whatever were gains to me I now consider loss for the sake of Christ. ⁸ What is more, I consider everything a loss because of the surpassing worth of knowing Christ Jesus my Lord, for whose sake I have lost all things. I consider them garbage, that I may gain Christ.

The Restoration Business

Adam Minter is in the junk business. The son of a junkyard owner, he circles the globe researching junk. In his book *Junkyard Planet,* he chronicles the multibillion-dollar industry of waste recycling. He notes that entrepreneurs around the world devote themselves to locating discarded materials such as copper wire, dirty rags, and plastics and repurposing them to make something new and useful.

After the apostle Paul turned his life over to the Savior, he realized his own achievements and abilities amounted to little more than trash. But Jesus transformed it all into something new and useful. Paul said, "Whatever were gains to me I now consider loss for the sake of Christ. What is more, I consider everything a loss because of the surpassing worth of know-

TODAY'S READING
Philippians 3:1–8

> **I have suffered the loss of all things, and count them as rubbish, that I may gain Christ.**
>
> Philippians 3:8 NKJV

ing Christ Jesus my Lord, for whose sake I have lost all things. I consider them garbage, that I may gain Christ" (PHIL. 3:7–8). Having been trained in Jewish religious law, he had been an angry and violent man toward those who followed Christ (ACTS 9:1–2). After being transformed by Christ, the tangled wreckage of his angry past was transformed into the love of Christ for others (2 COR. 5:14–17).

If you feel that your life is just an accumulation of junk, remember that God has always been in the restoration business. When we turn our lives over to Him, He makes us into something new and useful for Him and others. 🌀　　　*DENNIS FISHER*

Are you wondering how to become a new person? Romans 3:23 and 6:23 tell us that when we admit we are sinners and ask for God's forgiveness, He gives us the free gift of eternal life that was paid for by the death and resurrection of Jesus. Talk to him about your need.

Christ makes all things new.

[13] "You are the salt of the earth. But if the salt loses its saltiness, how can it be made salty again? It is no longer good for anything, except to be thrown out and trampled underfoot.

[14] "You are the light of the world. A town built on a hill cannot be hidden. [15] Neither do people light a lamp and put it under a bowl. Instead they put it on its stand, and it gives light to everyone in the house. [16] In the same way, let your light shine before others, that they may see your good deeds and glorify your Father in heaven.

Shine Through

A **little girl wondered** what a saint might be. One day her mother took her to a great cathedral to see the gorgeous stained-glass windows with scenes from the Bible. When she saw the beauty of it all she cried out loud, "Now I know what saints are. They are people who let the light shine through!"

> **TODAY'S READING**
> Matthew 5:13–16
>
> **Let your light shine before others.**
> Matthew 5:16

Some of us might think that saints are people of the past who lived perfect lives and did Jesus-like miracles. But when a translation of Scripture uses the word *saint*, it is actually referring to anyone who belongs to God through faith in Christ. In other words, saints are people like us who have the high calling of serving God while reflecting our relationship with Him wherever we are and in whatever we do. That is why the apostle Paul prayed that the eyes and understanding of his readers would be opened to think of themselves as the treasured inheritance of Christ and saints of God (EPH. 1:18).

So what then do we see in the mirror? No halos or stained glass. But if we are fulfilling our calling, we will look like people who, maybe even without realizing it, are letting the rich colors of the love, joy, peace, patience, kindness, gentleness, faithfulness, and self-control of God shine through.    *KEILA OCHOA*

Lord, You are the light of the world.
Thank You for wanting to shine that light in our lives.
Cleanse me today so that I may let Your light shine through.

Saints are people through whom God's light shines.

³ Praise be to the God and Father of our Lord Jesus Christ, the Father of compassion and the God of all comfort, ⁴ who comforts us in all our troubles, so that we can comfort those in any trouble with the comfort we ourselves receive from God. ⁵ For just as we share abundantly in the sufferings of Christ, so also our comfort abounds through Christ. ⁶ If we are distressed, it is for your comfort and salvation; if we are comforted, it is for your comfort, which produces in you patient endurance of the same sufferings we suffer. ⁷ And our hope for you is firm, because we know that just as you share in our sufferings, so also you share in our comfort.

Just What I Need

As I stood in the back of the room at a senior citizens' center in Palmer, Alaska, listening to my daughter's high school choir sing "It Is Well with My Soul," I wondered why she, the choir director, had chosen that song. It had been played at her sister Melissa's funeral, and Lisa knew it was always tough for me to hear it without having an emotional response.

My musings were interrupted when a man sidled up next to me and said, "This is just what I need to hear." I introduced myself and then asked why he needed this song. "I lost my son Cameron last week in a motorcycle accident," he said.

TODAY'S READING
2 Corinthians 1:3–7

We can comfort those in any trouble with the comfort we ourselves receive from God.

2 Corinthians 1:4

Wow! I was so focused on myself that I never considered the needs of others, and God was busy using that song exactly where He wanted it to be used. I took my new friend Mac, who worked at the center, aside, and we talked about God's care in this toughest time in his life.

All around us are people in need, and sometimes we have to set aside our own feelings and agendas to help them. One way we can do that is to remember how God has comforted us in our trials and troubles "so that we can comfort those in any trouble with the comfort we ourselves receive from God" (2 COR. 1:4). How easy it is to be engrossed in our own concerns and forget that someone right next to us might need a prayer, a word of comfort, a hug, or gift of mercy in Jesus's name. ❧

DAVE BRANON

Lord, help me to see where help is needed, and help me to provide
that help. Thank You for the comfort You give; help me to share it.
Comfort received should be comfort shared.

⁸ Slaves rule over us,
   and there is no one to free us from their hands.
⁹ We get our bread at the risk of our lives
   because of the sword in the desert.
¹⁰ Our skin is hot as an oven,
   feverish from hunger.
¹¹ Women have been violated in Zion,
   and virgins in the towns of Judah.
¹² Princes have been hung up by their hands;
   elders are shown no respect.
¹³ Young men toil at the millstones;
   boys stagger under loads of wood.
¹⁴ The elders are gone from the city gate;
   the young men have stopped their music.
¹⁵ Joy is gone from our hearts;
   our dancing has turned to mourning.
¹⁶ The crown has fallen from our head.
   Woe to us, for we have sinned!
¹⁷ Because of this our hearts are faint,
   because of these things our eyes grow dim
¹⁸ for Mount Zion, which lies desolate,
   with jackals prowling over it.
¹⁹ You, LORD, reign forever;
   your throne endures from generation to generation.
²⁰ Why do you always forget us?
   Why do you forsake us so long?
²¹ Restore us to yourself, LORD, that we may return;
   renew our days as of old
²² unless you have utterly rejected us
   and are angry with us beyond measure.

Out of the Ruins

I n the Jewish Quarter of Jerusalem you'll find Tiferet Yisrael Synagogue. Built in the 19th century, the synagogue was dynamited by commandos during the 1948 Arab-Israeli War.

For years the site lay in ruins. Then, in 2014, rebuilding began. As city officials set a piece of rubble as the cornerstone, one of them quoted from Lamentations: "Restore us to yourself, Lord, that we may return; renew our days as of old" (5:21).

TODAY'S READING
Lamentations 5:8–22

He has granted us new life to rebuild the house of our God and repair its ruins. Ezra 9:9

Lamentations is Jeremiah's funeral song for Jerusalem. With graphic imagery the prophet describes the impact of war on his city. Verse 21 is his heartfelt prayer for God to intervene. Still, the prophet wonders if that is even possible. He concludes his anguished song with this fearful caveat: "unless you have utterly rejected us and are angry with us beyond measure" (v. 22). Decades later, God did answer that prayer as the exiles returned to Jerusalem.

Our lives too may seem to be in ruins. Troubles of our own making and conflicts we can't avoid may leave us devastated. But we have a Father who understands. Gently, patiently, He clears away the rubble, repurposes it, and builds something better. It takes time, but we can always trust Him. He specializes in rebuilding projects. 🌿

TIM GUSTAFSON

Lord, You have reclaimed us, and You are remaking us.
Thank You for Your love and Your care despite our self-centered and
destructive ways. Thank You for true forgiveness and unity in You.

God will one day restore all the beauty lost before.

¹⁶ Rejoice always, ¹⁷ pray continually, ¹⁸ give thanks in all circumstances; for this is God's will for you in Christ Jesus.

¹⁹ Do not quench the Spirit. ²⁰ Do not treat prophecies with contempt ²¹ but test them all; hold on to what is good, ²² reject every kind of evil.

²³ May God himself, the God of peace, sanctify you through and through. May your whole spirit, soul and body be kept blameless at the coming of our Lord Jesus Christ. ²⁴ The one who calls you is faithful, and he will do it.

²⁵ Brothers and sisters, pray for us. ²⁶ Greet all God's people with a holy kiss. ²⁷ I charge you before the Lord to have this letter read to all the brothers and sisters.

²⁸ The grace of our Lord Jesus Christ be with you.

Prayer Marathon

Do you struggle to maintain a consistent prayer life? Many of us do. We know that prayer is important, but it can also be downright difficult. We have moments of deep communion with God and then we have times when it feels like we're just going through the motions. Why do we struggle so in our prayers?

The life of faith is a marathon. The ups, the downs, and the plateaus in our prayer life are a reflection of this race. And just as in a marathon we need to keep running, so we keep praying. The point is: Don't give up!

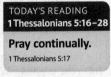

TODAY'S READING
1 Thessalonians 5:16–28

Pray continually.
1 Thessalonians 5:17

That is God's encouragement too. The apostle Paul said, "pray continually" (1 THESS. 5:17), "keep on praying" (ROM. 12:12 NLT), and "devote yourselves to prayer" (COL. 4:2). All of these statements carry the idea of remaining steadfast and continuing in the work of prayer.

And because God, our heavenly Father, is a personal being, we can develop a time of close communion with Him, just as we do with our close human relationships. A. W. Tozer writes that as we learn to pray, our prayer life can grow "from the initial most casual brush to the fullest, most intimate communion of which the human soul is capable." And that's what we really want—deep communication with God. It happens when we keep praying. 🌱

POH FANG CHIA

Dear Father, we often struggle to spend time with You.
Help us to make the time, and help us sense Your goodness
and presence.

There is never a day when we don't need to pray.

¹ The elder,

To my dear friend Gaius, whom I love in the truth.

² Dear friend, I pray that you may enjoy good health and that all may go well with you, even as your soul is getting along well. ³ It gave me great joy when some believers came and testified about your faithfulness to the truth, telling how you continue to walk in it. ⁴ I have no greater joy than to hear that my children are walking in the truth.

⁵ Dear friend, you are faithful in what you are doing for the brothers and sisters, even though they are strangers to you. ⁶ They have told the church about your love. Please send them on their way in a manner that honors God. ⁷ It was for the sake of the Name that they went out, receiving no help from the pagans. ⁸ We ought therefore to show hospitality to such people so that we may work together for the truth.

No Greater Joy

Bob and Evon Potter were a fun-loving couple with three young sons when their life took a wonderful new direction. In 1956 they attended a Billy Graham Crusade in Oklahoma City and gave their lives to Christ. Before long, they wanted to reach out to others to share their faith and the truth about Christ, so they opened their home every Saturday night to high school and college students who had a desire to study the Bible. A friend invited me and I became a regular at the Potters' house.

TODAY'S READING
3 John 1:1–8

I have no greater joy than to hear that my children are walking in the truth. 3 John 1:4

This was a serious Bible study that included lesson preparation and memorizing Scripture. Surrounded by an atmosphere of friendship, joy, and laughter, we challenged each other and the Lord changed our lives during those days.

I stayed in touch with the Potters over the years and received many cards and letters from Bob who always signed them with these words: "I have no greater joy than to hear that my children are walking in the truth" (3 JOHN 1:4). Like John writing to his "dear friend Gaius" (V. 1), Bob encouraged everyone who crossed his path to keep walking with the Lord.

A few years ago I attended Bob's memorial service. It was a joyful occasion filled with people still walking the road of faith—all because of a young couple who opened their home and their hearts to help others find the Lord. 🌑 DAVID MCCASLAND

Thank You, Lord, for the people who have encouraged me to keep walking in Your truth. May I honor them by helping someone along that road today.

Be a voice of encouragement to someone today.

⁵ The company of the prophets at Jericho went up to Elisha and asked him, "Do you know that the LORD is going to take your master from you today?"

"Yes, I know," he replied, "so be quiet."

⁶ Then Elijah said to him, "Stay here; the LORD has sent me to the Jordan."

And he replied, "As surely as the LORD lives and as you live, I will not leave you." So the two of them walked on.

⁷ Fifty men from the company of the prophets went and stood at a distance, facing the place where Elijah and Elisha had stopped at the Jordan. ⁸ Elijah took his cloak, rolled it up and struck the water with it. The water divided to the right and to the left, and the two of them crossed over on dry ground.

⁹ When they had crossed, Elijah said to Elisha, "Tell me, what can I do for you before I am taken from you?"

"Let me inherit a double portion of your spirit," Elisha replied.

¹⁰ "You have asked a difficult thing," Elijah said, "yet if you see me when I am taken from you, it will be yours—otherwise, it will not."

¹¹ As they were walking along and talking together, suddenly a chariot of fire and horses of fire appeared and separated the two of them, and Elijah went up to heaven in a whirlwind. ¹² Elisha saw this and cried out, "My father! My father! The chariots and horsemen of Israel!" And Elisha saw him no more. Then he took hold of his garment and tore it in two.

The Promised Spirit

Tenacity and audacity—Elisha had heaps of both. Having spent time with Elijah, he witnessed the Lord working through the prophet by performing miracles and by speaking truth in an age of lies. Second Kings 2:1 tells us that Elijah is about to be taken "up to heaven," and Elisha doesn't want him to leave.

The time came for the dreaded separation, and Elisha knew he needed what Elijah had if he was going to successfully continue the ministry. So he made a daring demand: "Let me inherit a double portion of your spirit" (2 KINGS 2:9). His bold request was a reference to the double portion given the firstborn son or heir under the law (DEUT. 21:17). Elisha wanted to be recognized as the heir of Elijah. And God said yes.

> **TODAY'S READING**
> **2 Kings 2:5–12**
>
> **"Let me inherit a double portion of your spirit," Elisha replied.** 2 Kings 2:9

Recently one of my mentors—a woman who spread the good news of Jesus—died. Having battled ill health for years, she was ready to enjoy her eternal feast with the Lord. Those of us who loved her were grateful at the thought of her newfound freedom from pain and that she could enjoy God's presence, but we grieved the loss of her love and example. Despite her departure, she did not leave us alone. We too had God's presence.

Elisha gained a double portion of Elijah's spirit—a tremendous privilege and blessing. We who live after the life, death, and resurrection of Jesus have the promised Holy Spirit. The triune God makes His home with us!   *AMY BOUCHER PYE*

Dear Lord, we want to be more like You.
Help us to be witnesses of Your Spirit within us.

When Jesus ascended to His Father, He sent His Spirit.

¹ Peter, an apostle of Jesus Christ,

To God's elect, exiles scattered throughout the provinces of Pontus, Galatia, Cappadocia, Asia and Bithynia, ² who have been chosen according to the foreknowledge of God the Father, through the sanctifying work of the Spirit, to be obedient to Jesus Christ and sprinkled with his blood:

Grace and peace be yours in abundance.

³ Praise be to the God and Father of our Lord Jesus Christ! In his great mercy he has given us new birth into a living hope through the resurrection of Jesus Christ from the dead, ⁴ and into an inheritance that can never perish, spoil or fade. This inheritance is kept in heaven for you, ⁵ who through faith are shielded by God's power until the coming of the salvation that is ready to be revealed in the last time. ⁶ In all this you greatly rejoice, though now for a little while you may have had to suffer grief in all kinds of trials. ⁷ These have come so that the proven genuineness of your faith—of greater worth than gold, which perishes even though refined by fire—may result in praise, glory and honor when Jesus Christ is revealed. ⁸ Though you have not seen him, you love him; and even though you do not see him now, you believe in him and are filled with an inexpressible and glorious joy, ⁹ for you are receiving the end result of your faith, the salvation of your souls.

Unseen, Yet Loved

Like others in the blogging community, I'd never met the man known to us as BruceC. Yet when his wife posted a note to the group to let us know that her husband had died, a string of responses from distant places showed we all knew we had lost a friend.

BruceC had often opened his heart to us. He talked freely about his concern for others and what was important to him. Many of us felt like we knew him. We would miss the gentle wisdom that came from his years in law enforcement and his faith in Christ.

TODAY'S READING
1 Peter 1:1–9

Though you have not seen him, you love him. 1 Peter 1:8

In recalling our online conversations with BruceC, I gained a renewed appreciation for words written by a first-century witness of Jesus. In the first New Testament letter the apostle Peter wrote, he addressed readers scattered throughout the Roman Empire: "Though you have not seen [Christ], you love him" (1 PETER 1:8).

Peter, as a personal friend of Jesus, was writing to people who had only heard about the One who had given them reason for so much hope in the middle of their troubles. Yet, as a part of the larger community of believers, they loved Him. They knew that at the price of His own life, He had brought them into the everlasting family of God. ❧ 		*MART DEHAAN*

Lord, we have never seen You, yet we believe in You and love You.
Strengthen our love for our brothers and sisters in Christ
who love You as well. Make us one community in You.

Our love for Christ is only as real as our love for our neighbor.

[1] As for other matters, brothers and sisters, we instructed you how to live in order to please God, as in fact you are living. Now we ask you and urge you in the Lord Jesus to do this more and more. [2] For you know what instructions we gave you by the authority of the Lord Jesus.

[3] It is God's will that you should be sanctified: that you should avoid sexual immorality; [4] that each of you should learn to control your own body in a way that is holy and honorable, [5] not in passionate lust like the pagans, who do not know God; [6] and that in this matter no one should wrong or take advantage of a brother or sister. The Lord will punish all those who commit such sins, as we told you and warned you before. [7] For God did not call us to be impure, but to live a holy life. [8] Therefore, anyone who rejects this instruction does not reject a human being but God, the very God who gives you his Holy Spirit.

[9] Now about your love for one another we do not need to write to you, for you yourselves have been taught by God to love each other. [10] And in fact, you do love all of God's family throughout Macedonia. Yet we urge you, brothers and sisters, to do so more and more, [11] and to make it your ambition to lead a quiet life: You should mind your own business and work with your hands, just as we told you, [12] so that your daily life may win the respect of outsiders and so that you will not be dependent on anybody.

Keep Climbing!

Richard needed a push, and he got one. He was rock climbing with his friend Kevin who was the belayer (the one who secures the rope). Exhausted and ready to quit, Richard asked Kevin to lower him to the ground. But Kevin urged him on, saying he had come too far to quit. Dangling in midair, Richard decided to keep trying. Amazingly, he was able to reconnect with the rock and complete the climb because of his friend's encouragement.

TODAY'S READING
1 Thessalonians 4:1–12

Encourage one another daily.
Hebrews 3:13

In the early church, followers of Jesus encouraged one another to continue to follow their Lord and to show compassion. In a culture riddled with immorality, they passionately appealed to one another to live pure lives (ROM. 12:1; 1 THESS. 4:1). Believers encouraged one another daily, as God prompted them to do so (ACTS 13:15). They urged each other to intercede for the body (ROM. 15:30), to help people stay connected to the church (HEB. 10:25), and to love more and more (1 THESS. 4:10).

Through His death and resurrection, Jesus has connected us to one another. Therefore, we have the responsibility and privilege with God's enablement to encourage fellow believers to finish the climb of trusting and obeying Him. ✒ *MARVIN WILLIAMS*

When was the last time you needed to urge someone to keep following Jesus? Who has encouraged you or stirred you to pursue holiness, to keep praying, or to enlarge your love for Jesus and others?

Encourage one another and build each other up. 1 THESSALONIANS 5:11

⁷ But when Sanballat, Tobiah, the Arabs, the Ammonites and the people of Ashdod heard that the repairs to Jerusalem's walls had gone ahead and that the gaps were being closed, they were very angry. ⁸ They all plotted together to come and fight against Jerusalem and stir up trouble against it. ⁹ But we prayed to our God and posted a guard day and night to meet this threat.

¹⁰ Meanwhile, the people in Judah said, "The strength of the laborers is giving out, and there is so much rubble that we cannot rebuild the wall."

¹¹ Also our enemies said, "Before they know it or see us, we will be right there among them and will kill them and put an end to the work."

¹² Then the Jews who lived near them came and told us ten times over, "Wherever you turn, they will attack us."

¹³ Therefore I stationed some of the people behind the lowest points of the wall at the exposed places, posting them by families, with their swords, spears and bows. ¹⁴ After I looked things over, I stood up and said to the nobles, the officials and the rest of the people, "Don't be afraid of them. Remember the LORD, who is great and awesome, and fight for your families, your sons and your daughters, your wives and your homes."

¹⁵ When our enemies heard that we were aware of their plot and that God had frustrated it, we all returned to the wall, each to our own work.

¹⁶ From that day on, half of my men did the work, while the other half were equipped with spears, shields, bows and armor. The officers posted themselves behind all the people of Judah ¹⁷ who were building the wall. Those who carried materials did their work with one hand and held a weapon in the other, ¹⁸ and each of the builders wore his sword at his side as he worked. But the man who sounded the trumpet stayed with me.

Our Divine Defense

Under Nehemiah's supervision, the Israelite workers were rebuilding the wall around Jerusalem. When they were nearly half finished, however, they learned that their enemies were plotting to attack Jerusalem. This news demoralized the already exhausted workers.

Nehemiah had to do something. First, he prayed and posted numerous guards in strategic places. Then, he armed his workers. "Those who carried materials did their work with one hand and held a weapon in the other, and each of the builders wore his sword at his side as he worked" (NEH. 4:17–18).

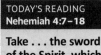

TODAY'S READING
Nehemiah 4:7–18

Take . . . the sword of the Spirit, which is the word of God.
Ephesians 6:17

We who are building God's kingdom need to arm ourselves against the attack of our spiritual enemy, Satan. Our protection is the sword of the Spirit, which is God's Word. Memorizing Scripture and meditating on it enable us to "take [our] stand against the devil's schemes" (EPH. 6:11). If we think that working for God doesn't matter, we should turn to the promise that what we do for Jesus will last for eternity (1 COR. 3:11–15). If we fear we've sinned too greatly for God to use us, we must remember we've been forgiven by the power of Jesus's blood (MATT. 26:28). And if we're worried we might fail if we try to serve God, we can recall that Jesus said we will bear fruit as we abide in Him (JOHN 15:5).

God's Word is our divine defense! ❖   *JENNIFER BENSON SCHULDT*

God, thank You for the Bible. I believe that Your Word is alive and active.
Please help me to remember it when I am worried or fearful,
when I need encouragement and inspiration.

God's Word is a divine defense against attacks from the Enemy.

⁵ You, LORD, are forgiving and good,
   abounding in love to all who call to you.
⁶ Hear my prayer, LORD;
   listen to my cry for mercy.
⁷ When I am in distress, I call to you,
   because you answer me.
⁸ Among the gods there is none like you, LORD;
   no deeds can compare with yours.
⁹ All the nations you have made
   will come and worship before you, LORD;
   they will bring glory to your name.
¹⁰ For you are great and do marvelous deeds;
   you alone are God.
¹¹ Teach me your way, LORD,
   that I may rely on your faithfulness;
give me an undivided heart,
   that I may fear your name.
¹² I will praise you, LORD my God, with all my heart;
   I will glorify your name forever.
¹³ For great is your love toward me;
   you have delivered me from the depths,
   from the realm of the dead.
¹⁴ Arrogant foes are attacking me, O God;
   ruthless people are trying to kill me—
   they have no regard for you.
¹⁵ But you, LORD, are a compassionate and gracious God,
   slow to anger, abounding in love and faithfulness.

Start Afresh

When I was growing up, one of my favorite books was *Anne of Green Gables* by Lucy Maud Montgomery. In one amusing passage, young Anne, by mistake, adds a skin medication instead of vanilla to the cake she is making. Afterward, she exclaims hopefully to her stern-faced guardian, Marilla, "Isn't it nice to think that tomorrow is a new day with no mistakes in it yet?"

I like that thought: tomorrow is a new day—a new day when we can start afresh. We all make mistakes. But when it comes to sin, God's forgiveness is what enables us to start each morning with a clean slate. When we repent, He chooses to remember our sins no more (JER. 31:34; HEB. 8:12).

TODAY'S READING
Psalm 86:5–15

His compassions never fail. They are new every morning; great is your faithfulness.
Lamentations 3:22–23

Some of us have made wrong choices in our lives, but our past words and deeds need not define our future in God's eyes. There is always a fresh start. When we ask for His forgiveness, we take a first step toward restoring our relationship with Him and with others. "If we confess our sins, he is faithful and just and will forgive us our sins and purify us from all unrighteousness" (1 JOHN 1:9).

God's compassion and faithfulness are new every morning (LAM. 3:23), so we can start afresh each day. 🕊️ *CINDY HESS KASPER*

Thank You for this new day, Lord. Forgive me for doing those things in the past that I shouldn't have done, and for not doing those things that I should have done. Set my feet on Your right path today.

Each new day gives us new reasons to praise the Lord.

⁹ "How can this be?" Nicodemus asked.

¹⁰ "You are Israel's teacher," said Jesus, "and do you not understand these things? ¹¹ Very truly I tell you, we speak of what we know, and we testify to what we have seen, but still you people do not accept our testimony.

¹² I have spoken to you of earthly things and you do not believe; how then will you believe if I speak of heavenly things? ¹³ No one has ever gone into heaven except the one who came from heaven—the Son of Man. ¹⁴ Just as Moses lifted up the snake in the wilderness, so the Son of Man must be lifted up, ¹⁵ that everyone who believes may have eternal life in him."

¹⁶ For God so loved the world that he gave his one and only Son, that whoever believes in him shall not perish but have eternal life. ¹⁷ For God did not send his Son into the world to condemn the world, but to save the world through him.

¹⁸ Whoever believes in him is not condemned, but whoever does not believe stands condemned already because they have not believed in the name of God's one and only Son.

¹⁹ This is the verdict: Light has come into the world, but people loved darkness instead of light because their deeds were evil. ²⁰ Everyone who does evil hates the light, and will not come into the light for fear that their deeds will be exposed. ²¹ But whoever lives by the truth comes into the light, so that it may be seen plainly that what they have done has been done in the sight of God.

Ambassador of Love

I n my work as a chaplain, some people occasionally ask if I am willing to give them some additional spiritual help. While I'm happy to spend time with anyone who asks for help, I often find myself doing more learning than teaching. This was especially true when one painfully honest new Christian said to me with resignation, "I don't think it's a good idea for me to read the Bible. The more I read what God expects from me, the more I judge others who aren't doing what it says."

As he said this, I realized that I was at least partly responsible for instilling this judgmental spirit in him. At that time, one of the first things I did with those new to faith in Jesus was to introduce them to things they should no longer be doing. In other words, instead of showing them God's love and letting the Holy Spirit reshape them, I urged them to "behave like a believer."

TODAY'S READING
John 3:9–21

For God did not send his Son into the world to condemn the world, but to save the world through him. John 3:17

Now I was gaining a new appreciation for John 3:16-17. Jesus's invitation to believe in Him in verse 16 is followed by these words. "For God did not send his Son into the world to condemn the world, but to save the world through him."

Jesus didn't come to condemn us. But by giving these new Christians a checklist of behaviors, I was teaching them to condemn themselves, which then led them to judge others. Instead of being agents of condemnation, we are to be ambassadors of God's love and mercy.   *RANDY KILGORE*

Father, help me not to judge others today. Let me learn this until it changes me into someone more like You.

If Jesus didn't come to condemn the world, that's probably not our mission either!

¹³ Shout for joy, you heavens;
    rejoice, you earth;
    burst into song, you mountains!
For the LORD comforts his people
    and will have compassion on his afflicted ones.
¹⁴ But Zion said, "The LORD has forsaken me,
    the LORD has forgotten me."
¹⁵ "Can a mother forget the baby at her breast
    and have no compassion on the child she has borne?
Though she may forget,
    I will not forget you!
¹⁶ See, I have engraved you on the palms of my hands;
    your walls are ever before me.
¹⁷ Your children hasten back,
    and those who laid you waste depart from you.
¹⁸ Lift up your eyes and look around;
    all your children gather and come to you.
As surely as I live," declares the LORD,
    "you will wear them all as ornaments;
    you will put them on, like a bride.
¹⁹ "Though you were ruined and made desolate
    and your land laid waste,
now you will be too small for your people,
    and those who devoured you will be far away.
²⁰ The children born during your bereavement
    will yet say in your hearing,
'This place is too small for us;
    give us more space to live in.'
²¹ Then you will say in your heart,
    'Who bore me these?
I was bereaved and barren;
    I was exiled and rejected.
Who brought these up?
I was left all alone,
    but these—where have they come from?'"

Not Forgotten

At her mother's 50th birthday celebration with hundreds of people present, firstborn daughter Kukua recounted what her mother had done for her. The times were hard, Kukua remembered, and funds were scarce in the home. But her single mother deprived herself of personal comfort, selling her precious jewelry and other possessions in order to put Kukua through high school. With tears in her eyes, Kukua said that no matter how difficult things were, her mother never abandoned her or her siblings.

TODAY'S READING
Isaiah 49:13–21

I will not forget you! Isaiah 49:15

God compared His love for His people with a mother's love for her child. When the people of Israel felt abandoned by God during their exile, they complained: "The LORD has forsaken me, the Lord has forgotten me" (ISA. 49:14). But God said, "Can a mother forget the baby at her breast and have no compassion on the child she has borne? Though she may forget, I will not forget you!" (V. 15).

When we are distressed or disillusioned, we may feel abandoned by society, family, and friends, but God does not abandon us. It is a great encouragement that the Lord says, "I have engraved you on the palms of my hands" (V. 16) to indicate how much He knows and protects us. Even if people forsake us, God will never forsake His own. 🌱 *LAWRENCE DARMANI*

Thank You, Lord, that I am Yours forever.
I'm thankful that I won't have to walk through any experience alone.

God never forgets us.

⁴ Now he had to go through Samaria. ⁵ So he came to a town in Samaria called Sychar, near the plot of ground Jacob had given to his son Joseph. ⁶ Jacob's well was there, and Jesus, tired as he was from the journey, sat down by the well. It was about noon.

⁷ When a Samaritan woman came to draw water, Jesus said to her, "Will you give me a drink?" ⁸ (His disciples had gone into the town to buy food.)

⁹ The Samaritan woman said to him, "You are a Jew and I am a Samaritan woman. How can you ask me for a drink?" (For Jews do not associate with Samaritans.)

¹⁰ Jesus answered her, "If you knew the gift of God and who it is that asks you for a drink, you would have asked him and he would have given you living water."

¹¹ "Sir," the woman said, "you have nothing to draw with and the well is deep. Where can you get this living water? ¹² Are you greater than our father Jacob, who gave us the well and drank from it himself, as did also his sons and his livestock?"

¹³ Jesus answered, "Everyone who drinks this water will be thirsty again, ¹⁴ but whoever drinks the water I give them will never thirst. Indeed, the water I give them will become in them a spring of water welling up to eternal life."

Resting and Waiting

I **t was high noon.** Jesus, foot-weary from His long journey, was resting beside Jacob's well. His disciples had gone into the city of Sychar to buy bread. A woman came out of the city to draw water . . . and found her Messiah. The account tells us that she quickly went into the city and invited others to come hear "a man who told me everything I ever did" (JOHN 4:29).

The disciples came back bringing bread. When they urged Jesus to eat, He said to them, "My food . . . is to do the will of him who sent me and to finish his work" (V. 34).

Now I ask you: What work had Jesus been doing? He'd been resting and waiting by the well.

> TODAY'S READING
> **John 4:4–14**
>
> **"My food," said Jesus, "is to do the will of him who sent me and to finish his work."**
>
> John 4:34

I find great encouragement in this story for I am living with physical limitations. This passage tells me that I do not have to scurry about—worrying myself about doing the will of my Father and getting His work done. In this season of life, I can rest and wait for Him to bring His work to me.

Similarly, your tiny apartment, your work cubicle, your prison cell, or your hospital bed can become a "Jacob's well," a place to rest and to wait for your Father to bring His work to you. I wonder who He'll bring to you today? ❤ *DAVID ROPER*

Lord, our circumstances can often threaten to overwhelm us. Today, help us to see You in all of life. We are learning to trust You as You do Your work.

If you want a field of service, look around you.

¹ You have searched me, LORD, and you know me.
² You know when I sit and when I rise;
   you perceive my thoughts from afar.
³ You discern my going out and my lying down;
   you are familiar with all my ways.
⁴ Before a word is on my tongue you, LORD, know it completely.
⁵ You hem me in behind and before,
   and you lay your hand upon me.
⁶ Such knowledge is too wonderful for me, too lofty for me to attain.
⁷ Where can I go from your Spirit?
   Where can I flee from your presence?
⁸ If I go up to the heavens, you are there;
   if I make my bed in the depths, you are there.
⁹ If I rise on the wings of the dawn,
   if I settle on the far side of the sea,
¹⁰ even there your hand will guide me,
   your right hand will hold me fast.
¹¹ If I say, "Surely the darkness will hide me
   and the light become night around me,"
¹² even the darkness will not be dark to you;
   the night will shine like the day,
   for darkness is as light to you.
¹³ For you created my inmost being;
   you knit me together in my mother's womb.
¹⁴ I praise you because I am fearfully and wonderfully made;
   your works are wonderful, I know that full well.
¹⁵ My frame was not hidden from you
   when I was made in the secret place,
   when I was woven together in the depths of the earth.
¹⁶ Your eyes saw my unformed body;
   all the days ordained for me were written in your book
   before one of them came to be.
¹⁷ How precious to me are your thoughts, God!
   How vast is the sum of them!
¹⁸ Were I to count them,
   they would outnumber the grains of sand—
   when I awake, I am still with you.

Always In His Care

Veteran news reporter Scott Pelley never goes on assignment without his travel essentials—a shortwave radio, camera, indestructible suitcase, laptop computer, phone, and an emergency locator beacon that works anywhere. "You extend the antenna, push two buttons, and it sends a signal to a satellite connected to the National Oceanic and Atmospheric Administration," Pelley says. "It tells them who and where I am. Depending on what country you're in, they'll either send a rescue team—or not" (*AARP The Magazine*). Pelley has never needed to use the beacon, but he never travels without it.

TODAY'S READING
Psalm 139:1–18

You know when I sit and when I rise; you perceive my thoughts from afar.

Psalm 139:2

But when it comes to our relationship with God, we don't need radios, phones, or emergency beacons. No matter how precarious our circumstances become, He already knows who and where we are. The psalmist celebrated this as he wrote, "You have searched me, Lord, and you know me. . . . You are familiar with all my ways" (PS. 139:1–3). Our needs are never hidden from God, and we are never separated from His care.

Today, we can say with confidence, "If I rise on the wings of the dawn, if I settle on the far side of the sea, even there your hand will guide me, your right hand will hold me fast" (VV. 9–10).

The Lord knows who we are, where we are, and what we need. We are always in His care.

DAVID MCCASLAND

O Lord, we praise You for Your never-ending love and your never-failing care.

We are always in His care.

¹ Now the serpent was more crafty than any of the wild animals the Lᴏʀᴅ God had made. He said to the woman, "Did God really say, 'You must not eat from any tree in the garden'?"

² The woman said to the serpent, "We may eat fruit from the trees in the garden, ³ but God did say, 'You must not eat fruit from the tree that is in the middle of the garden, and you must not touch it, or you will die.'"

⁴ "You will not certainly die," the serpent said to the woman. ⁵ "For God knows that when you eat from it your eyes will be opened, and you will be like God, knowing good and evil."

⁶ When the woman saw that the fruit of the tree was good for food and pleasing to the eye, and also desirable for gaining wisdom, she took some and ate it. She also gave some to her husband, who was with her, and he ate it. ⁷ Then the eyes of both of them were opened, and they realized they were naked; so they sewed fig leaves together and made coverings for themselves.

⁸ Then the man and his wife heard the sound of the Lᴏʀᴅ God as he was walking in the garden in the cool of the day, and they hid from the Lᴏʀᴅ God among the trees of the garden.

Is He Good?

" **I** don't think God is good," my friend told me. She had been praying for years about some difficult issues, but nothing had improved. Her anger and bitterness over God's silence grew. Knowing her well, I sensed that deep down she believed God is good, but the continual pain in her heart and God's seeming lack of interest caused her to doubt. It was easier for her to get angry than to bear the sadness.

TODAY'S READING
Genesis 3:1–8

He said to the woman, "Did God really say … ?"

Genesis 3:1

Doubting God's goodness is as old as Adam and Eve (GEN. 3). The serpent put that thought in Eve's mind when he suggested that God was withholding the fruit from her because "God knows that when you eat from it your eyes will be opened, and you will be like God, knowing good and evil" (V. 5). In pride, Adam and Eve thought they, rather than God, should determine what was good for them.

Years after losing a daughter in death, James Bryan Smith found he was able to affirm God's goodness. In his book *The Good and Beautiful God,* Smith wrote, "God's goodness is not something I get to decide upon. I am a human being with limited understanding." Smith's amazing comment isn't naïve; it arises out of years of processing his grief and seeking God's heart.

In times of discouragement, let's listen well to each other and help each other see the truth that God is good.  *ANNE CETAS*

Lord, we will praise You in our difficult times like the psalmist did. You know us, and we turn to You because we know You are good.

The LORD is good to all; he has compassion on all he has made. PSALM 145:9

¹ Brothers and sisters, if someone is caught in a sin, you who live by the Spirit should restore that person gently. But watch yourselves, or you also may be tempted. ² Carry each other's burdens, and in this way you will fulfill the law of Christ. ³ If anyone thinks they are something when they are not, they deceive themselves. ⁴ Each one should test their own actions. Then they can take pride in themselves alone, without comparing themselves to someone else, ⁵ for each one should carry their own load. ⁶ Nevertheless, the one who receives instruction in the word should share all good things with their instructor.

⁷ Do not be deceived: God cannot be mocked. A man reaps what he sows. ⁸ Whoever sows to please their flesh, from the flesh will reap destruction; whoever sows to please the Spirit, from the Spirit will reap eternal life. ⁹ Let us not become weary in doing good, for at the proper time we will reap a harvest if we do not give up. ¹⁰ Therefore, as we have opportunity, let us do good to all people, especially to those who belong to the family of believers.

Time to Grow

I n Debbie's new home, she discovered an abandoned plant in a dark corner of the kitchen. The dusty and ragged leaves looked like those of a moth orchid, and she imagined how pretty the plant would look once it had sent up new bloom-bearing stems. She moved the pot into a spot by the window, cut off the dead leaves, and watered it thoroughly. She bought plant food and applied it to the roots. Week after week she inspected the plant, but no new shoots appeared. "I'll give it another month," she told her husband, "and if nothing has happened by then, out it goes."

TODAY'S READING
Galatians 6:1-10

At the proper time we will reap a harvest if we do not give up.

Galatians 6:9

When decision day came, she could hardly believe her eyes. Two small stems were poking out from among the leaves! The plant she'd almost given up on was still alive.

Do you ever get discouraged by your apparent lack of spiritual growth? Perhaps you frequently lose your temper or enjoy that spicy piece of gossip you just can't resist passing on. Or perhaps you get up too late to pray and read your Bible, in spite of resolving to set the alarm earlier.

Why not tell a trusted friend about the areas of your life in which you want to grow spiritually and ask that person to pray for and encourage you to be accountable? Be patient. You will grow as you allow the Holy Spirit to work in you. ✸ *MARION STROUD*

Please give me patience, dear Lord, with myself and with others. Help me to cooperate with the Holy Spirit as He shapes my desires and helps me to grow.

Each small step of faith is a giant step of growth.

¹⁰:³⁸ As Jesus and his disciples were on their way, he came to a village where a woman named Martha opened her home to him. ³⁹ She had a sister called Mary, who sat at the Lord's feet listening to what he said. ⁴⁰ But Martha was distracted by all the preparations that had to be made. She came to him and asked, "Lord, don't you care that my sister has left me to do the work by myself? Tell her to help me!"

⁴¹ "Martha, Martha," the Lord answered, "you are worried and upset about many things, ⁴² but few things are needed—or indeed only one. Mary has chosen what is better, and it will not be taken away from her."

¹¹:¹ One day Jesus was praying in a certain place. When he finished, one of his disciples said to him, "Lord, teach us to pray, just as John taught his disciples."

² He said to them, "When you pray, say:

"'Father,
hallowed be your name,
your kingdom come.
³ Give us each day our daily bread.
⁴ Forgive us our sins,
    for we also forgive everyone who sins against us.
And lead us not into temptation.'"

The Bread That Satisfies

learned to recite the Lord's Prayer as a boy in primary school. Every time I said the line, "Give us today our daily bread" (MATT. 6:11), I couldn't help but think about the bread that we got only occasionally at home. Only when my father returned from his trip into town did we have a loaf of bread. So asking God to give us our daily bread was a relevant prayer to me.

How curious I was when years later I discovered the booklet *Our Daily Bread*. I knew the title came from the Lord's Prayer, but I also knew it couldn't be talking about the loaf of bread from the baker's shop. I discovered as I read the booklet regularly that this "bread," full of Scripture portions and helpful notes, was spiritual food for the soul.

TODAY'S READING
Luke 10:38–11:4

Give us each day our daily bread.
Luke 11:3

It was spiritual food that Mary chose when she sat at the feet of Jesus and listened attentively to His words (LUKE 10:39). While Martha wearied herself with concern about physical food, Mary was taking time to be near their guest, the Lord Jesus, and to listen to Him. May we take that time as well. He is the Bread of Life (JOHN 6:35), and He feeds our hearts with spiritual food. He is the Bread that satisfies. ❂ *LAWRENCE DARMANI*

I sit before You now, Lord, and want to learn from You.
My heart is open to hear from You in Your Word.

"I am the bread of life." JESUS

> [97] Oh, how I love your law!
>   I meditate on it all day long.
> [98] Your commands are always with me
>   and make me wiser than my enemies.
> [99] I have more insight than all my teachers,
>   for I meditate on your statutes.
> [100] I have more understanding than the elders,
>   for I obey your precepts.
> [101] I have kept my feet from every evil path
>   so that I might obey your word.
> [102] I have not departed from your laws,
>   for you yourself have taught me.
> [103] How sweet are your words to my taste,
>   sweeter than honey to my mouth!
> [104] I gain understanding from your precepts;
>   therefore I hate every wrong path.

Great Literature

Recently I came across an article describing what constitutes great literature. The author suggested that great literature "changes you. When you are done reading, you're a different person."

In that light, the Word of God will always be classified as great literature. Reading the Bible challenges us to be better. Stories of biblical heroes inspire us to be courageous and persevering. The wisdom and prophetic books warn of the danger of living by our fallen instincts. God spoke through various writers to pen life-changing psalms for our benefit. The teachings of Jesus shape our character to become more like

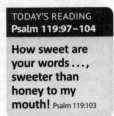

TODAY'S READING
Psalm 119:97–104

How sweet are your words . . . , sweeter than honey to my mouth! Psalm 119:103

Him. The writings of Paul orient our minds and lives to holy living. As the Holy Spirit brings these Scriptures to our minds, they become powerful agents for change in our lives.

The writer of Psalm 119 loved God's Word for its transforming influence in his life. He recognized that the ancient Scriptures handed down from Moses made him wise and more understanding than his teachers (V. 99). It kept him from evil (V. 101). No wonder he exclaimed, "Oh, how I love your law! I meditate on it all day long," and "How sweet are your words to my taste, sweeter than honey to my mouth!" (VV. 97, 103).

Welcome to the joy of loving great literature, especially the life-changing power of God's Word! 🍂 *JOE STOWELL*

Lord, thank You for Your Word and its powerful influence in my life.
Help me learn to put its truth into practice.

The Spirit of God uses the Word of God to change the people of God.

²² Do not merely listen to the word, and so deceive yourselves. Do what it says. ²³ Anyone who listens to the word but does not do what it says is like someone who looks at his face in a mirror ²⁴ and, after looking at himself, goes away and immediately forgets what he looks like. ²⁵ But whoever looks intently into the perfect law that gives freedom, and continues in it—not forgetting what they have heard, but doing it—they will be blessed in what they do.

²⁶ Those who consider themselves religious and yet do not keep a tight rein on their tongues deceive themselves, and their religion is worthless. ²⁷ Religion that God our Father accepts as pure and faultless is this: to look after orphans and widows in their distress and to keep oneself from being polluted by the world.

Chili Peppers

"**My mother gave us** chili peppers before we went to bed," said Samuel, recalling his difficult childhood in sub-Saharan Africa. "We drank water to cool our mouths, and then we would feel full." He added, "It did not work well."

Government upheaval had forced Samuel's father to flee for his life, leaving their mother as the family's sole provider. Sam's brother had sickle cell anemia, and they couldn't afford medical care. Their mother took them to church, but it didn't mean much to Sam. *How could God allow our family to suffer like this?* he wondered.

TODAY'S READING
James 1:22–27

Religion that God our Father accepts as pure and faultless is this: to look after orphans and widows in their distress.

James 1:27

Then one day a man learned about their plight and brought them some medicine to help with treatment. "On Sunday we will go to this man's church," his mother announced. Right away Sam sensed something different about this church. They celebrated their relationship with Jesus by living His love.

That was three decades ago. Today in this part of the world, Sam has started more than 20 churches, a large school, and a home for orphans. He's continuing the legacy of true religion taught by James, the brother of Jesus, who urged us not to "merely listen to the word" but to "do what it says" (JAMES 1:22). "Religion that God our Father accepts as pure and faultless is this: to look after orphans and widows in their distress" (V. 27).

There's no telling what a simple act of kindness done in Jesus's name can do. 🌢   *TIM GUSTAFSON*

Sometimes the best witness is kindness.

¹ Then I saw "a new heaven and a new earth," for the first heaven and the first earth had passed away, and there was no longer any sea. ² I saw the Holy City, the new Jerusalem, coming down out of heaven from God, prepared as a bride beautifully dressed for her husband.

³ And I heard a loud voice from the throne saying, "Look! God's dwelling place is now among the people, and he will dwell with them. They will be his people, and God himself will be with them and be their God. ⁴ 'He will wipe every tear from their eyes. There will be no more death' or mourning or crying or pain, for the old order of things has passed away."

⁵ He who was seated on the throne said, "I am making everything new!" Then he said, "Write this down, for these words are trustworthy and true."

⁶ He said to me: "It is done. I am the Alpha and the Omega, the Beginning and the End. To the thirsty I will give water without cost from the spring of the water of life. ⁷ Those who are victorious will inherit all this, and I will be their God and they will be my children.

God's Dwelling Place

James Oglethorpe (1696-1785) was a British general and member of Parliament who had a vision for a great city. Charged with settling the state of Georgia in North America, he planned the city of Savannah according to that vision. He designed a series of squares, each having a green space and designated areas for churches and shops, with the rest reserved for housing. The visionary thinking of Oglethorpe is seen today in a beautiful, well-organized city that is considered a jewel of the American South.

TODAY'S READING
Revelation 21:1-7

There will be no more death or mourning or crying or pain. Revelation 21:4

In Revelation 21, John received a vision of a different city—the New Jerusalem. What he said of this city was less about its design and more about the character of who was there. When John described our eternal home, he wrote, "I heard a loud voice from the throne saying, 'Look! God's dwelling place is now among the people, and he will dwell with them'" (V. 3). And because of *who* was there—God Himself—this dwelling place would be notable for what was *not* there. Quoting from Isaiah 25:8, John wrote, "He will wipe every tear from their eyes. There will be no more death" (V. 4).

No more death! Nor will there be any more "mourning or crying or pain." All our sorrow will be replaced by the wonderful, healing presence of the God of the universe. This is the home Jesus is preparing for all who turn to Him for forgiveness. ✒

BILL CROWDER

Thank You, Father, that Your Son is preparing a place for us to live with You. Thank You that it will be more than just a wonderful place. It is where we will live with You and know You forever.

While You prepare a place for us, Lord, prepare us for that place.

¹² Not that I have already obtained all this, or have already arrived at my goal, but I press on to take hold of that for which Christ Jesus took hold of me. ¹³ Brothers and sisters, I do not consider myself yet to have taken hold of it. But one thing I do: Forgetting what is behind and straining toward what is ahead, ¹⁴ I press on toward the goal to win the prize for which God has called me heavenward in Christ Jesus.

¹⁵ All of us, then, who are mature should take such a view of things. And if on some point you think differently, that too God will make clear to you. ¹⁶ Only let us live up to what we have already attained.

Paddling Home

like Reepicheep, C. S. Lewis's tough little talking mouse in the Chronicles of Narnia series. Determined to reach the "utter East" and join the great lion Aslan [symbolic of Christ], Reepicheep declares his resolve: "While I may, I sail East in *Dawn Treader*. When she fails me, I row East in my coracle [small boat]. When that sinks, I shall paddle East with my four paws. Then, when I can swim no longer, if I have not yet reached Aslan's Country, there shall I sink with my nose to the sunrise."

Paul put it another way: "I press on toward the goal" (PHIL. 3:14). His goal was to be like Jesus. Nothing else mattered. He admitted that he had much ground to cover but he would not give up until he attained that to which Jesus had called him.

> **TODAY'S READING**
> **Philippians 3:12–16**
>
> **One thing I do: Forgetting what is behind and straining toward what is ahead.**
>
> Philippians 3:13

None of us are what we should be, but we can, like the apostle, press and pray toward that goal. Like Paul we will always say, "I have not yet arrived." Nevertheless, despite weakness, failure, and weariness we must press on (V. 12). But everything depends on God. Without Him we can do nothing!

God is with you, calling you onward. Keep paddling! ❧

DAVID ROPER

Lord, help us learn that we do not press on toward our goal by our own effort but through prayer and the guidance of the Holy Spirit. Apart from You, we can do nothing. Work in us today, we pray.

God provides the power we need to persevere.

¹ Now Naomi had a relative on her husband's side, a man of standing from the clan of Elimelek, whose name was Boaz.

² And Ruth the Moabite said to Naomi, "Let me go to the fields and pick up the leftover grain behind anyone in whose eyes I find favor."

Naomi said to her, "Go ahead, my daughter." ³ So she went out, entered a field and began to glean behind the harvesters. As it turned out, she was working in a field belonging to Boaz, who was from the clan of Elimelek.

⁴ Just then Boaz arrived from Bethlehem and greeted the harvesters, "The LORD be with you!"

"The LORD bless you!" they answered.

⁵ Boaz asked the overseer of his harvesters, "Who does that young woman belong to?"

⁶ The overseer replied, "She is the Moabite who came back from Moab with Naomi. ⁷ She said, 'Please let me glean and gather among the sheaves behind the harvesters.' She came into the field and has remained here from morning till now, except for a short rest in the shelter."

⁸ So Boaz said to Ruth, "My daughter, listen to me. Don't go and glean in another field and don't go away from here. Stay here with the women who work for me. ⁹ Watch the field where the men are harvesting, and follow along after the women. I have told the men not to lay a hand on you. And whenever you are thirsty, go and get a drink from the water jars the men have filled."

¹⁰ At this, she bowed down with her face to the ground. She asked him, "Why have I found such favor in your eyes that you notice me—a foreigner?"

¹¹ Boaz replied, "I've been told all about what you have done for your mother-in-law since the death of your husband—how you left your father and mother and your homeland and came to live with a people you did not know before.

Why Me?

Ruth was a foreigner. She was a widow. She was poor. In many parts of the world today she would be considered a nobody—someone whose future doesn't hold any hope.

However, Ruth found favor in the eyes of a relative of her deceased husband, a rich man and the owner of the fields where she chose to ask for permission to glean grain. In response to his kindness, Ruth asked, "What have I done to deserve such kindness? . . . I am only a foreigner" (RUTH 2:10 NLT).

> **TODAY'S READING**
> Ruth 2:1–11
>
> **Why have I found such favor in your eyes?** Ruth 2:10

Boaz, the good man who showed Ruth such compassion, answered her truthfully. He had heard about her good deeds toward her mother-in-law, Naomi, and how she chose to leave her country and follow Naomi's God. Boaz prayed that God, "under whose wings" she had come for refuge, would bless her (1:16; 2:11–12; SEE PS. 91:4). As her kinsman redeemer (RUTH 3:9), when Boaz married Ruth he became her protector and part of the answer to his prayer.

Like Ruth, we were foreigners and far from God. We may wonder why God would choose to love us when we are so undeserving. The answer is not in us, but in Him. "God showed his great love for us by sending Christ to die for us while we were still sinners" (ROM. 5:8 NLT). Christ has become our Redeemer. When we come to Him in salvation, we are under His protective wings. ❧

KEILA OCHOA

Dear Lord, I don't know why You love me, but I don't doubt Your love. I thank You and worship You!

Gratefulness is the heart's response to God's undeserved love.

4:35 That day when evening came, he said to his disciples, "Let us go over to the other side." 36 Leaving the crowd behind, they took him along, just as he was, in the boat. There were also other boats with him.

37 A furious squall came up, and the waves broke over the boat, so that it was nearly swamped. 38 Jesus was in the stern, sleeping on a cushion. The disciples woke him and said to him, "Teacher, don't you care if we drown?"

39 He got up, rebuked the wind and said to the waves, "Quiet! Be still!" Then the wind died down and it was completely calm.

40 He said to his disciples, "Why are you so afraid? Do you still have no faith?"

41 They were terrified and asked each other, "Who is this? Even the wind and the waves obey him!"

5:1 They went across the lake to the region of the Gerasenes.

No Worries

A **comfortable plane ride** was about to get bumpy. The voice of the captain interrupted in-flight beverage service and asked passengers to make sure their seatbelts were fastened. Soon the plane began to roll and pitch like a ship on a wind-whipped ocean. While the rest of the passengers were doing their best to deal with the turbulence, a little girl sat through it all reading her book. After the plane landed, she was asked why she had been able to be so calm. She responded, "My daddy is the pilot and he's taking me home."

TODAY'S READING
Mark 4:35–5:1

Let us go over to the other side.

Mark 4:35

Though Jesus's disciples were seasoned fishermen, they were terrified the day a storm threatened to swamp their boat. They were following Jesus's instructions. Why was this happening? (MARK 4:35–38). He was with them but He was asleep at the stern of the craft. They learned that day that it is not true that when we do as our Lord says there will be no storms in our lives. Yet because He was with them, they also learned that storms don't stop us from getting to where our Lord wants us to go (5:1).

Whether the storm we encounter today is the result of a tragic accident, a loss of employment, or some other trial, we can be confident that all is not lost. Our Pilot can handle the storm. He will get us home. 🍃   *C. P. HIA*

What storms are you encountering today? Perhaps you have lost a loved one or are facing a serious illness. Perhaps you are having difficulty finding a job. Ask the Lord to strengthen your faith and take you safely through the storm to the other side.

We don't need to fear the storm with Jesus as our anchor.

¹⁴ So then he told them plainly, "Lazarus is dead, ¹⁵ and for your sake I am glad I was not there, so that you may believe. But let us go to him."

¹⁶ Then Thomas (also known as Didymus) said to the rest of the disciples, "Let us also go, that we may die with him."

¹⁷ On his arrival, Jesus found that Lazarus had already been in the tomb for four days. ¹⁸ Now Bethany was less than two miles from Jerusalem, ¹⁹ and many Jews had come to Martha and Mary to comfort them in the loss of their brother. ²⁰ When Martha heard that Jesus was coming, she went out to meet him, but Mary stayed at home.

²¹ "Lord," Martha said to Jesus, "if you had been here, my brother would not have died. ²² But I know that even now God will give you whatever you ask."

²³ Jesus said to her, "Your brother will rise again."

²⁴ Martha answered, "I know he will rise again in the resurrection at the last day."

²⁵ Jesus said to her, "I am the resurrection and the life. The one who believes in me will live, even though they die; ²⁶ and whoever lives by believing in me will never die. Do you believe this?"

²⁷ "Yes, Lord," she replied, "I believe that you are the Messiah, the Son of God, who is to come into the world."

When the Woods Wake Up

Through cold, snowy winters, the hope of spring sustains those of us who live in Michigan. May is the month when that hope is rewarded. The transformation is remarkable. Limbs that look lifeless on May 1 turn into branches that wave green leafy greetings by month's end. Although the change each day is imperceptible, by the end of the month the woods in my yard have changed from gray to green.

God has built into creation a cycle of rest and renewal. What looks like death to us is rest to God. And just as rest is preparation for renewal, death is preparation for resurrection.

I love watching the woods awaken every spring, for it reminds me that death is a temporary condition and that its purpose is to prepare for new life, a new beginning, for something even better. "Unless a kernel of wheat falls to the ground and dies, it remains only a single seed. But if it dies, it produces many seeds" (JOHN 12:24).

> **TODAY'S READING**
> **John 11:14–27**
>
> I am the resurrection and the life. The one who believes in me will live, even though they die.
> John 11:25

While pollen is a springtime nuisance when it coats my furniture and makes people sneeze, it reminds me that God is in the business of keeping things alive. And after the pain of death, He promises a glorious resurrection for those who believe in His Son. ❧ 　　　　　　　　　*JULIE ACKERMAN LINK*

Read these encouraging verses that remind us of the hope of resurrection: 1 Corinthians 15:35–58.

Every new leaf of springtime is a reminder of our promised resurrection.

¹ Who has believed our message
  and to whom has the arm of the LORD been revealed?
² He grew up before him like a tender shoot,
  and like a root out of dry ground.
He had no beauty or majesty to attract us to him,
  nothing in his appearance that we should desire him.
³ He was despised and rejected by mankind,
  a man of suffering, and familiar with pain.
Like one from whom people hide their faces
  he was despised, and we held him in low esteem.
⁴ Surely he took up our pain
  and bore our suffering,
yet we considered him punished by God,
  stricken by him, and afflicted.
⁵ But he was pierced for our transgressions,
  he was crushed for our iniquities;
the punishment that brought us peace was on him,
  and by his wounds we are healed.
⁶ We all, like sheep, have gone astray,
  each of us has turned to our own way;
and the LORD has laid on him
  the iniquity of us all.

Like Sheep

One of my daily chores when I lived with my grandfather in northern Ghana was taking care of sheep. Each morning I took them out to pasture and returned by evening. That was when I first noticed how stubborn sheep can be. Whenever they saw a farm, for instance, their instinct drove them right into it, getting me in trouble with the farmers on a number of occasions.

TODAY'S READING
Isaiah 53:1–6

We all, like sheep, have gone astray, each of us has turned to our own way. Isaiah 53:6

Sometimes when I was tired from the heat and resting under a tree, I observed the sheep dispersing into the bushes and heading for the hills, causing me to chase after them and scratching my skinny legs in the shrubs. I had a hard time directing the animals away from danger and trouble, especially when robbers sometimes raided the field and stole stray sheep.

So I quite understand when Isaiah says, "We all, like sheep, have gone astray, each of us has turned to our own way" (53:6). We stray in many ways: desiring and doing what displeases our Lord, hurting other people by our conduct, and being distracted from spending time with God and His Word because we are too busy or lack interest. We behave like sheep in the field.

Fortunately for us, we have the Good Shepherd who laid down His life for us (JOHN 10:11) and who carries our sorrows and our sins (ISA. 53:4–6). And as our shepherd, He calls us back to safe pasture that we might follow Him more closely. 🌱

LAWRENCE DARMANI

Shepherd of my soul, I do wander at times. I'm grateful that You're always seeking me to bring me back to Your side.

If you want God to lead you, be willing to follow.

¹⁶ And I will ask the Father, and he will give you another advocate to help you and be with you forever— ¹⁷ the Spirit of truth. The world cannot accept him, because it neither sees him nor knows him. But you know him, for he lives with you and will be in you. ¹⁸ I will not leave you as orphans; I will come to you. ¹⁹ Before long, the world will not see me anymore, but you will see me. Because I live, you also will live. ²⁰ On that day you will realize that I am in my Father, and you are in me, and I am in you. ²¹ Whoever has my commands and keeps them is the one who loves me. The one who loves me will be loved by my Father, and I too will love them and show myself to them."

²² Then Judas (not Judas Iscariot) said, "But, Lord, why do you intend to show yourself to us and not to the world?"

²³ Jesus replied, "Anyone who loves me will obey my teaching. My Father will love them, and we will come to them and make our home with them. ²⁴ Anyone who does not love me will not obey my teaching. These words you hear are not my own; they belong to the Father who sent me.

²⁵ "All this I have spoken while still with you. ²⁶ But the Advocate, the Holy Spirit, whom the Father will send in my name, will teach you all things and will remind you of everything I have said to you. ²⁷ Peace I leave with you; my peace I give you. I do not give to you as the world gives. Do not let your hearts be troubled and do not be afraid.

Flowing Peace

"I'm not surprised you lead retreats," said an acquaintance in my exercise class. "You have a good aura." I was jolted but pleased by her comment, because I realized that what she saw as an "aura" in me, I understood to be the peace of Christ. As we follow Jesus, He gives us the peace that transcends understanding (PHIL. 4:7) and radiates from within—though we may not even be aware of it.

TODAY'S READING
John 14:16–27

Peace I leave with you; my peace I give you. John 14:27

Jesus promised His followers this peace when, after their last supper together, He prepared them for His death and resurrection. He told them that though they would have trouble in the world, the Father would send them the Spirit of truth to live with them and be in them (JOHN 14:16–17). The Spirit would teach them, bringing to mind His truths; the Spirit would comfort them, bestowing on them His peace. Though soon they would face trials—including fierce opposition from the religious leaders and seeing Jesus executed—He told them not to be afraid. The Holy Spirit's presence would never leave them.

Although as God's children we experience hardship, we too have His Spirit living within and flowing out of us. God's peace can be His witness to everyone we meet—whether at a local market, at school or work, or in the gym. ❡ *AMY BOUCHER PYE*

Father, Son, and Holy Spirit, thank You for welcoming me into Your circle of love. May I share Your peace with someone in my community today.

When we keep our mind on God, His Spirit keeps our mind at peace.

¹⁰ In bringing many sons and daughters to glory, it was fitting that God, for whom and through whom everything exists, should make the pioneer of their salvation perfect through what he suffered. ¹¹ Both the one who makes people holy and those who are made holy are of the same family. So Jesus is not ashamed to call them brothers and sisters. ¹² He says,

"I will declare your name to my brothers and sisters;
   in the assembly I will sing your praises."

¹³ And again,

"I will put my trust in him."

And again he says,

"Here am I, and the children God has given me."

¹⁴ Since the children have flesh and blood, he too shared in their humanity so that by his death he might break the power of him who holds the power of death—that is, the devil— ¹⁵ and free those who all their lives were held in slavery by their fear of death. ¹⁶ For surely it is not angels he helps, but Abraham's descendants. ¹⁷ For this reason he had to be made like them, fully human in every way, in order that he might become a merciful and faithful high priest in service to God, and that he might make atonement for the sins of the people. ¹⁸ Because he himself suffered when he was tempted, he is able to help those who are being tempted.

He Walked in Our Shoes

To **help his staff** of young architects understand the needs of those for whom they design housing, David Dillard sends them on "sleepovers." They put on pajamas and spend 24 hours in a senior living center in the same conditions as people in their 80s and 90s. They wear earplugs to simulate hearing loss, tape their fingers together to limit manual dexterity, and exchange eyeglasses to replicate vision problems. Dillard says, "The biggest benefit is [that] when I send 27-year-olds out, they come back with a heart 10 times as big. They meet people and understand their plights" (RODNEY BROOKS, *USA TODAY*).

TODAY'S READING
Hebrews 2:10–18

Because he himself suffered when he was tempted, he is able to help those who are being tempted. Hebrews 2:18

Jesus lived on this earth for 33 years and shared in our humanity. He was made like us, "fully human in every way" (HEB. 2:17), so He knows what it's like to live in a human body on this earth. He understands the struggles we face and comes alongside with understanding and encouragement.

"Because [Jesus] himself suffered when he was tempted, he is able to help those who are being tempted" (V. 18). The Lord could have avoided the cross. Instead, He obeyed His Father. Through His death, He broke the power of Satan and freed us from our fear of death (VV. 14–15).

In every temptation, Jesus walks beside us to give us courage, strength, and hope along the way. ✿ *DAVID MCCASLAND*

Lord Jesus, thank You for "walking in our shoes" on this earth and for being with us. May we experience Your presence today.

Jesus understands.

²⁶ "So do not be afraid of them, for there is nothing concealed that will not be disclosed, or hidden that will not be made known. ²⁷ What I tell you in the dark, speak in the daylight; what is whispered in your ear, proclaim from the roofs. ²⁸ Do not be afraid of those who kill the body but cannot kill the soul. Rather, be afraid of the One who can destroy both soul and body in hell. ²⁹ Are not two sparrows sold for a penny? Yet not one of them will fall to the ground outside your Father's care. ³⁰ And even the very hairs of your head are all numbered. ³¹ So don't be afraid; you are worth more than many sparrows.

³² "Whoever acknowledges me before others, I will also acknowledge before my Father in heaven.

Can't Die But Once

Born into slavery and badly treated as a young girl, Harriet Tubman (C. 1822–1913) found a shining ray of hope in the Bible stories her mother told. The account of Israel's escape from slavery under Pharaoh showed her a God who desired freedom for His people.

Harriet found freedom when she slipped over the Maryland state line and out of slavery. She couldn't remain content, however, knowing so many were still trapped in captivity. So she led more than a dozen rescue missions to free those still in slavery, dismissing the personal danger. "I can't die but once," she said.

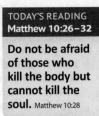

TODAY'S READING
Matthew 10:26–32

Do not be afraid of those who kill the body but cannot kill the soul. Matthew 10:28

Harriet knew the truth of the statement: "Do not be afraid of those who kill the body but cannot kill the soul" (MATT. 10:28). Jesus spoke those words as He sent His disciples on their first mission. He knew they would face danger, and not everyone would receive them warmly. So why expose the disciples to the risk? The answer is found in the previous chapter. "When he saw the crowds, [Jesus] had compassion on them, because they were harassed and helpless, like sheep without a shepherd" (9:36).

When Harriet Tubman couldn't forget those still trapped in slavery, she showed us a picture of Christ, who did not forget us when we were trapped in our sins. Her courageous example inspires us to remember those who remain without hope in the world. 🕊

TIM GUSTAFSON

May we find our peace and purpose in You, Lord,
and share You with others.

True freedom is found in knowing and serving Christ.

⁷ Cleanse me with hyssop, and I will be clean;
  wash me, and I will be whiter than snow.
⁸ Let me hear joy and gladness;
  let the bones you have crushed rejoice.
⁹ Hide your face from my sins
  and blot out all my iniquity.
¹⁰ Create in me a pure heart, O God,
  and renew a steadfast spirit within me.
¹¹ Do not cast me from your presence
  or take your Holy Spirit from me.
¹² Restore to me the joy of your salvation
  and grant me a willing spirit, to sustain me.
¹³ Then I will teach transgressors your ways,
  so that sinners will turn back to you.
¹⁴ Deliver me from the guilt of bloodshed, O God,
  you who are God my Savior,
  and my tongue will sing of your righteousness.
¹⁵ Open my lips, Lord,
  and my mouth will declare your praise.
¹⁶ You do not delight in sacrifice, or I would bring it;
  you do not take pleasure in burnt offerings.
¹⁷ My sacrifice, O God, is a broken spirit;
  a broken and contrite heart
  you, God, will not despise.

Praise from Pure Hearts

During my friend Myrna's travels to another country, she visited a church for worship. She noticed that as people entered the sanctuary they immediately knelt and prayed, facing away from the front of the church. My friend learned that people in that church confessed their sin to God before they began the worship service.

TODAY'S READING
Psalm 51:7–17

A broken and contrite heart you, God, will not despise. Psalm 51:17

This act of humility is a picture to me of what David said in Psalm 51: "My sacrifice, O God, is a broken spirit; a broken and contrite heart you, God, will not despise" (V. 17). David was describing his own remorse and repentance for his sin of adultery with Bathsheba. Real sorrow for sin involves adopting God's view of what we've done—seeing it as clearly wrong, disliking it, and not wanting it to continue.

When we are truly broken over our sin, God lovingly puts us back together. "If we confess our sins, he is faithful and just and will forgive us our sins and purify us from all unrighteousness" (1 JOHN 1:9). This forgiveness produces a fresh sense of openness with Him and is the ideal starting point for praise. After David repented, confessed, and was forgiven by God, he responded by saying, "Open my lips, Lord, and my mouth will declare your praise" (PS. 51:15).

Humility is the right response to God's holiness. And praise is our heart's response to His forgiveness. *JENNIFER BENSON SCHULDT*

Dear God, help me never to excuse or minimize my sin.
Please meet me in my brokenness, and let nothing hold me back
from praising Your name.

Praise is the song of a soul set free.

¹⁷ As Jesus started on his way, a man ran up to him and fell on his knees before him. "Good teacher," he asked, "what must I do to inherit eternal life?"

¹⁸ "Why do you call me good?" Jesus answered. "No one is good—except God alone. ¹⁹ You know the commandments: 'You shall not murder, you shall not commit adultery, you shall not steal, you shall not give false testimony, you shall not defraud, honor your father and mother.'"

²⁰ "Teacher," he declared, "all these I have kept since I was a boy."

²¹ Jesus looked at him and loved him. "One thing you lack," he said. "Go, sell everything you have and give to the poor, and you will have treasure in heaven. Then come, follow me."

²² At this the man's face fell. He went away sad, because he had great wealth.

²³ Jesus looked around and said to his disciples, "How hard it is for the rich to enter the kingdom of God!"

²⁴ The disciples were amazed at his words. But Jesus said again, "Children, how hard it is to enter the kingdom of God! ²⁵ It is easier for a camel to go through the eye of a needle than for someone who is rich to enter the kingdom of God."

²⁶ The disciples were even more amazed, and said to each other, "Who then can be saved?"

²⁷ Jesus looked at them and said, "With man this is impossible, but not with God; all things are possible with God."

Knowing and Doing

Chinese philosopher Han Feizi made this observation about life: "Knowing the facts is easy. Knowing how to act based on the facts is difficult."

A rich man with that problem once came to Jesus. He knew the law of Moses and believed he had kept the commandments since his youth (MARK 10:20). But he seems to be wondering what additional facts he might hear from Jesus. " 'Good teacher,' he asked, 'what must I do to inherit eternal life?' " (V. 17).

Jesus's answer disappointed the rich man. He told him to sell his possessions, give the money to the poor, and follow Him (V. 21). With these few words Jesus exposed a fact the man didn't want to hear. He loved and relied on his wealth more than he trusted Jesus. Abandoning the security of his money to follow Jesus was too great a risk, and he went away sad (V. 22).

> **TODAY'S READING**
> Mark 10:17–27
>
> **With man this is impossible, but not with God; all things are possible with God.** Mark 10:27

What was the Teacher thinking? His own disciples were alarmed and asked, "Who then can be saved?" He replied, "With man this is impossible, but not with God; all things are possible with God" (V. 27). It takes courage and faith. "If you declare with your mouth, 'Jesus is Lord,' and believe in your heart that God raised him from the dead, you will be saved" (ROM. 10:9). 🌱

POH FANG CHIA

God, thank You for the good news of Jesus. Give us the courage to act on what we know to be true, and to accept the salvation offered through Jesus. Thank You that You will give us the strength to act on the facts.

Believe in the Lord Jesus, and you will be saved. ACTS 16:31

⁷ At that time Hanani the seer came to Asa king of Judah and said to him: "Because you relied on the king of Aram and not on the LORD your God, the army of the king of Aram has escaped from your hand. ⁸ Were not the Cushites and Libyans a mighty army with great numbers of chariots and horsemen? Yet when you relied on the LORD, he delivered them into your hand. ⁹ For the eyes of the LORD range throughout the earth to strengthen those whose hearts are fully committed to him. You have done a foolish thing, and from now on you will be at war."

¹⁰ Asa was angry with the seer because of this; he was so enraged that he put him in prison. At the same time Asa brutally oppressed some of the people.

¹¹ The events of Asa's reign, from beginning to end, are written in the book of the kings of Judah and Israel. ¹² In the thirty-ninth year of his reign Asa was afflicted with a disease in his feet. Though his disease was severe, even in his illness he did not seek help from the LORD, but only from the physicians. ¹³ Then in the forty-first year of his reign Asa died and rested with his ancestors. ¹⁴ They buried him in the tomb that he had cut out for himself in the City of David. They laid him on a bier covered with spices and various blended perfumes, and they made a huge fire in his honor.

Not a Simple Story

Life seems straightforward in the laws of the Old Testament. Obey God and get blessed. Disobey Him and expect trouble. It's a satisfying theology. But is it that simple?

King Asa's story seems to fit the pattern. He led his people away from false gods and his kingdom thrived (2 CHRON. 15:1–19). Then late in his reign, he depended on himself instead of God (16:2–7) and the rest of his life was marked by war and illness (V. 12).

It's easy to look at that story and draw a simple conclusion. But when the prophet Hanani warned Asa, he said that God will "strengthen those whose hearts are fully committed to him" (16:9). Why do our hearts need strengthening? Because doing the right thing may require courage and perseverance.

> **TODAY'S READING**
> **2 Chronicles 16:7–14**
>
> **The eyes of the LORD range throughout the earth to strengthen those whose hearts are fully committed to him.**
>
> 2 Chronicles 16:9

Job got the starring role in a cosmic tragedy. His crime? "He [was] blameless and upright" (JOB 1:8). Joseph, falsely accused of attempted rape, languished in prison for years—to serve God's good purposes (GEN. 39:19–41:1). And Jeremiah was beaten and put in stocks (JER. 20:2). What was the prophet's offense? Telling the truth to rebellious people (26:15).

Life is not simple, and God's ways are not our ways. Making the right decision may come at a cost. But in God's eternal plan, His blessings arrive in due time. 🌿

TIM GUSTAFSON

Lord, thank You for the examples of courage and obedience in Your Word. Help us learn from their mistakes and from their wise choices, as we make our choice to serve You.

God helps those who depend on Him.

14 Therefore, since we have a great high priest who has ascended into heaven, Jesus the Son of God, let us hold firmly to the faith we profess. 15 For we do not have a high priest who is unable to empathize with our weaknesses, but we have one who has been tempted in every way, just as we are—yet he did not sin. 16 Let us then approach God's throne of grace with confidence, so that we may receive mercy and find grace to help us in our time of need.

Lord, Help!

was so happy for my friend when she told me she was going to be a mum! Together we counted the days until the birth. But when the baby suffered a brain injury during delivery, my heart broke and I didn't know *how* to pray. All I knew was *who* I should pray to—God. He is our Father, and He hears us when we call.

I knew that God was capable of miracles. He brought Jairus's daughter back to life (LUKE 8:49–55) and in so doing also healed the girl of whatever disease had robbed her of life. So I asked Him to bring healing for my friend's baby too.

TODAY'S READING
Hebrews 4:14–16

But what if God doesn't heal? I wondered. *Surely He doesn't lack the power. Could it be He doesn't care?* I thought of Jesus's suffering on the cross and the explanation that "God demonstrates his own love for us in this: While we were still sinners, Christ died for us" (ROM. 5:8). Then I remembered the questions of Job and how he learned to see the wisdom of God as shown in the creation around him (JOB 38–39).

> Let us then approach God's throne of grace with confidence, so that we may receive mercy and find grace to help us in our time of need. Hebrews 4:16

Slowly I saw how God calls us to Him in the details of our lives. In God's grace, my friend and I learned together what it means to call on the Lord and to trust Him—whatever the outcome.

POH FANG CHIA

Lord, to whom can I go but You! I trust You with my life and the lives of my loved ones. I'm grateful You always hear my cry.

When life knocks you down, you're in the perfect position to pray!

²⁷ Why do you complain, Jacob?
   Why do you say, Israel,
"My way is hidden from the LORD;
   my cause is disregarded by my God"?
²⁸ Do you not know?
   Have you not heard?
The LORD is the everlasting God,
   the Creator of the ends of the earth.
He will not grow tired or weary,
   and his understanding no one can fathom.
²⁹ He gives strength to the weary
   and increases the power of the weak.
³⁰ Even youths grow tired and weary,
   and young men stumble and fall;
³¹ but those who hope in the LORD
   will renew their strength.
They will soar on wings like eagles;
   they will run and not grow weary,
   they will walk and not be faint.

Strength for the Weary

On a beautiful, sunny day, I was walking in a park and feeling very weary in spirit. It wasn't just one thing weighing me down—it seemed to be everything. When I stopped to sit on a bench, I noticed a small plaque placed there in loving memory of a "devoted husband, father, brother, and friend." Also on the plaque were these words, "But they who wait for the Lord shall renew their strength; they shall mount up with wings like eagles; they shall run and not be weary, they shall walk and not faint" (ISA. 40:31 ESV).

TODAY'S READING
Isaiah 40:27–31

Those who hope in the LORD will renew their strength. Isaiah 40:31

Those familiar words came to me as a personal touch from the Lord. Weariness—whether physical, emotional, or spiritual—comes to us all. Isaiah reminds us that although we become tired, the Lord, the everlasting God, the Creator of the ends of the earth "will not grow tired or weary" (V. 28). How easily I had forgotten that in every situation "[the Lord] gives strength to the weary and increases the power of the weak" (V. 29).

What's it like on your journey today? If fatigue has caused you to forget God's presence and power, why not pause and recall His promise. "Those who hope in the LORD will renew their strength" (V. 31). Here. Now. Right where we are. 🌱

DAVID MCCASLAND

Lord, thank You that You do not grow weary.
Give me the strength to face whatever situation I am in today.

When life's struggles make you weary, find strength in the Lord.

⁷ The end of all things is near. Therefore be alert and of sober mind so that you may pray. ⁸ Above all, love each other deeply, because love covers over a multitude of sins. ⁹ Offer hospitality to one another without grumbling. ¹⁰ Each of you should use whatever gift you have received to serve others, as faithful stewards of God's grace in its various forms. ¹¹ If anyone speaks, they should do so as one who speaks the very words of God. If anyone serves, they should do so with the strength God provides, so that in all things God may be praised through Jesus Christ. To him be the glory and the power for ever and ever. Amen.

You Have Purpose

On a hot day in western Texas, my niece Vania saw a woman standing by a stoplight and holding up a sign. As she drove closer, she tried to read what the sign said, assuming it was a request for food or money. Instead, she was surprised to see these three words:

"You Have Purpose"

God has created each of us for a specific purpose. Primarily that purpose is to bring honor to Him, and one way we do that is by meeting the needs of others (1 PETER 4:10–11).

A mother of young children may find purpose in wiping runny noses and telling her kids about Jesus. An employee in an unsatisfying job might find his purpose in doing his work conscientiously, remembering it is the Lord he is serving (COL. 3:23-24). A woman who has lost her sight still finds purpose in praying for her children and grandchildren and influencing them to trust God.

Psalm 139 says that before we were born "all the days ordained for [us] were written in [His] book" (V. 16). We are "fearfully and wonderfully made" to bring glory to our Creator (V. 14).

Never forget: You have purpose! 🌼

CINDY HESS KASPER

> **TODAY'S READING**
> **1 Peter 4:7–11**
>
> If anyone serves, they should do so with the strength God provides, so that in all things God may be praised through Jesus Christ.
> 1 Peter 4:11

Lord, it often seems that our lives swing from drudgery to challenges we don't want. Today help us to see You in the midst of whatever faces us. Show us a small glimpse of the purpose and meaning You bring to everything.

Even when everything seems meaningless,
God still has a purpose for your life.

¹ After Jesus said this, he looked toward heaven and prayed:

"Father, the hour has come. Glorify your Son, that your Son may glorify you. ² For you granted him authority over all people that he might give eternal life to all those you have given him. ³ Now this is eternal life: that they know you, the only true God, and Jesus Christ, whom you have sent. ⁴ I have brought you glory on earth by finishing the work you gave me to do. ⁵ And now, Father, glorify me in your presence with the glory I had with you before the world began.

The Beauty of Rome

The glory of the Roman Empire offered an expansive backdrop for the birth of Jesus. In 27 BC Rome's first emperor, Caesar Augustus, ended 200 years of civil war and began to replace rundown neighborhoods with monuments, temples, arenas, and government complexes. According to Roman historian Pliny the Elder, they were "the most beautiful buildings the world has ever seen."

TODAY'S READING
John 17:1–5

> Now this is eternal life: that they may know you, the only true God. John 17:3

Yet even with her beauty, the Eternal City and its empire had a history of brutality that continued until Rome fell. Thousands of slaves, foreigners, revolutionaries, and army deserters were crucified on roadside poles as a warning to anyone who dared to defy the power of Rome.

What irony that Jesus's death on a Roman cross turned out to reveal an eternal glory that made the pride of Rome look like the momentary beauty of a sunset!

Who could have imagined that in the public curse and agony of the cross we would find the eternal glory of the love, presence, and kingdom of our God?

Who could have foreseen that all heaven and earth would one day sing, "Worthy is the Lamb, who was slain, to receive power and wealth and wisdom and strength and honor and glory and praise!" (REV. 5:12).

MART DEHAAN

Father in heaven, please help us to reflect the heart of Your sacrifice for the world. May Your love become our love, Your life our life, and Your glory our never-ending joy.

The Lamb who died is the Lord who lives!

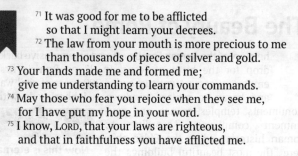

71 It was good for me to be afflicted
    so that I might learn your decrees.
72 The law from your mouth is more precious to me
    than thousands of pieces of silver and gold.
73 Your hands made me and formed me;
    give me understanding to learn your commands.
74 May those who fear you rejoice when they see me,
    for I have put my hope in your word.
75 I know, LORD, that your laws are righteous,
    and that in faithfulness you have afflicted me.

Broken to Be Made New

During World War II my dad served with the US Army in the South Pacific. During that time Dad rejected any idea of religion, saying, "I don't need a crutch." Yet the day came when his attitude toward spiritual things would change forever. Mom had gone into labor with their third child, and my brother and I went to bed with the excitement of soon seeing our new brother or sister. When I got out of bed the next morning, I excitedly asked Dad, "Is it a boy or a girl?" He replied, "It was a little girl but she was born dead." We began to weep together at our loss.

TODAY'S READING
Psalm 119:71–75

I know, LORD, that your laws are righteous, and that in faithfulness you have afflicted me.

Psalm 119:75

For the first time, Dad took his broken heart to Jesus in prayer. At that moment he felt an overwhelming sense of peace and comfort from God, though his daughter would always be irreplaceable. Soon he began to take an interest in the Bible and continued to pray to the One who was healing his broken heart. His faith grew through the years. He became a strong follower of Jesus—serving Him as a Bible-study teacher and a leader in his church.

Jesus is not a crutch for the weak. He is the source of new spiritual life! When we're broken, He can make us new and whole (PS. 119:75). ❧ *DENNIS FISHER*

What is on your heart that you need to talk with God about?
Bring Him your brokenness and ask Him to make you whole.

Brokenness can lead to wholeness.

¹ They went across the lake to the region of the Gerasenes.
² When Jesus got out of the boat, a man with an impure spirit came from the tombs to meet him.

³ This man lived in the tombs, and no one could bind him anymore, not even with a chain. ⁴ For he had often been chained hand and foot, but he tore the chains apart and broke the irons on his feet. No one was strong enough to subdue him. ⁵ Night and day among the tombs and in the hills he would cry out and cut himself with stones.

⁶ When he saw Jesus from a distance, he ran and fell on his knees in front of him. ⁷ He shouted at the top of his voice, "What do you want with me, Jesus, Son of the Most High God? In God's name don't torture me!" ⁸ For Jesus had said to him, "Come out of this man, you impure spirit!"

⁹ Then Jesus asked him, "What is your name?"

"My name is Legion," he replied, "for we are many." ¹⁰ And he begged Jesus again and again not to send them out of the area. ¹¹ A large herd of pigs was feeding on the nearby hillside.

¹² The demons begged Jesus, "Send us among the pigs; allow us to go into them." ¹³ He gave them permission, and the impure spirits came out and went into the pigs. The herd, about two thousand in number, rushed down the steep bank into the lake and were drowned.

¹⁴ Those tending the pigs ran off and reported this in the town and countryside, and the people went out to see what had happened.
¹⁵ When they came to Jesus, they saw the man who had been possessed by the legion of demons, sitting there, dressed and in his right mind; and they were afraid.

¹⁶ Those who had seen it told the people what had happened to the demon-possessed man—and told about the pigs as well. ¹⁷ Then the people began to plead with Jesus to leave their region.

¹⁸ As Jesus was getting into the boat, the man who had been demon-possessed begged to go with him. ¹⁹ Jesus did not let him, but said, "Go home to your own people and tell them how much the Lord has done for you, and how he has had mercy on you." ²⁰ So the man went away and began to tell in the Decapolis how much Jesus had done for him. And all the people were amazed.

Tell It!

The year was 1975 and something significant had just happened to me. I needed to find my friend Francis, with whom I shared a lot of personal matters, and tell him about it. I found him in his apartment hurriedly preparing to go out, but I slowed him down. The way he stared at me, he must have sensed that I had something important to tell him. "What is it?" he asked. So I told him simply, "Yesterday I surrendered my life to Jesus!"

TODAY'S READING
Mark 5:1–20

The man went away and began to tell . . . how much Jesus had done for him. Mark 5:20

Francis looked at me, sighed heavily, and said, "I've felt like doing the same for a long time now." He asked me to share what happened, and I told him how the previous day someone had explained the gospel to me and how I asked Jesus to come into my life. I still remember the tears in his eyes as he too prayed to receive Jesus's forgiveness. No longer in a hurry, he and I talked and talked about our new relationship with Christ.

After Jesus healed the man with an evil spirit, He told him, "Go home to your own people and tell them how much the Lord has done for you, and how he has had mercy on you" (MARK 5:19). The man didn't need to preach a powerful sermon; he simply needed to share his story.

No matter what our conversion experience is, we can do what that man did: "[He] went away and began to tell . . . how much Jesus had done for him." 🌐

LAWRENCE DARMANI

What has Jesus done for you? Tell it!

Let the redeemed of the Lord tell their story. PSALM 107:2

¹² Now I want you to know, brothers and sisters, that what has happened to me has actually served to advance the gospel. ¹³ As a result, it has become clear throughout the whole palace guard and to everyone else that I am in chains for Christ. ¹⁴ And because of my chains, most of the brothers and sisters have become confident in the Lord and dare all the more to proclaim the gospel without fear.

¹⁵ It is true that some preach Christ out of envy and rivalry, but others out of goodwill. ¹⁶ The latter do so out of love, knowing that I am put here for the defense of the gospel. ¹⁷ The former preach Christ out of selfish ambition, not sincerely, supposing that they can stir up trouble for me while I am in chains. ¹⁸ But what does it matter? The important thing is that in every way, whether from false motives or true, Christ is preached. And because of this I rejoice.

Yes, and I will continue to rejoice, ¹⁹ for I know that through your prayers and God's provision of the Spirit of Jesus Christ what has happened to me will turn out for my deliverance. ²⁰ I eagerly expect and hope that I will in no way be ashamed, but will have sufficient courage so that now as always Christ will be exalted in my body, whether by life or by death. ²¹ For to me, to live is Christ and to die is gain. ²² If I am to go on living in the body, this will mean fruitful labor for me. Yet what shall I choose? I do not know! ²³ I am torn between the two: I desire to depart and be with Christ, which is better by far; ²⁴ but it is more necessary for you that I remain in the body. ²⁵ Convinced of this, I know that I will remain, and I will continue with all of you for your progress and joy in the faith, ²⁶ so that through my being with you again your boasting in Christ Jesus will abound on account of me.

Better By Far

A siren wailed outside a little boy's house. Unfamiliar with the sound, he asked his mother what it was. She explained that it was meant to alert people of a dangerous storm. She said that if people did not take cover, they might die as a result of the tornado. The boy replied, "Mommy, why is that a bad thing? If we die, don't we meet Jesus?"

Little children don't always understand what it means to die. But Paul, who had a lifetime of experience, wrote something similar: "I desire to depart and be with Christ, which is better by far" (PHIL. 1:23). The apostle was under house arrest at the time, but his statement wasn't fueled by despair. He was rejoicing because his suffering was causing the gospel to spread (VV. 12-14).

TODAY'S READING
Philippians 1:12-26

**I desire to depart
and be with Christ,
which is better
by far.** Philippians 1:23

So why would Paul be torn between a desire for life and death? Because to go on living would mean "fruitful labor." But if he died he knew he would enjoy a special kind of closeness with Christ. To be absent from our bodies is to be home with the Lord (2 COR. 5:6-8).

People who believe in the saving power of Jesus's death and resurrection will be with Him forever. It's been said, "All's well that ends in heaven." Whether we live or die, we win. "For to me, to live is Christ and to die is gain" (PHIL. 1:21). 🖋

JENNIFER BENSON SCHULDT

Dear Jesus, help me to keep my eyes on You, whether I face difficulty
in life or death. Let me find security and peace in You.

*Belief in Jesus's death and resurrection brings
the assurance of life with Him forever.*

¹ Therefore if you have any encouragement from being united with Christ, if any comfort from his love, if any common sharing in the Spirit, if any tenderness and compassion, ² then make my joy complete by being like-minded, having the same love, being one in spirit and of one mind. ³ Do nothing out of selfish ambition or vain conceit. Rather, in humility value others above yourselves, ⁴ not looking to your own interests but each of you to the interests of the others.

⁵ In your relationships with one another, have the same mindset as Christ Jesus:

⁶ Who, being in very nature God,
    did not consider equality with God something to be used to his own advantage;

⁷ rather, he made himself nothing
    by taking the very nature of a servant,
    being made in human likeness.

⁸ And being found in appearance as a man,
    he humbled himself
    by becoming obedient to death—
        even death on a cross!

⁹ Therefore God exalted him to the highest place
    and gave him the name that is above every name,

¹⁰ that at the name of Jesus every knee should bow,
    in heaven and on earth and under the earth,

¹¹ and every tongue acknowledge that Jesus Christ is Lord,
    to the glory of God the Father.

What Really Matters

Two men sat down to review their business trip and its results. One said he thought the trip had been worthwhile because some meaningful new relationships had begun through their business contacts. The other said, "Relationships are fine, but selling is what matters most." Obviously they had very different agendas.

It is all too easy—whether in business, family, or church—to view others from the perspective of how they can benefit us. We value them for what we can get from them, rather than focusing on how we can serve them in Jesus's name. In his letter to the Philippians, Paul wrote, "Do nothing out of selfish ambition or vain conceit. Rather, in humility value others above yourselves, not looking to your own interests but each of you to the interests of the others" (PHIL. 2:3-4).

> **TODAY'S READING**
> **Philippians 2:1–11**
>
> **In humility value others above yourselves, not looking to your own interests but each of you to the interests of others.**
> Philippians 2:3–4

People are not to be used for our own benefit. Because they are loved by God and we are loved by Him, we love one another. His love is the greatest love of all. ❧

BILL CROWDER

Teach me, Lord, to see people as You do—bearing Your image,
being worthy of Your love, and needing Your care.
May Your great love find in my heart a vessel
through which that love can be displayed.

Joy comes from putting another's needs ahead of our own.

12 "To the angel of the church in Pergamum write:
These are the words of him who has the sharp, double-edged sword. 13 I know where you live—where Satan has his throne. Yet you remain true to my name. You did not renounce your faith in me, not even in the days of Antipas, my faithful witness, who was put to death in your city—where Satan lives.

14 Nevertheless, I have a few things against you: There are some among you who hold to the teaching of Balaam, who taught Balak to entice the Israelites to sin so that they ate food sacrificed to idols and committed sexual immorality.
15 Likewise, you also have those who hold to the teaching of the Nicolaitans. 16 Repent therefore! Otherwise, I will soon come to you and will fight against them with the sword of my mouth.

17 Whoever has ears, let them hear what the Spirit says to the churches. To the one who is victorious, I will give some of the hidden manna. I will also give that person a white stone with a new name written on it, known only to the one who receives it.

Our New Name

She called herself a worrier, but when her child was hurt in an accident, she learned how to escape that restricting label. As her child was recovering, she met each week with friends to talk and pray, asking God for help and healing. Through the months as she turned her fears and concerns into prayer, she realized that she was changing from being a *worrier* to a prayer *warrior*. She sensed that the Lord was giving her a new name. Her identity in Christ was deepening through the struggle of unwanted heartache.

> **TODAY'S READING**
> Revelation 2:12–17
>
> **I will also give that person a white stone with a new name written on it.**
> Revelation 2:17

In Jesus's letter to the church at Pergamum, the Lord promises to give to the faithful a white stone with a new name on it (REV. 2:17). Biblical commentators have debated over the meaning, but most agree that this white stone points to our freedom in Christ. In biblical times, juries in a court of law used a white stone for a not-guilty verdict and a black stone for guilty. A white stone also gained the bearer entrance into such events as banquets; likewise, those who receive God's white stone are welcomed to the heavenly feast. Jesus's death brings us freedom and new life—and a new name.

What new name do you think God might give to you? ❦

AMY BOUCHER PYE

May I live out my new identity, sharing Your love and joy.
Show me how You have made me into a new creation.

Followers of Christ have a brand-new identity.

43 "You have heard that it was said, 'Love your neighbor and hate your enemy.' 44 But I tell you, love your enemies and pray for those who persecute you,

45 that you may be children of your Father in heaven. He causes his sun to rise on the evil and the good, and sends rain on the righteous and the unrighteous. 46 If you love those who love you, what reward will you get? Are not even the tax collectors doing that? 47 And if you greet only your own people, what are you doing more than others? Do not even pagans do that? 48 Be perfect, therefore, as your heavenly Father is perfect.

Safety Net

For years I thought of the Sermon on the Mount (MATT. 5–7) as a blueprint for human behavior, a standard no one could possibly meet. How could I have missed the true meaning? Jesus spoke these words not to frustrate us, but to tell us what God is like.

Why should we love our enemies? Because our merciful Father causes His sun to rise on the evil and the good. Why store up treasures in heaven? Because the Father lives there and will lavishly reward us. Why live without fear and worry? Because the same God who

TODAY'S READING
Matthew 5:43–48

Be perfect, therefore, as your heavenly Father is perfect. Matthew 5:48

clothes the lilies and the grass of the field has promised to take care of us. Why pray? If an earthly father gives his son bread or fish, how much more will the Father in heaven give good gifts to those who ask?

Jesus gave the Sermon on the Mount (MATT. 5–7) not only to explain God's ideal toward which we should never stop striving but also to show that in this life none of us will ever reach that ideal.

Before God, we all stand on level ground: murderers and tantrum-throwers, adulterers and lusters, thieves and coveters. We are all desperate, and that is the only state appropriate to a human being who wants to know God. Having fallen from the absolute ideal, we have nowhere to land but in the safety net of absolute grace. ❡   *PHILIP YANCEY*

Dear Lord, I am a sinner and I need Your forgiveness. I believe that You died on the cross to pay the penalty for my sin. You did what I could not do for myself, and in humility I accept Your gift of grace. Help me to live a life that is pleasing to You.

Only God can transform a sinful soul into a masterpiece of grace.

⁷ Then they gave money to the masons and carpenters, and gave food and drink and olive oil to the people of Sidon and Tyre, so that they would bring cedar logs by sea from Lebanon to Joppa, as authorized by Cyrus king of Persia.

⁸ In the second month of the second year after their arrival at the house of God in Jerusalem, Zerubbabel son of Shealtiel, Joshua son of Jozadak and the rest of the people (the priests and the Levites and all who had returned from the captivity to Jerusalem) began the work. They appointed Levites twenty years old and older to supervise the building of the house of the LORD. ⁹ Joshua and his sons and brothers and Kadmiel and his sons (descendants of Hodaviah) and the sons of Henadad and their sons and brothers—all Levites—joined together in supervising those working on the house of God.

¹⁰ When the builders laid the foundation of the temple of the LORD, the priests in their vestments and with trumpets, and the Levites (the sons of Asaph) with cymbals, took their places to praise the Lord, as prescribed by David king of Israel. ¹¹ With praise and thanksgiving they sang to the LORD:

"He is good;
    his love toward Israel endures forever."

And all the people gave a great shout of praise to the LORD, because the foundation of the house of the LORD was laid. ¹² But many of the older priests and Levites and family heads, who had seen the former temple, wept aloud when they saw the foundation of this temple being laid, while many others shouted for joy. ¹³ No one could distinguish the sound of the shouts of joy from the sound of weeping, because the people made so much noise. And the sound was heard far away.

Tears and Laughter

ast year at a retreat I reconnected with some friends I hadn't seen in a long time. I laughed with them as we enjoyed the reunion, but I also cried because I knew how much I had missed them.

On the last day of our time together we celebrated the Lord's Supper. More smiles and tears! I rejoiced over the grace of God, who had given me eternal life and these beautiful days with my friends. But again I cried as I was sobered by what it had cost Jesus to deliver me from my sin.

TODAY'S READING
Ezra 3:7–13

No one could distinguish the sound of the shouts of joy from the sound of weeping. Ezra 3:13

I thought about Ezra and that wonderful day in Jerusalem. The exiles had returned from captivity and had just completed rebuilding the foundation of the Lord's temple. The people sang for joy, but some of the older priests cried (EZRA 3:10–12). They were likely remembering Solomon's temple and its former glory. Or were they grieving over their sins that had led to the captivity in the first place?

Sometimes when we see God at work we experience a wide range of emotions, including joy when we see God's wonders and sorrow as we remember our sins and the need for His sacrifice.

The Israelites were singing and weeping, the noise was heard far away (V. 13). May our emotions be expressions of our love and worship to our Lord, and may they touch those around us. 🌱

KEILA OCHOA

Lord, You welcome our sorrow and our joy, our tears and our laughter. We bring all of our emotions in their raw honesty to You. May we praise You with our whole being.

Both tears and smiles bring God praise.

¹ I call to you, LORD, come quickly to me;
    hear me when I call to you.
² May my prayer be set before you like incense;
    may the lifting up of my hands be like the evening
sacrifice.
³ Set a guard over my mouth, LORD;
    keep watch over the door of my lips.
⁴ Do not let my heart be drawn to what is evil
    so that I take part in wicked deeds
along with those who are evildoers;
    do not let me eat their delicacies.
⁵ Let a righteous man strike me—that is a kindness;
    let him rebuke me—that is oil on my head.
My head will not refuse it,
    for my prayer will still be against the deeds of evildoers.
⁶ Their rulers will be thrown down from the cliffs,
    and the wicked will learn that my words were well spoken.
⁷ They will say, "As one plows and breaks up the earth,
    so our bones have been scattered at the mouth of the
grave."
⁸ But my eyes are fixed on you, Sovereign LORD;
    in you I take refuge—do not give me over to death.
⁹ Keep me safe from the traps set by evildoers,
    from the snares they have laid for me.
¹⁰ Let the wicked fall into their own nets,
    while I pass by in safety.

Repeat After Me

When Rebecca stood on stage to speak at a conference, her first sentence into the microphone echoed around the room. It was a bit unsettling for her to hear her own words come back at her, and she had to adjust to the faulty sound system and try to ignore the echo of every word she spoke.

Imagine what it would be like to hear everything we say repeated! It wouldn't be so bad to hear ourselves repeat "I love you" or "I was wrong" or "Thank You, Lord" or "I'm praying for you." But not all of our words are beautiful or gentle or kind. What about those angry outbursts or demeaning comments that no one wants to hear once, let alone twice—those words that we would really rather take back?

TODAY'S READING
Psalm 141

Take control of what I say, O LORD, and guard my lips.

Psalm 141:3 NLT

Like the psalmist David, we long to have the Lord's control over our words. He prayed, "Take control of what I say, O LORD, and guard my lips" (PS. 141:3 NLT). And thankfully, the Lord wants to do that. He can help us control what we say. He can guard our lips.

As we learn to adjust to our own sound system by paying careful attention to what we say and praying about the words we speak, the Lord will patiently teach us and even empower us to have self-control. And best of all, He forgives us when we fail and is pleased with our desire for His help. *ANNE CETAS*

Can you think of something you said recently that you would like to take back? Ask the Lord to help you become aware of careless words.

Part of self-control is mouth-control.

^{12:1} The LORD had said to Abram, "Go from your country, your people and your father's household to the land I will show you.

² "I will make you into a great nation,
 and I will bless you;
I will make your name great,
 and you will be a blessing.
³ I will bless those who bless you,
 and whoever curses you I will curse;
and all peoples on earth
 will be blessed through you."

⁴ So Abram went, as the LORD had told him; and Lot went with him. Abram was seventy-five years old when he set out from Harran.

^{17:1} When Abram was ninety-nine years old, the LORD appeared to him and said, "I am God Almighty; walk before me faithfully and be blameless. ² Then I will make my covenant between me and you and will greatly increase your numbers."

God of the Ordinary

Hearing testimonies about how God did something spectacular in someone else's life can challenge us. While we may rejoice to hear about answers to prayer, we may also wonder why God hasn't done anything amazing for us lately.

It's easy to think that if God showed up in astonishing ways for us like He did for Abraham, then we would be more inspired to be faithful servants of God. But then we remember that God showed up for Abraham every 12 to 14 years, and most of Abraham's journey was rather ordinary (SEE GEN. 12:1–4; 15:1–6; 16:16–17:12).

TODAY'S READING
Genesis 12:1–4; 17:1–2

He will not let you be tempted beyond what you can bear.

1 Corinthians 10:13

God's work is usually done behind the scenes in the ordinary things of life. As our text says, "He will not let you be tempted beyond what you can bear. But when you are tempted, he will also provide a way out" (1 COR. 10:13). Every day God is busy shielding us from devastating onslaughts of Satan that would otherwise leave us helplessly defeated. And when temptation hits, He is making exit ramps for us so we can escape.

When we put our head on the pillow at night, we should pause to thank God for the amazing things He has done for us that day in the midst of our ordinary lives. So, instead of longing for Him to do something spectacular for you, thank Him! He already has. 🌱 *JOE STOWELL*

Lord, help me to be constantly aware that Your power and presence are with me even in the ordinary times in my life. Thank You for Your amazing work on my behalf that I know nothing about.

God is always in control behind the scenes, even on "ordinary" days.

¹ When the day of Pentecost came, they were all together in one place. ² Suddenly a sound like the blowing of a violent wind came from heaven and filled the whole house where they were sitting. ³ They saw what seemed to be tongues of fire that separated and came to rest on each of them. ⁴ All of them were filled with the Holy Spirit and began to speak in other tongues as the Spirit enabled them.

⁵ Now there were staying in Jerusalem God-fearing Jews from every nation under heaven. ⁶ When they heard this sound, a crowd came together in bewilderment, because each one heard their own language being spoken. ⁷ Utterly amazed, they asked: "Aren't all these who are speaking Galileans? ⁸ Then how is it that each of us hears them in our native language? ⁹ Parthians, Medes and Elamites; residents of Mesopotamia, Judea and Cappadocia, Pontus and Asia, ¹⁰ Phrygia and Pamphylia, Egypt and the parts of Libya near Cyrene; visitors from Rome ¹¹ (both Jews and converts to Judaism); Cretans and Arabs—we hear them declaring the wonders of God in our own tongues!" ¹² Amazed and perplexed, they asked one another, "What does this mean?"

True Communication

Walking in my North London neighborhood, I can hear snatches of conversation in many languages—Polish, Japanese, Hindi, Croatian, and Italian, to name a few. This diversity feels like a taste of heaven, yet I can't understand what they're saying. As I step into the Russian café or the Polish market and hear the different accents and sounds, I sometimes reflect on how wonderful it must have been on the day of Pentecost when people of many nations could understand what the disciples were saying.

On that day, pilgrims gathered together in Jerusalem to celebrate the festival of the harvest. The Holy Spirit rested on the believers so that when they spoke, the hearers (who had come from all over the known world) could understand them in their own languages (ACTS 2:5–6). What a miracle that these strangers from different lands could understand the praises to God in their own tongues! Many were spurred on to find out more about Jesus.

TODAY'S READING
Acts 2:1–12

A crowd came together in bewilderment, because each one heard their own language being spoken. Acts 2:6

We may not speak or understand many languages, but we know that the Holy Spirit equips us to connect with people in other ways. Amazingly, we are God's hands and feet—and mouth—to further His mission. Today, how might we—with the Spirit's help—reach out to someone unlike us? 🌱 *AMY BOUCHER PYE*

Lord, give us eyes to see those around us as You see them. Give us ears to hear their stories; give us hearts to share Your love.

Love is the language everybody understands.

⁷ The people served the LORD throughout the lifetime of Joshua and of the elders who outlived him and who had seen all the great things the LORD had done for Israel. ⁸ Joshua son of Nun, the servant of the LORD, died at the age of a hundred and ten. ⁹ And they buried him in the land of his inheritance, at Timnath Heres in the hill country of Ephraim, north of Mount Gaash. ¹⁰ After that whole generation had been gathered to their ancestors, another generation grew up who knew neither the LORD nor what he had done for Israel. ¹¹ Then the Israelites did evil in the eyes of the LORD and served the Baals. ¹² They forsook the LORD, the God of their ancestors, who had brought them out of Egypt. They followed and worshiped various gods of the peoples around them. They aroused the LORD's anger ¹³ because they forsook him and served Baal and the Ashtoreths. ¹⁴ In his anger against Israel the LORD gave them into the hands of raiders who plundered them. He sold them into the hands of their enemies all around, whom they were no longer able to resist. ¹⁵ Whenever Israel went out to fight, the hand of the LORD was against them to defeat them, just as he had sworn to them. They were in great distress. ¹⁶ Then the LORD raised up judges, who saved them out of the hands of these raiders. ¹⁷ Yet they would not listen to their judges but prostituted themselves to other gods and worshiped them. They quickly turned from the ways of their ancestors, who had been obedient to the LORD's commands. ¹⁸ Whenever the LORD raised up a judge for them, he was with the judge and saved them out of the hands of their enemies as long as the judge lived; for the LORD relented because of their groaning under those who oppressed and afflicted them. ¹⁹ But when the judge died, the people returned to ways even more corrupt than those of their ancestors, following other gods and serving and worshiping them. They refused to give up their evil practices and stubborn ways.

Some Assembly Required

Around our home, the words "some assembly required" have been the cause of great frustration (mine) and great humor (my family). When my wife and I first married, I attempted to make simple home repairs—with disastrous results. A repaired shower handle worked perfectly—if the plan was for the water to run between the walls. My fiascoes continued after we had children, when I assured my wife, Cheryl, I "don't need instructions" to put these "simple" toys together. Wrong!

Gradually, I learned my lesson and began to pay strict attention to the instructions and things went together as they should. Unfortunately, the longer things went well, the more confident I became, and soon I was again ignoring instructions with predictably disastrous results.

TODAY'S READING
Judges 2:7–19

Whenever the LORD raised up a judge for them, he was with the judge and saved them out of the hands of their enemies. Judges 2:18

The ancient Israelites struggled with a similar tendency: they would forget God, ignoring His instructions to avoid following after Baal and the other gods of the region (JUDG. 2:12). This produced disastrous results, until God, in His mercy, raised up judges to rescue them and bring them back to Himself (2:18).

God has reasons for all of the instructions He's given us to keep our affections on Him. Only by a daily awareness of His loving presence can we resist the temptation to "construct" our lives our own way. What great gifts He has given us in His Word and His presence! ✒

RANDY KILGORE

Lord, keep me close to You this day. Remind me of Your presence through Your Word and prayer and the leading of the Holy Spirit.

Our greatest privilege is to enjoy God's presence.

¹² Therefore, brothers and sisters, we have an obligation—but it is not to the flesh, to live according to it. ¹³ For if you live according to the flesh, you will die; but if by the Spirit you put to death the misdeeds of the body, you will live.

¹⁴ For those who are led by the Spirit of God are the children of God. ¹⁵ The Spirit you received does not make you slaves, so that you live in fear again; rather, the Spirit you received brought about your adoption to sonship. And by him we cry, "Abba, Father." ¹⁶ The Spirit himself testifies with our spirit that we are God's children. ¹⁷ Now if we are children, then we are heirs—heirs of God and co-heirs with Christ, if indeed we share in his sufferings in order that we may also share in his glory.

Abba, Father

The scene belonged on a funny Father's Day card. As a dad muscled a lawn mower ahead of him with one hand, he expertly towed a child's wagon behind him with the other. In the wagon sat his three-year-old daughter, delighted at the noisy tour of their yard. This might not be the safest choice, but who says men can't multitask?

If you had a good dad, a scene like that can invoke fantastic memories. But for many, "Dad" is an incomplete concept. Where are we to turn if our fathers are gone, or if they fail us, or even if they wound us?

King David certainly had his short-comings as a father, but he understood the paternal nature of God. "A father to the fatherless," he wrote, "a defender of widows, is God in his holy dwelling. God sets the lonely in families" (PS. 68:5–6). The apostle Paul expanded on that idea: "The Spirit you received brought about your adoption to sonship." Then, using the Aramaic word for father—a term young children would use for their dad—Paul added, "By him we cry, '*Abba*, Father'" (ROM. 8:15). This is the same word Jesus used when He prayed in anguish to His Father the night He was betrayed (MARK 14:36).

What a privilege to come to God using the same intimate term for "father" that Jesus used! Our *Abba* Father welcomes into His family anyone who will turn to Him. 🌀   TIM GUSTAFSON

> **TODAY'S READING**
> Romans 8:12–17
>
> **A father to the fatherless, a defender of widows, is God in his holy dwelling.**
> Psalm 68:5

Heavenly Father, I want to be part of Your family. I believe that Your only Son Jesus died for my sins. Please forgive me and help me.

A good father reflects the love of the heavenly Father.

¹ Everyone who believes that Jesus is the Christ is born of God, and everyone who loves the father loves his child as well. ² This is how we know that we love the children of God: by loving God and carrying out his commands. ³ In fact, this is love for God: to keep his commands. And his commands are not burdensome, ⁴ for everyone born of God overcomes the world. This is the victory that has overcome the world, even our faith. ⁵ Who is it that overcomes the world? Only the one who believes that Jesus is the Son of God.

⁶ This is the one who came by water and blood—Jesus Christ. He did not come by water only, but by water and blood. And it is the Spirit who testifies, because the Spirit is the truth. ⁷ For there are three that testify: ⁸ the Spirit, the water and the blood; and the three are in agreement. ⁹ We accept human testimony, but God's testimony is greater because it is the testimony of God, which he has given about his Son. ¹⁰ Whoever believes in the Son of God accepts this testimony. Whoever does not believe God has made him out to be a liar, because they have not believed the testimony God has given about his Son. ¹¹ And this is the testimony: God has given us eternal life, and this life is in his Son. ¹² Whoever has the Son has life; whoever does not have the Son of God does not have life.

¹³ I write these things to you who believe in the name of the Son of God so that you may know that you have eternal life.

Defeat or Victory?

Each year on June 18 the great Battle of Waterloo is recalled in what is now Belgium. On that day in 1815, Napoleon's French army was defeated by a multinational force commanded by the Duke of Wellington. Since then, the phrase "to meet your Waterloo" has come to mean "to be defeated by someone who is too strong for you or by a problem that is too difficult for you."

When it comes to our spiritual lives, some people feel that ultimate failure is inevitable and it's only a matter of time until each of us will "meet our Waterloo." But John refuted that pessimistic view when he wrote to followers of Jesus: "Everyone born of God overcomes the world. This is the victory that has overcome the world, even our faith" (1 JOHN 5:4).

> **TODAY'S READING**
> **1 John 5:1–13**
>
> **Everyone born of God overcomes the world. This is the victory that has overcome the world, even our faith.** 1 John 5:4

John weaves this theme of spiritual victory throughout his first letter as he urges us not to love the things this world offers, which will soon fade away (2:15–17). Instead, we are to love and please God, "And this is what he promised us—eternal life" (2:25).

While we may have ups and downs in life, and even some battles that feel like defeats, the ultimate victory is ours in Christ as we trust in His power. 🍃   *DAVID MCCASLAND*

Lord Jesus, Your ultimate victory in this fallen world is assured, and You ask us to share in it each day of our lives. By Your grace, enable us to overcome the world through faith and obedience to You.

When it comes to problems, the way out is to trust God on the way through.

¹ All the people came together as one in the square before the Water Gate. They told Ezra the teacher of the Law to bring out the Book of the Law of Moses, which the LORD had commanded for Israel.

² So on the first day of the seventh month Ezra the priest brought the Law before the assembly, which was made up of men and women and all who were able to understand. ³ He read it aloud from daybreak till noon as he faced the square before the Water Gate in the presence of the men, women and others who could understand. And all the people listened attentively to the Book of the Law.

⁴ Ezra the teacher of the Law stood on a high wooden platform built for the occasion. Beside him on his right stood Mattithiah, Shema, Anaiah, Uriah, Hilkiah and Maaseiah; and on his left were Pedaiah, Mishael, Malkijah, Hashum, Hashbaddanah, Zechariah and Meshullam.

⁵ Ezra opened the book. All the people could see him because he was standing above them; and as he opened it, the people all stood up. ⁶ Ezra praised the LORD, the great God; and all the people lifted their hands and responded, "Amen! Amen!" Then they bowed down and worshiped the LORD with their faces to the ground.

⁷ The Levites—Jeshua, Bani, Sherebiah, Jamin, Akkub, Shabbethai, Hodiah, Maaseiah, Kelita, Azariah, Jozabad, Hanan and Pelaiah—instructed the people in the Law while the people were standing there. ⁸ They read from the Book of the Law of God, making it clear and giving the meaning so that the people understood what was being read.

Marathon Reading

When the sun came up on the first day of the seventh month in 444 BC, Ezra started reading the law of Moses (what we know as the first five books of the Bible). Standing on a platform in front of the people in Jerusalem, he read it straight through for the next six hours.

Men, women, and children had gathered at the entrance to the city known as the Water Gate to observe the Festival of Trumpets—one of the feasts prescribed for them by God. As they listened, four reactions stand out.

They stood up in reverence for the Book of the Law (NEH. 8:5). They praised God by lifting their hands and saying "Amen." They bowed down in humble worship (V. 6). Then they listened carefully as the Scriptures were both read and explained to them (V. 8). What an amazing

> **TODAY'S READING**
> **Nehemiah 8:1–8**
>
> **They read from the Book of the Law of God, making it clear and giving the meaning so that the people understood what was being read.**
>
> Nehemiah 8:8

day as the book that "the Lord had commanded for Israel" (V. 1) was read aloud inside Jerusalem's newly rebuilt walls!

Ezra's marathon reading session can remind us that God's words to us are still meant to be a source of praise, worship, and learning. When we open the Bible and learn more about Christ, let's praise God, worship Him, and seek to discover what He is saying to us now. ❧

DAVE BRANON

Lord, thank You for this amazing book we call the Bible. Thank You for inspiring its creation by the writers You chose to pen its words. Thank You for preserving this book through the ages so we can learn Your people's story and the good news of Your love.

The goal of Bible study is not just learning but living.

⁷ When you, God, went out before your people,
   when you marched through the wilderness,
⁸ the earth shook, the heavens poured down rain,
   before God, the One of Sinai,
before God, the God of Israel.
⁹ You gave abundant showers, O God;
   you refreshed your weary inheritance.
¹⁰ Your people settled in it,
   and from your bounty, God, you provided for the poor.

¹⁹ Praise be to the LORD, to God our Savior,
   who daily bears our burdens.
²⁰ Our God is a God who saves;
   from the Sovereign LORD comes escape from death.

Hoo-ah!

The US Army's expression "hoo-ah" is a guttural response barked when troops voice approval. Its original meaning is lost to history, but some say it is derived from an old acronym HUA—Heard, Understood, and Acknowledged. I first heard the word in basic training.

TODAY'S READING
Psalm 68:7–10,19–20

Many years later it found its way into my vocabulary again when I began to meet on Wednesday mornings with a group of men to study the Scriptures. One morning one of the men—a former member of the 82nd Airborne Division—was reading one of the psalms and came to the notation *selah* that occurs throughout the psalms. Instead of reading "*selah*," however, he growled *hoo-ah*, and that became our word for *selah* ever after.

> **Blessed be the Lord, who daily loads us with benefits, the God of our salvation!** *Selah.* Psalm 68:19 NKJV

No one knows for certain what *selah* actually means. Some say it is only a musical notation. It often appears after a truth that calls for a deep-seated, emotional response. In that sense *hoo-ah* works for me.

This morning I read Psalm 68:19: "Blessed be the Lord, who daily [day to day] loads us with benefits, the God of our salvation! *Selah*" (NKJV).

Imagine that! Every single morning God loads us up on His shoulders and carries us through the day. *He* is our salvation. Thus safe and secure in Him, we've no cause for worry or for fear. "Hoo-ah!" I say. ❷

DAVID ROPER

Day by day and with each passing moment, strength I find to meet my trials here. Trusting in my Father's wise bestowment, I've no cause for worry or for fear. *LINA SANDELL BERG*

Worship is giving God the best that He has given you. OSWALD CHAMBERS

¹ If I speak in the tongues of men or of angels, but do not have love, I am only a resounding gong or a clanging cymbal. ² If I have the gift of prophecy and can fathom all mysteries and all knowledge, and if I have a faith that can move mountains, but do not have love, I am nothing. ³ If I give all I possess to the poor and give over my body to hardship that I may boast, but do not have love, I gain nothing.

⁴ Love is patient, love is kind. It does not envy, it does not boast, it is not proud. ⁵ It does not dishonor others, it is not self-seeking, it is not easily angered, it keeps no record of wrongs. ⁶ Love does not delight in evil but rejoices with the truth. ⁷ It always protects, always trusts, always hopes, always perseveres.

⁸ Love never fails. But where there are prophecies, they will cease; where there are tongues, they will be stilled; where there is knowledge, it will pass away. ⁹ For we know in part and we prophesy in part, ¹⁰ but when completeness comes, what is in part disappears. ¹¹ When I was a child, I talked like a child, I thought like a child, I reasoned like a child. When I became a man, I put the ways of childhood behind me. ¹² For now we see only a reflection as in a mirror; then we shall see face to face. Now I know in part; then I shall know fully, even as I am fully known.

¹³ And now these three remain: faith, hope and love. But the greatest of these is love.

Learning to Love

Love does more than make "the world go round," as an old song says. It also makes us immensely vulnerable. From time to time, we may say to ourselves: "Why love when others do not show appreciation?" or "Why love and open myself up to hurt?" But the apostle Paul gives a clear and simple reason to pursue love: "These three remain: faith, hope and love. But the greatest of these is love. Follow the way of love" (1 COR. 13:13–14:1).

TODAY'S READING
1 Corinthians 13

Follow the way of love. 1 Corinthians 14:1

"Love is an activity, the essential activity of God himself," writes Bible commentator C. K. Barrett, "and when men love either Him or their fellow-men, they are doing (however imperfectly) what God does." And God is pleased when we act like Him.

To begin following the way of love, think about how you might live out the characteristics listed in 1 Corinthians 13:4–7. For example, how can I show my child the same patience God shows me? How can I show kindness and respect for my parents? What does it mean to look out for the interests of others when I am at work? When something good happens to my friend, do I rejoice with her or am I envious?

As we "follow the way of love," we'll find ourselves often turning to God, the source of love, and to Jesus, the greatest example of love. Only then will we gain a deeper knowledge of what true love is and find the strength to love others like God loves us. 🌱

POH FANG CHIA

God, thank You that You are love and that You love me so much. Help me to love others the way Jesus showed us so that the whole world will know I am Your child.

Love comes from God. Everyone who loves has been born of God and knows God. 1 JOHN 4:7

¹ During those days another large crowd gathered. Since they had nothing to eat, Jesus called his disciples to him and said, ² "I have compassion for these people; they have already been with me three days and have nothing to eat. ³ If I send them home hungry, they will collapse on the way, because some of them have come a long distance."

⁴ His disciples answered, "But where in this remote place can anyone get enough bread to feed them?"

⁵ "How many loaves do you have?" Jesus asked.

"Seven," they replied.

⁶ He told the crowd to sit down on the ground. When he had taken the seven loaves and given thanks, he broke them and gave them to his disciples to distribute to the people, and they did so. ⁷ They had a few small fish as well; he gave thanks for them also and told the disciples to distribute them. ⁸ The people ate and were satisfied. Afterward the disciples picked up seven basketfuls of broken pieces that were left over. ⁹ About four thousand were present. After he had sent them away, ¹⁰ he got into the boat with his disciples and went to the region of Dalmanutha.

¹¹ The Pharisees came and began to question Jesus. To test him, they asked him for a sign from heaven. ¹² He sighed deeply and said, "Why does this generation ask for a sign? Truly I tell you, no sign will be given to it." ¹³ Then he left them, got back into the boat and crossed to the other side.

A Remote Location

Tristan da Cunha Island is famous for its isolation. It is the most remote inhabited island in the world, thanks to the 288 people who call it home. The island is located in the South Atlantic Ocean, 1,750 miles from South Africa—the nearest mainland. Anyone who might want to drop by for a visit has to travel by boat for seven days because the island has no airstrip.

Jesus and His followers were in a somewhat remote area when He produced a miraculous meal for thousands of hungry people. Before His miracle, Jesus said to His disciples, "[These people] have already been with me three days and have nothing to eat. If I send them home hungry, they will collapse on the way" (MARK 8:2–3). Because they were in the countryside where food was not readily available, they had to depend fully on Jesus. They had nowhere else to turn.

Sometimes God allows us to end up in desolate places where He is our only source of help. His ability to provide for us is not necessarily linked with our circumstances. If He created the entire world out of nothing, God can certainly meet our needs—whatever our circumstances—out of the riches of His glory, in Christ Jesus (PHIL. 4:19). 🌱

JENNIFER BENSON SCHULDT

> **TODAY'S READING**
> Mark 8:1–13
>
> My God will meet all your needs according to the riches of his glory in Christ Jesus.
> Philippians 4:19

Dear God, thank You for all that You have provided through Your Son, Jesus Christ. You know what my needs are. Please reassure me of Your care and power.

We can trust God to do what we cannot do.

⁵ Slaves, obey your earthly masters with respect and fear, and with sincerity of heart, just as you would obey Christ. ⁶ Obey them not only to win their favor when their eye is on you, but as slaves of Christ, doing the will of God from your heart. ⁷ Serve wholeheartedly, as if you were serving the Lord, not people, ⁸ because you know that the Lord will reward each one for whatever good they do, whether they are slave or free.

⁹ And masters, treat your slaves in the same way. Do not threaten them, since you know that he who is both their Master and yours is in heaven, and there is no favoritism with him.

Serving Christ

"I'm a secretary," a friend told me. "When I tell people this, they sometimes look at me with a certain pity. But when they find out who I am secretary for, they open their eyes with admiration!" In other words, society often defines some jobs as less important than others, unless those jobs happen to relate in some way to rich or famous people.

For the child of God, however, any occupation, regardless of the earthly boss, can be held proudly because we serve the Lord Jesus.

In Ephesians 6, Paul talks to servants and masters. He reminds both groups that we serve one Master who is in heaven. So we need to do everything with

TODAY'S READING
Ephesians 6:5–9

Obey [your earthly masters] . . . as slaves of Christ, doing the will of God from your heart. Ephesians 6:6

sincerity of heart, integrity, and respect because we are serving and working for Christ Himself. As the apostle Paul reminds us, "Serve wholeheartedly, as if you were serving the Lord, not people" (EPH. 6:7).

What a privilege to serve God in everything we do, whether answering a phone or driving a car or doing house-work or running a business. Let us work with a smile today, remembering that no matter what we are doing, we are serving God. 🌿

KEILA OCHOA

> **Lord Jesus,** I want to serve You in everything I do.
> Help me, as I begin each day, to remember this.

Serving shows our love for God.

¹ Keep on loving one another as brothers and sisters. ² Do not forget to show hospitality to strangers, for by so doing some people have shown hospitality to angels without knowing it. ³ Continue to remember those in prison as if you were together with them in prison, and those who are mistreated as if you yourselves were suffering.

⁴ Marriage should be honored by all, and the marriage bed kept pure, for God will judge the adulterer and all the sexually immoral. ⁵ Keep your lives free from the love of money and be content with what you have, because God has said,

"Never will I leave you;
   never will I forsake you."

⁶ So we say with confidence,

"The Lord is my helper; I will not be afraid.
   What can mere mortals do to me?"

His Loving Presence

Our hearts sank when we learned that our good friend Cindy had been diagnosed with cancer. Cindy was a vibrant person whose life blessed all who crossed her path. My wife and I rejoiced when she went into remission, but a few months later her cancer returned with a vengeance. In our minds she was too young to die. Her husband told me about her last hours. When she was weak and hardly able to talk, Cindy whispered to him, "Just be with me." What she wanted more than anything in those dark moments was his loving presence.

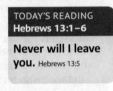

TODAY'S READING
Hebrews 13:1–6

Never will I leave you. Hebrews 13:5

The writer to the Hebrews comforted his readers by quoting Deuteronomy 31:6, where God told His people: "Never will I leave you; never will I forsake you" (HEB. 13:5). In the darkest moments of life, the assurance of His loving presence gives us confidence that we are not alone. He gives us the grace to endure, the wisdom to know He is working, and the assurance that Christ can "empathize with our weaknesses" (4:15).

Together let's embrace the blessing of His loving presence so we can confidently say, "The Lord is my helper; I will not be afraid" (13:6). 🌱   JOE STOWELL

Lord, thank You for the promise that You will never leave me.
May the reality of Your constant supporting presence fill my heart with comfort, confidence, and courage.

There is peace in the presence of God.

¹ I waited patiently for the LORD;
    he turned to me and heard my cry.
² He lifted me out of the slimy pit,
    out of the mud and mire;
he set my feet on a rock
    and gave me a firm place to stand.
³ He put a new song in my mouth,
    a hymn of praise to our God.
Many will see and fear the LORD
    and put their trust in him.
⁴ Blessed is the one
    who trusts in the LORD,
who does not look to the proud,
    to those who turn aside to false gods.
⁵ Many, LORD my God,
    are the wonders you have done,
    the things you planned for us.
None can compare with you;
    were I to speak and tell of your deeds,
    they would be too many to declare.

A Firm Place to Stand

The historic riverwalk area of Savannah, Georgia, is paved with mismatched cobblestones. Local residents say that centuries ago the stones provided ballast for ships as they crossed the Atlantic Ocean. When cargo was loaded in Georgia, the ballast stones were no longer needed, so they were used to pave the streets near the docks. Those stones had accomplished their primary job—stabilizing the ship through dangerous waters.

TODAY'S READING
Psalm 40:1–5

He lifted me out of the slimy pit; out of the mud and mire, he set my feet on a rock and gave me a firm place to stand.

Psalm 40:2

The days in which we live can feel as turbulent as the high seas. Like sailing ships of old, we need stability to help us navigate our way through the storms of life. David faced danger as well, and he celebrated the character of God for providing him with stability after he had endured a desperate time. He declared, "He lifted me out of the slimy pit; out of the mud and mire, he set my feet on a rock, and gave me a firm place to stand" (PS. 40:2). David's experience was one of conflict, personal failure, and family strife, yet God gave him a place to stand. So David sang "a hymn of praise to our God" (V. 3).

In times of difficulty, we too can look to our powerful God for the stability only He brings. His faithful care inspires us to say with David, "Many, Lord my God, are the wonders you have done, the things you planned for us" (V. 5). 🌱   *BILL CROWDER*

My hope is built on nothing less than Jesus' blood and righteousness;
I dare not trust the sweetest frame, but wholly lean on Jesus' name.
On Christ, the solid rock, I stand—all other ground is sinking sand.
EDWARD MOTE

When the world around us is crumbling,
Christ is the solid Rock on which we stand.

⁷ Husbands, in the same way be considerate as you live with your wives, and treat them with respect as the weaker partner and as heirs with you of the gracious gift of life, so that nothing will hinder your prayers.

⁸ Finally, all of you, be like-minded, be sympathetic, love one another, be compassionate and humble. ⁹ Do not repay evil with evil or insult with insult. On the contrary, repay evil with blessing, because to this you were called so that you may inherit a blessing. ¹⁰ For,

"Whoever would love life
    and see good days
must keep their tongue from evil
    and their lips from deceitful speech.
¹¹ They must turn from evil and do good;
    they must seek peace and pursue it.
¹² For the eyes of the Lord are on the righteous
    and his ears are attentive to their prayer,
but the face of the Lord is against those who do evil."

Shocking Honesty

When the minister asked one of his elders to lead the congregation in prayer, the man shocked everyone. "I'm sorry, Pastor," he said, "but I've been arguing with my wife all the way to church, and I'm in no condition to pray." The next moment was *awkward*. The minister prayed. The service moved on. Later, the pastor vowed never to ask anyone to pray publicly without first asking privately.

TODAY'S READING
1 Peter 3:7–12

Treat her as you should so your prayers will not be hindered.

1 Peter 3:7 NLT

That man demonstrated astonishing honesty in a place where hypocrisy would have been easier. But there is a larger lesson about prayer here. God is a loving Father. If I as a husband do not respect and honor my wife—a cherished daughter of God—why would her heavenly Father hear my prayers?

The apostle Peter made an interesting observation about this. He instructed husbands to treat their wives with respect and as equal heirs in Christ "so that nothing will hinder your prayers" (1 PETER 3:7). The underlying principle is that our relationships affect our prayer life.

What would happen if we exchanged the Sunday smiles and the façade of religiosity for refreshing honesty with our brothers and sisters? What might God do through us when we pray and learn to love each other as we love ourselves? ✿

TIM GUSTAFSON

Father, You love all of Your children, but so often we fight and disagree. Help us learn to interact with love and respect in all our relationships so the world will see the difference You make. Teach us to pray.

Prayer is simply an honest conversation with God.

¹ We must pay the most careful attention, therefore, to what we have heard, so that we do not drift away. ² For since the message spoken through angels was binding, and every violation and disobedience received its just punishment, ³ how shall we escape if we ignore so great a salvation? This salvation, which was first announced by the Lord, was confirmed to us by those who heard him. ⁴ God also testified to it by signs, wonders and various miracles, and by gifts of the Holy Spirit distributed according to his will.

No Drifting

At the end of one school semester, my wife and I picked up our daughter from her school 100 kilometers (60 miles) away. On our way back home we detoured to a nearby beach resort for snacks. While enjoying our time there, we watched the boats at the seashore. Usually they are anchored to prevent them from drifting away, but I noticed one boat drifting unhindered among the others—slowly and steadily making its way out to sea.

As we drove home, I reflected on the timely caution given to believers in the book of Hebrews: "We must pay the most careful attention, therefore, to what we have heard, so that we do not drift away"

TODAY'S READING
Hebrews 2:1–4

We must pay the most careful attention...so that we do not drift away. Hebrews 2:1

(HEB. 2:1). We have good reason to stay close. The author of Hebrews says that while the Mosaic law was reliable and needed to be obeyed, the message of the Son of God is far superior. Our salvation is "so great" in Jesus that He shouldn't be ignored (V. 3).

Drifting in our relationship with God is hardly noticeable at first; it happens gradually. However, spending time talking with Him in prayer and reading His Word, confessing our wrongs to Him, and interacting with other followers of Jesus can help us stay anchored in Him. As we connect with the Lord regularly, He will be faithful to sustain us, and we can avoid drifting away. 🌼

LAWRENCE DARMANI

What do you know about Jesus that keeps you wanting to be near Him?

To avoid drifting away from God, stay anchored to the Rock.

¹² We are not trying to commend ourselves to you again, but are giving you an opportunity to take pride in us, so that you can answer those who take pride in what is seen rather than in what is in the heart. ¹³ If we are "out of our mind," as some say, it is for God; if we are in our right mind, it is for you. ¹⁴ For Christ's love compels us, because we are convinced that one died for all, and therefore all died. ¹⁵ And he died for all, that those who live should no longer live for themselves but for him who died for them and was raised again.

¹⁶ So from now on we regard no one from a worldly point of view. Though we once regarded Christ in this way, we do so no longer. ¹⁷ Therefore, if anyone is in Christ, the new creation has come: The old has gone, the new is here! ¹⁸ All this is from God, who reconciled us to himself through Christ and gave us the ministry of reconciliation: ¹⁹ that God was reconciling the world to himself in Christ, not counting people's sins against them. And he has committed to us the message of reconciliation. ²⁰ We are therefore Christ's ambassadors, as though God were making his appeal through us. We implore you on Christ's behalf: Be reconciled to God. ²¹ God made him who had no sin to be sin for us, so that in him we might become the righteousness of God.

Leaving the Past Behind

Chris Baker is a tattoo artist who transforms symbols of pain and enslavement into works of art. Many of his clients are former gang members and victims of human trafficking who have been marked with identifying names, symbols, or codes. Chris transforms these into beautiful art by tattooing over them with new images.

Jesus does for the soul what Chris Baker does for the skin—He takes us as we are and transforms us. The Bible says, "Anyone who belongs to Christ has become a new person. The old life is gone; a new life has begun!" (2 COR. 5:17 NLT). Before knowing Christ, we follow our desires wherever they lead us, and our

TODAY'S READING
2 Corinthians 5:12–21

Anyone who belongs to Christ has become a new person.

2 Corinthians 5:17 NLT

lifestyles reflect this. When we repent and begin to walk with Christ, the passions and pitfalls that once dominated our lives is the "old life" (1 COR. 6:9–11) that fades away as we are transformed. "All this is from God, who reconciled us to himself through Christ" (2 COR. 5:18).

Still, life as a "new person" isn't always easy. It can take time to disconnect from old habits. We may struggle with ideas that were foundational to our old way of life. Yet over time, God's Holy Spirit works in us, giving us inner strength and an understanding of Christ's love. As God's beautiful new creations, we're free to leave the past behind. 🌑

JENNIFER BENSON SCHULDT

Jesus, thank You for the power of Your death and resurrection. Your victory over sin means that I can be forgiven and can enjoy a new life in You.

To enjoy the future, accept God's forgiveness for the past.

¹ As for you, you were dead in your transgressions and sins, ² in which you used to live when you followed the ways of this world and of the ruler of the kingdom of the air, the spirit who is now at work in those who are disobedient. ³ All of us also lived among them at one time, gratifying the cravings of our flesh and following its desires and thoughts. Like the rest, we were by nature deserving of wrath. ⁴ But because of his great love for us, God, who is rich in mercy, ⁵ made us alive with Christ even when we were dead in transgressions—it is by grace you have been saved. ⁶ And God raised us up with Christ and seated us with him in the heavenly realms in Christ Jesus, ⁷ in order that in the coming ages he might show the incomparable riches of his grace, expressed in his kindness to us in Christ Jesus. ⁸ For it is by grace you have been saved, through faith—and this is not from yourselves, it is the gift of God— ⁹ not by works, so that no one can boast. ¹⁰ For we are God's handiwork, created in Christ Jesus to do good works, which God prepared in advance for us to do.

Our Way of Life

was struck by a phrase I heard quoted from a contemporary Bible translation. When I Googled the phrase "our way of life" to locate the passage, many of the results focused on things people felt were threatening their expected way of living. Prominent among the perceived threats were climate change, terrorism, and government policies.

What really is our way of life as followers of Jesus? I wondered. Is it what makes us comfortable, secure, and happy, or is it something more?

Paul reminded the Christians in Ephesus of the remarkable way God had transformed their lives. "God, who is rich in mercy, out of the great love with which he loved us even when we were dead through our trespasses, made us alive together with Christ—by grace you have been saved" (EPH. 2:4–5 NRSV). The result is that we are "created in Christ Jesus for good works, which God prepared beforehand to be our way of life" (V. 10 NRSV).

> TODAY'S READING
> **Ephesians 2:1–10**
>
> **We are what he has made us, created in Christ Jesus for good works, which God prepared beforehand to be our way of life.**
> Ephesians 2:10 NRSV

Doing good works, helping others, giving, loving, and serving in Jesus's name—these are to be our way of life. They are not optional activities for believers, but the very reason God has given us life in Christ.

In a changing world, God has called and empowered us to pursue a life that reaches out to others and honors Him.

DAVID MCCASLAND

Father, thank You for the incredible riches of Your love and mercy. You rescued us from our dead way of living and made us alive with Christ.

Let your light shine before others, that they may see your good deeds and glorify your Father in heaven. MATTHEW 5:16

¹ "Very truly I tell you Pharisees, anyone who does not enter the sheep pen by the gate, but climbs in by some other way, is a thief and a robber. ² The one who enters by the gate is the shepherd of the sheep. ³ The gatekeeper opens the gate for him, and the sheep listen to his voice. He calls his own sheep by name and leads them out. ⁴ When he has brought out all his own, he goes on ahead of them, and his sheep follow him because they know his voice. ⁵ But they will never follow a stranger; in fact, they will run away from him because they do not recognize a stranger's voice." ⁶ Jesus used this figure of speech, but the Pharisees did not understand what he was telling them.

⁷ Therefore Jesus said again, "Very truly I tell you, I am the gate for the sheep. ⁸ All who have come before me are thieves and robbers, but the sheep have not listened to them. ⁹ I am the gate; whoever enters through me will be saved. They will come in and go out, and find pasture. ¹⁰ The thief comes only to steal and kill and destroy; I have come that they may have life, and have it to the full.

¹¹ "I am the good shepherd. The good shepherd lays down his life for the sheep.

Called by Name

When I first meet a new group of students in the college composition class I teach, I already know their names. I take the time to familiarize myself with their names and photos on my student roster, so when they walk into my classroom I can say, "Hello, Jessica," or "Welcome, Trevor." I do this because I know how meaningful it is when someone knows and calls us by name.

TODAY'S READING
John 10:1–11

He calls his own sheep by name.
John 10:3

Yet to truly know someone, we need to know more than that person's name. In John 10, we can sense the warmth and care Jesus, the Good Shepherd, has for us when we read that He "calls his own sheep by name" (V. 3). He knows even more than our name. He knows our thoughts, longings, fears, wrongs, and deepest needs. Because He knows our deepest needs, He has given us our very life—our eternal life—at the cost of His own. As He says in verse 11, He "lays down his life for the sheep."

You see, our sin separated us from God. So Jesus, the Good Shepherd, became the Lamb and sacrificed Himself, taking our sin on Himself. When He gave His life for us and then was resurrected, He redeemed us. As a result, when we accept His gift of salvation through faith, we are no longer separated from God.

Give thanks to Jesus! He knows your name and your needs!

DAVE BRANON

Dear Lord, thank You for knowing my name and for knowing exactly what I need. Thank You for dying for my sin and for rising from the grave to defeat death and give me eternal life with You.

God's knowledge of us knows no bounds.

God Moves
Through Prayer

God has chosen to move through our praying to accomplish things that would not have happened through any other means. As we seek God's presence, He gives us light for the path ahead and makes His purposes known.

Many people struggle with spending time in prayer because they believe that God would have them *do* something. But Scripture shows us in multiple places that praying *is* doing something. Yet it's hard for us to grasp that because we're conditioned to equate sitting still (in this case, stillness before God) with laziness and inactivity. So when do you pray, and when do you *do something* about what you're praying for?

Praying or Doing?

Our family struggled with that question in a heart-rending way. Though our daughter received Jesus when she was a small child, with adolescence came a gathering storm of rebellion and trouble at home. In spite of our best efforts, the world and the influence of friends without faith gradually took their toll. The distance between us and the daughter we dearly loved became so great that one day she simply walked away.

The urgency in my wife's voice reached through the cell phone and grabbed me by the throat. "She's *gone*," she said, choking back tears. "Katie's *gone*."

"What do you mean, *gone*?" I asked. "What happened?

Where did she go?"

What followed was every parent's nightmare. Day after day, night after night, Katie was out on the street in our city known for its violent crime and drug abuse. We scoured the city looking for her. Police and sheriff's departments were notified, parents and friends alerted, reports filed, and Katie's name and picture circulated to law enforcement agencies throughout the state and country. Members of our church joined in the search, sending Katie's name out on prayer chains. Out late at night and up early in the morning, we followed every clue we could find.

The sleepless nights and long hours of worry took their toll. Days stretched into weeks. Like any passionate mother, Cari was so consumed with finding her daughter that she was teetering on the edge. One day, she called me from an armed drug dealer's apartment where she had gone *alone*, trying to find out anything she could about Katie. The minutes in the car as I made my way there through traffic were the longest of my life.

> Scripture shows us in multiple places that praying *is* doing something. Yet . . . we're conditioned to equate stillness before God with laziness and inactivity.

After that, I told Cari that we needed to be less frantic and spend more time praying. Her response was, "I pray while I am looking." But something didn't feel right. No matter how hard we looked or how hard we prayed *while* we were looking, it led nowhere.

By now, she had been gone for over three weeks. One night one of our son's friends who was helping us look for her saw her at a convenience store. She was hanging out with a girl who had been a runaway for months and a young man newly released from jail. The store clerk told us they had asked about bus tickets out of state.

For the next twenty-four hours we hardly slept. I sent fliers to every bus terminal in the area. I sat outside the bus station, watching and waiting. We did everything we could think of. Only then did we begin to realize that this was just too much, more than anyone can handle on their own.

The truth had finally sunk in. God alone knew exactly where she was, and He could help us find her better than anyone else.

In the end, that's how it happened. The next Sunday, difficult as it was, we took a step back from our frantic search. It was Father's Day. We spent some time with our son that afternoon and made a special effort to pray together for Katie. That evening I took Cari out to dinner in a nearby town. We heard Katie had been seen there, and we thought that we might even run into her. But when we arrived, we discovered the restaurants were already closed for the day. So we started back home.

Then the phone rang. It was a server at a diner we liked to visit just two blocks away. Katie was there. God had led us directly to where she was. Within two minutes, we were standing in front of her. With a lot of love and hard work, Katie was soon on the road to recovery at home. And Cari and I discovered the difference praying can make.

Walking at God's Pace

Our time in the crucible taught us a life lesson. *Prayer must precede action.* We must learn how to walk at God's pace if we desire to truly hear God and discern His best for our lives.

Walking at God's pace does not exclude action. We act on what God gives us and go no further. We pray and we wait, then we act. This is rarely easy, especially in a crisis when we feel like we have to do something, but we learn to be sensitive to the Spirit and move with God's promptings. We act on what God gives us and do no more. Then we wait again. This rhythm of praying, waiting, and acting brings a new level of effectiveness to our lives, because we are staying in step with the Holy Spirit (GAL. 5:22–25).

Praying IS Action

Nehemiah provides a great example of the rhythm of prayer and action in a challenging time. While exiled with the Jewish people in Babylon, Nehemiah hears that the wall of Jerusalem is in ruins. His immediate response is to fast and pray (NEH. 1:4). God then gives him direction through the personal interest and response of the Persian King Artaxerxes.

All the while, Nehemiah continues to pray (2:1–6). As the rebuilding begins in Jerusalem, he encounters opposition from Israel's enemies. Nehemiah immediately gathers the exiles who have returned with him. What does he want them to do together? Pray (4:8–9). God then directs them to divide the people into those who will work on the wall and those who will guard the workers (4:16).

There's the rhythm again: Pray. Wait. Act.
Action follows prayer.
Prayer discovers what action to take.

Prayer and action should never exclude each other. But in the busyness of the world around us, we often live that way and end up living disconnected from our real source of direction and peace.

Making Prayer a Priority

Prayer not only should precede action, it is action of the highest kind because it gives God the priority He deserves. Prayer must permeate our actions by being a continual part of them as we consciously live in God's presence. We are easily distracted, and we must fight to keep this perspective continually. It is not just a matter of "making time" for God; it is the realization that all of our time is in His hands and that we are constantly before Him wherever we are and whatever we do. This is what it means to live day by day in a relationship with Him, and this realization helps us pray increasingly "without ceasing" (1 THESS. 5:17 NKJV).

Learning to give prayer higher priority takes time. It rarely happens immediately because we're steeped in self-reliance. We have to unlearn old habits and patterns of thought. At the beginning of the Welsh Revival, Evan Roberts prayed with real anguish, "Oh Lord, bend me!" Roberts was trained as a blacksmith, and his words painted a picture of what happens when metal is forged on an anvil. Taking more time for prayer can be like that. God works with our wills and bends us in new directions. But gently, over time, we find new peace and strength in His presence.

> God desires us to be prayerful people of action: people who pray first and then act in response to His leading.

God desires us to be prayerful people of action: people who pray first and then act in response to His leading. All of us are at varying degrees of keeping this balance. Sometimes we tell ourselves, "I am not much of a praying person." But because Jesus was a praying person, you and I are intended to become like Him. Because God loves us, sooner or later He will bring us to our knees.

Prayer and action are two sides of the same coin of a mature and Christlike faith. You can't have one without the other. Action without prayer, even if it's done for God, too often misses the mark.

A missionary to India during the early 1900s learned this balance in a beautiful way. She had been frustrated by a lack of results in her work. She then decided that instead of asking God to bless what she was already doing, she would give prayer a new priority in her ministry. This wasn't easy at first, because she continually thought of things she "should" be doing as she started each morning on her knees. She often felt guilty, as if she wasn't working hard enough. But soon she discovered her prayer was work. It required special effort in a way she had never known before.

She was astounded by the transformation that followed. She wrote a friend, "Every department of the work now is in a more prosperous condition than I have ever known it to be. The stress and strain have gone out of my life. The joy of feeling that my life is easily balanced, the life of communion on the one hand and the life of work on the other, brings constant rest and peace. I could not go back to the old life, and God grant that it may always be impossible."

This is the work that changes the world. Prayer is the vehicle God uses to take us to new places of grace. When we pray, we willfully remove ourselves from the driver's seat. But our Father pulls us close and whispers His will to us. ✿

He will steer us in the direction we need to go. ✿

Excerpted and adapted from *Praying Together: Kindling Passion for Prayer*
©2009, 2016 by James Banks. Used by permission of Discovery House.

Why Read the Bible?

The Bible has been given to us so that we may know its author and grow to love Him. To get to know someone we need to communicate with them. We need to talk with them and listen to them.

It's the same with our relationship with God. If we want to get to know Him, we need to communicate with Him. We can talk to Him through prayer. But how can we hear His voice?

The way we can hear what God has to say is to read His message to us . . . the Bible. Paul, one of the writers, actually says it's "God-breathed." Think of it, the very breath of God is somehow infused in those words. But how do we know those words are really His? How do we know they can be trusted?

Jesus Himself believed in the Bible and referred to it often. He didn't quote the New Testament; that hadn't even been written yet. He believed and quoted the Old Testament. So Jesus trusted the Bible. But there's plenty of evidence that supports the accuracy of the Bible too.

> If we want to get to know [God], we need to communicate with Him. We can talk to Him through prayer. But how can we hear His voice?

Hundreds of archaeological sites have uncovered the exact locations of biblical events. Then there's the way the Bible lines up with other historical documents. Did you know you can trace the life of Jesus through historical documents without ever once going to the Bible? Four writers of different backgrounds and personalities, Matthew (a tax collector), Mark (an investigative reporter), Luke (a doctor), and John (a fisherman), all wrote the same account but from their own unique viewpoints.

But isn't it boring and confusing? The Bible is an epic thriller that contains the all-time best love story. But some portions of it can seem boring. It's important to remember that the Bible is not just one book; it's many different books put together over the centuries. And not every book is to be read like a novel. Some are historical events written for study. Some even contain a census. (Imagine curling up in bed at night to read a nice, long census!) Those sections are included in the Bible for very good reasons, but they are best read along with a book that can explain the historical context.

Other books in the Bible contain firsthand descriptions of God's magnificence and His creativity. Some are insightful poetry. Others honestly explore doubt and every possible aspect of the human condition. Still others are full of wisdom and no-nonsense approaches on how to succeed in life. Finally, there are the prophetic books that point to what we can expect in the future. When combined, these books from the Creator of Life show us how to best understand life.

God wants to use His Word in our lives to . . .

GIVE US FAITH. *"For it is by grace you have been saved, through faith—and this is not from yourselves, it is the gift of God—not by works, so that no one can boast"* (EPHESIANS 2:8–9).

"Faith comes from hearing the message, and the message is heard through the word about Christ" (ROMANS 10:17).

ENCOURAGE US. *"For everything that was written in the past was written to teach us, so that through the endurance taught in the Scriptures and the encouragement they provide we might have hope"* (ROMANS 15:4).

EQUIP US. *"All Scripture . . . is useful for teaching, rebuking,* *correcting and training in righteousness, so that the servant of God may be thoroughly equipped for every good work"* (2 TIMOTHY 3:16–17).

GUIDE US. In this chaotic world where there no longer seem to be absolutes, no right or wrong, the Bible is an unwavering compass always pointing us to True North. And it is that truth that guides and directs our steps. According to Psalm 119, it lights the path for our feet so we know where to walk.

The Next Step

Jesus declared, "I am the bread of life. Whoever comes to me will never go hungry, and whoever believes in me will never be thirsty" (JOHN 6:35). Jesus says that human beings don't just live on physical food "but on every word that comes from the mouth of God" (MATTHEW 4:4).

Our bodies would cry out if we only fed them once a day. How can we do any less for our souls? Yes, the world constantly demands our attention. But if we intentionally set aside time to regularly feed our soul by reading God's Word, we will grow.

For me the best time to read is in the still of the morning while having a cup of coffee with God. For other folks it may be just before bed. I read slowly and ask the Holy Spirit to bring out truths. I've learned over the years that the only way I can know God is by taking the time to hear what He says through His Word. And as I get to know Him, I can't help but fall deeper and deeper in love with Him. ✿

Bill Myers, author and filmmaker, www.billmyers.com

Why Do We Pray?

Any thoughtful person wrestling with prayer asks, "Why pray at all?" Is the basic purpose of prayer to get things from God? George MacDonald offered this rationale for prayer: "What if God knows prayer to be the thing we need first and most? What if the main object in God's idea of prayer is a supplying of our great, our endless need—the need of Himself? . . . Communion with God is the one need of the soul beyond all other need. Prayer is the beginning of that communion, of talking with God, a coming-to-one with Him, which is the sole end of prayer, yea, of existence itself."

God wants us for Himself. He desires communion with us. His purpose in prayer is not to make us sit up and beg. He wants us to know Him.

For that reason, God has made Himself known through His Son Jesus Christ, who died on the cross and rose again to pay the penalty for our sin. If you don't know Christ as your Savior, go to Him in prayer—maybe for the first time—confess your sin, and receive the forgiveness you need. "For God so loved the world that he gave his one and only Son, that whoever believes in him shall not perish but have eternal life" (JOHN 3:16).

Then you'll begin that all-important communication with God. 🍃

Adapted from *Jesus' Blueprint For Prayer*, © 2002 Our Daily Bread Ministries.

Making Hope-Filled Choices

squinted at the alarm clock as Gene reached for the phone. It was 12:35 a.m. Who would be calling at this hour? Gene put the receiver back and choked out the words. "Jason has been arrested for the murder of his wife's first husband. He's in jail in Orlando."

The next hours were a blur of tears, panic, fear, and erratic activity. Two parents in the grip of a nightmare. Our son was a disciplined and compassionate young man who had dedicated himself to serving his God and his country through military service. But without warning our dreams for Jason came crashing down in a thousand pieces.

There were multiple allegations of abuse about the biological father of our son's stepdaughters, and it appeared he was about to receive unsupervised visitation. Feeling powerless to protect them, he began to unravel until he did the unthinkable. How we grieved for the family of the deceased! While we were planning a murder trial, they were planning a funeral.

We were emotionally, financially, and spiritually challenged. Friends became the hands and feet of Jesus to us. We had never been so needy, but we had never felt so loved.

Our son was convicted of first-degree murder and sentenced to life without parole. In the middle of our new normal, we realized we needed to make hope-filled choices if we were going to bring God glory in our circumstances. We needed to choose life—instead of curling up and dying emotionally and spiritually. We memorized John 10:10: "I am come that they may have life, and have it to the full."

One day I asked my son how he keeps depression from enveloping him. He said, "Mom, I have a gratitude list. When I feel like I can't go on, I make a list of everything I have to be thankful for. I'm thankful I have parents who are my advocates. I'm thankful I have ministry opportunities every day in the prison."

Another hope-filled choice was vulnerability. I needed to be honest about our journey. After hearing of our son's arrest, a woman who had been in the Bible study I taught said, "Carol, I used to think you were perfect, but now I think we could be friends."

Choosing purposeful action in the middle of hopeless circumstances has been our most important step. With over two million people incarcerated in the US, our family was in a unique position to understand the needs of inmates and their families. One year after Jason's trial, we launched the nonprofit organization, Speak Up for Hope, to minister to others in practical ways.

All of us will need to make hope-filled choices at one time or another. You may need to reach out to other Christians with a spirit of vulnerability. Or you may need to focus on helping others in order to find purpose in each day. Whatever journey you are on, place your hope in God. You may, like Gene and me, discover the truth of Romans 5:5: "This hope will not lead to disappointment. For we know how dearly God loves us, because he has given us the Holy Spirit to fill our hearts with his love" (NLT). ❧

Carol Kent is an international public speaker and the author of *Waiting Together: Hope and Healing for Families of Prisoners*. For more information visit www.CarolKent.org

OUR DAILY BREAD FOR KIDS™

Coloring & Activity Book

For enquiries visit our facebook page **Our Daily Bread Ministries Philippines** or contact our office at **705 1355**

Your kids will use their imagination while coloring, bringing favorite Bible characters to life. They'll challenge their brains with fun activities that help them remember important Bible stories and concepts. The *Our Daily Bread for Kids Coloring and Activity Book* is great for kids to use by themselves—or to share with another person to double the fun. The best part is that they'll follow the big story of the Bible while they play!

Visit us on:

facebook

Our Daily Bread
Ministries Philippines, Inc.

- ☑ View our office information & profile.
- ☑ Ask questions.
- ☑ Read daily inspirational devotionals.
- ☑ View & share images & videos.
- ☑ Browse through our different resources.
- ☑ Give comments & suggestions.

Topic Index

Topic Index